6.99

98

88

)

20.
FEB

International Marketing

The book starts with an overview of basic marketing concepts and their applicability on an international basis. It then covers each ingredient of the marketing mix and explores them in relation to multinational markets. Each ingredient of the mix is studied in the light of the fundamental question: 'How far can it be standardised internationally or in a research-based cluster of countries?' Research, planning and organisation problems receive particular attention. A whole chapter is devoted to 'Creativity and innovation' on a global scale.

Simon Majaro has been described as one of this country's leading thinkers on marketing topics. Yet his approach is always practical and is based on years of experience in industry and a very successful consultancy practice.

Since 1968 he has combined an academic career with an active consultancy practice. He has taught many of Europe's managers in prominent training establishments such as Ashridge Management College, 'De Baak' in Holland, CEI in Geneva, the College of the Institute of Marketing, British Transport Staff College, Strategic Management Learning and many others. At the same time he has developed an international reputation as a management consultant, initially as a senior partner with Urwick Orr and Partners and now as the head of his own international consultancy firm.

Simon Majaro is also the author of '*Marketing in Perspective*'.

International Marketing
A Strategic Approach to World Markets

Simon Majaro

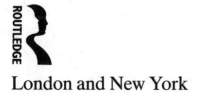

London and New York

First published 1977
by Unwin Hyman

Revised edition 1987
Seventh edition 1991

Reprinted 1993
by Routledge
11 New Fetter Lane, London EC4P 4EE

Simultaneously published in the USA and Canada
by Routledge
29 West 35th Street, New York, NY 10001

© 1993 Simon Majaro

Printed and bound in Great Britain by
Biddles Ltd, Guildford and King's Lynn

British Library Cataloguing in Publication Data
A catalogue record for this book is available from the British Library

Library of Congress Cataloging in Publication Data
Majaro, Simon.
    International marketing.
Bibliography: p.
Includes index.
1. Export marketing.   I. Title.
HF1009.5.M34   1982   658.8′48   82–8771
ISBN 0–415–10442–4 (pbk.)   AACR2

To My Parents

Preface

For many years I practised international marketing with some success. During this time it became clear that many of my problems stemmed from the fact that my skills and knowledge had been gained in a domestic marketing environment. I had assumed, as many managers do, that international marketing is the same as marketing in a domestic environment, but on a larger scale. I realise that I could have been spared many moments of anguish had I been better equipped with the tools and concepts which marketing on a global scale calls for.

On leaving industry I opted for a career which combined teaching businessmen with management consultancy. In the former capacity I have taught in a number of management development establishments in the UK and abroad. It gave me the privilege of teaching many hundreds of Europe's promising managers, some of whom have by now reached top positions in large and successful multinationals.

Working with these international managers taught me a lot about the problems firms face when seeking to internationalise their operations, and about the waste that can occur in the process. Many firms drift into international markets without proper plans, giving too little attention to the financial, organisational and infrastructural complexities. By the time they are entrenched in foreign markets the die is cast. An organisation is established; policies are defined and some kind of philosophy emerges. In most cases it works, but too often at a sub-optimal level.

This is not a book on techniques or procedures. It is an attempt to provide the reader with a conceptual framework for a systematic approach to international marketing. Against this framework the experienced practitioner can test his ideas or seek to develop a new approach. To the person who plans to enter world markets for the first time the framework may offer guidance towards a more analytical orientation. My basic aim throughout has been to look at international marketing problems from the vantage point of the strategic level of the firm. My experience has taught me that if managers at that level see the problems with clarity, performance at operational level is sure to be more effective.

The cases at the end of the book do not purport to illustrate examples of good or bad international marketing—they simply represent typical situations. They are provided for group discussion in the event that this book is used as a text for courses and seminars, either at academic establishments or on an in-house company basis.

To a large extent the ideas developed here are an outgrowth of discussions with students and clients, from whom I learnt as much as they learnt from me. It is obviously impractical to list them by name. However I wish to express a collective thank you to them all through these pages.

Simon Majaro

Preface to the Revised Edition

Since 1977 when my book on 'International Marketing' was first published international marketing has become more important not only to the success of firms but also for the welfare of nations. International trade has become extremely competitive and economic conditions throughout the world have presented the marketer with a daunting challenge. Nonetheless one encounters firms that have managed to thrive in spite of all these difficulties.

I have always believed that the main ingredient of success is a sound marketing strategy coupled with a well-structured organisation. The experience of the last few years has confirmed my conviction in this regard. If one attempts to identify the best performer in any sector of industry or commerce throughout the world one soon discovers that it is the level of effectiveness and creativity of its marketing effort that places a company in this role. The reverse also seems to be true: poor marketing appears to be the main source of failure.

The world is shrinking fast. Rapid travel and ease of communication have meant that wherever one refers to the word 'marketing' one should talk about 'international marketing'. Any company that endeavours to sell its products in more than one country is involved in international marketing and must plan its entry into foreign markets in an integrated and structured fashion. This is what this book has sought to cover.

The revised edition incorporates a number of changes necessitated by the passage of time. Most of these changes, though, are quite minor. Basic concepts and principles seem to remain intact over the years. A major addition is the chapter on 'The application of the business portfolio concept to international marketing decisions'. A new case Medi-systems International Inc has been added. The bibliography has been up-dated. The book as a whole has been revised to meet the needs of the '80's although the changes that were required to achieve this objective were not drastic. To most readers it is the emphasis which they will need to place on specific topics that will have probably changed.

Contents

Chapter 1

The Path Towards Internationalisation

Two major developments have imperceptibly become the vital forces that have determined the strategic route that modern firms have taken. They are:

The marketing concept
Internationalisation

Many writers have dealt with both subjects. The literature abounds with treatises on both marketing and internationalisation. However, these subjects are normally treated as two separate disciplines. It is seldom appreciated that marketing and internationalisation are not only related but interdependent. Many firms have accelerated the development of the international dimension to their activities through the stimulus of the international marketing vistas they had perceived. General Motors, Nestlé and IBM have become international companies in the main because at a certain stage in their respective development they identified promising opportunities in world markets. Having established that the domestic market offered limited scope for expansion in terms of growth and profits, these firms sought to exploit opportunities abroad and that meant marketing opportunities. This is probably the main reason why firms based in small countries like the Netherlands and Switzerland embarked on the road to internationalisation at an earlier date than their American counterparts.

Whilst firms claim to have initiated the internationalisation process for a host of reasons, it is not always recognised that probably the most convincing rationale is the desire to harness global marketing opportunities. A firm that is enjoying continuous growth and profitability in its domestic market is far less prone to the internationalising process than the firm that has encountered tough competition at home with eroding margins. In other words, 'internationalisation' is a corporate strategy with strong marketing 'inputs' rather than an inevitable evolution. A firm can be very successful and remain so without indulging in foreign adventures. On the other hand, with the ever-shortening product life cycle tendency, a firm may find that shunning international markets may in certain circumstances spell stagnation and vulnerability. The message implied in what has been said so far is that the internationalisation process can provide a firm with rich new pastures for planned growth and prosperity but it must be based on clearly thought out and quantified marketing justification. Without such information, the road to internationalisation can be a rocky one.

Too many writers seem to imply that the world enterprise is an end in itself. In his paper 'The Tortuous Evolution of the Multinational Corporation', Howard V. Perlmutter concludes:

'The geocentric enterprise offers an institutional and supranational framework which could conceivably make war less likely, on the assumption that bombing customers, suppliers and employees, is in nobody's interest. . . .'*

This sounds extremely idealistic. Ford Motor Company is operating in the UK and in many other parts of the world mainly because the marketing objectives of the firm are well served by this mode of operation. When Henry Ford II announced in public during a serious industrial dispute that he had no intention of authorising further investments in the UK he forgot why his firm had come to Britain in the first place. Ford came to Britain because it probably made good *marketing* sense to do so. Ford internationalised its operations because of an underlying marketing stimulus. If, for marketing reasons, the UK ceases to offer attractive opportunities, at that point Ford may cease to invest in that country. Of course there are other elements in such a decision: labour availability, logistics, infrastructure, location convenience, etc. However, in reality the marketing justification is the most powerful. As long as the UK remains a large and promising market for automobiles, marketing considerations will overrule Henry Ford's personal emotions regardless of the pain that industrial relations may inflict upon the firm's management. On the other hand, in the event that marketing opportunities melt away, Ford will probably refrain from sinking more funds in the UK however docile the British workers and the unions become. So much for a large multinational's idealism.

The hypothesis that emerges, therefore, is that the internationalisation of a firm is to a great extent the corollary to its marketing aspirations and needs. A firm becomes an international enterprise not because it desires to become one, but because it is forced to seek wider markets outside its domestic scene. Internationalisation is a corporate strategy, just like mergers, acquisitions and diversification. Marketing is the underlying justification for such a strategy. Unfortunately, the interdependence between marketing and internationalisation is often overlooked by management and decisions to internationalise are taken with inadequate marketing justification. This is probably why so many firms encounter severe difficulties in achieving success in their international operations. The domestic company that decides to seek its fortunes in world markets is well advised to approach its strategy with

*Howard V. Perlmutter, 'The Tortuous Evolution of the Multinational Corporation' *Columbia Journal of World Business,* vol. IV, 1969.

caution and systematic planning. The number of pitfalls is enormous; at the same time, the rewards for the manager who enters world markets with a full awareness of the tasks to be undertaken, coupled with a deep-rooted sensitivity towards the international consumer, can be very substantial.

Chapter 2

The Organisation of the International Firm—A Conceptual Framework

The so-called 'multinational' firm is frequently in the news nowadays. Anxieties over the growth and power of the multinational companies show no sign of fading away. The US Government has been seeking to establish how far such firms have been a contributing factor to the dollar decline. In Brussels EEC Commission officials have been discussing proposals for control procedures over multinationals including changes in tax treatment. In the UK Roche came into conflict with the Government on the question of pricing and profits of two drugs supplied to the National Health Service.

Many examples can be added to illustrate how the multinational firm has ceased to enjoy the kind of immunity that its international omnipresence had bestowed upon it previously. It is difficult to assess at the present moment how far this movement is likely to go and what are the longer term implications of this kind of agitation. The significant point to remember is that many firms operating internationally are contributing substantially, directly or indirectly, to the welfare of the communities in which they operate. A study conducted by the Conference Board in the USA covered the activities of 218 US companies which have foreign operations and listed the kind of aid that the companies in question contributed to local activities. Among the forms of aid were cash grants to technical schools and universities, part-time or vacation employment for students, exchange programmes for travel, study or work overseas, emergency relief operations and grants to hospitals and clinics.

In other words not all multinationals are as 'wicked' as the recent spate of adverse publicity seems to imply.

The realisation that mounting social, economic and moral pressures are also undergoing an internationalisation process must be recognised by companies wishing to operate on a multinational scale. Indeed it is difficult to see how any company operating on an international basis can hope to survive without paying full heed to the wind of change that is sweeping world markets.

The adjective 'multinational' will be avoided in this book. It evokes too much controversy among both academics and international businessmen. There are those who distinguish between an 'international' firm and a 'multinational' firm. The former, according to a number of writers is 'bad', the latter is 'good'. A most artificial and unsatisfactory classification. Others go as far as to claim that a domestic firm, say a British company with considerable overseas interests, is neither a multinational nor an international firm—it is, according to them, purely a domestic company which happens to have foreign interests! Thus Lord Kearton, when he was the Chairman of Courtaulds, insisted that his company was not multinational in so far as three-quarters of its sales emanated from the UK facilities. 'Investment in Britain is our first priority', he said, 'and investment overseas is complementary to this'. . . . We see once again the trap of semantics. Does it really matter what title one ascribes to a firm? Is Courtaulds in any way exonerated from the rigours of social responsiveness to the needs of the communities it serves just because the stigma of 'multinationalism' has been removed from it by its former Chairman's eloquence?

At the other extreme, one also meets the notion that a company that has foreign subsidiaries—with or without manufacturing facilities is automatically classified as an international firm.

Surely what one decides to call a company with international interests is immaterial. What is important is that a firm that has embarked on an internationalisation path rapidly develops the awareness of the need to consider and meet the expectations of the various communities in which it proposes to operate. This is the most fundamental principle of a successful international marketing effort.

At this point it may be appropriate to attempt to categorise the kind of organisational patterns that exist among companies operating internationally. The reader will note that the terminology multinational firms, international firms or even transnational firms is avoided. We are talking about firms with international operations or interests; whether these are companies with many manufacturing and distribution centres abroad or firms that have just embarked on the internationalisation path is quite immaterial. The conceptual framework described should apply to most situations and it is useful for a firm's management to try to understand the kind of 'culture' that the company has developed or is likely to develop in the future. A firm that has selected, knowingly or by accident, a certain organisational style must be aware of the implications both for the short-term and the longer-term development of its international effort. As we shall see later, a style which is inherently efficient in the use of men and resources may also contain elements of weakness in terms of sensitivity and responsiveness to markets and their special needs. No pattern is perfect, nor is it intended to suggest that one kind of structure is better than another. The options to be described are purely a conceptual classification based on an empirical observation of a large number of firms operating on the international scene. The acceptance of this framework is helpful in so far as it will provide a basis for subsequent discussions pertaining to the international marketing function. It must be emphasised that no recommendations are being made here as to correct solutions, nor is it being suggested that hybrid structures do not exist.

Background Concepts

The management of any activity normally calls for the following steps:

> *Information* gathering ('*input*')
> *Objectives* setting
> *Operations*
> *Control* procedures

The control procedures in turn constitute an 'input' for the next cycle.

The process, in this very simplified form, can be described diagrammatically as in Figure 1.

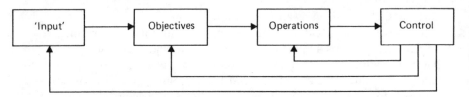

Fig. 1   The management of activities—a simple model

The concept applies not only to the management of business problems and activities, it applies to many decision areas in day-to-day life. This is how we manage the purchase of a car. This is how we select a holiday. This is how we choose a new job. Without information the choice of objectives may be ill-conceived and without objectives operations may be totally irrelevant. Finally, if we do not control what we have done, we cannot judge whether or not we have been successful in what we have set out to achieve. Furthermore, without control procedures we may repeat the same mistakes when we come to plan the next cycle.

In a firm we have an intricate conglomeration of decision levels. Whilst each level has a different task to perform it is important that everybody in the organisation functions in an integrated way. Once again to simplify the description we can divide the firm into three distinct levels:*

> Strategic
> Management
> Operational

Briefly, the *strategic* level has to identify the expectations of the stakeholders (e.g. shareholders, employees, the community, the bankers, the

---

*Adapted from: H. Igor Ansoff, *Corporate Strategy*, McGraw-Hill Book Company and Robert Anthony, 'Planning and Control Systems—A framework for Analysis', *Studies in Management Control*, Harvard University.

unions, the government etc.); determine the firm's objectives (the attainment of which will meet the stakeholders' expectations); decide on the type of resources that will be required if the firm is to attain its objectives and select the most appropriate corporate strategy for the firm to adopt.

The *management* level has the task of translating corporate objectives into functional and/or unit objectives and ensuring that resources placed at its disposal are used effectively in the pursuit of those activities which will make the achievement of the firm's goals possible.

The *operational* level is responsible for the effective performance of those tasks which underly the achievement of unit/functional objectives. The attainment of the latter will of course be the instrument through which the corporation as a whole can expect to achieve its overall objectives. Thus all three levels are interrelated to such an extent that failure at any level may affect adversely the firm's performance. Having an effective operational level is not enough; similarly having the brightest board of directors (assuming that in most instances the board represents the strategic level) does not guarantee success if the other levels are ineffectual.

Translating what was said about the three levels of a firm into the 'managerial model' shown earlier we can describe the firm's hierarchy as a pyramid. Functional activities transcend all levels. Thus, for example, the marketing function requires *strategic* planning as well as *management* activities, and finally the process is completed by the *operational* level undertaking the detailed tasks allotted to it such as selling, advertising, administering the warehousing procedures and so on. Each function and each level requires information, 'input', to be able to plan its activities and at the end of the day control procedures are also needed to measure the effectiveness of the performance. The 'input' and control are shown outside the pyramid They do not represent resource management activities in so far as their real role is to provide information which facilitates the managerial process or monitors performance. In other words, they constitute what is called in modern jargon *management information systems*. They are vitally important; they aid all levels of management and without them the firm can hardly survive. However, they are outside the pyramid because the pyramid represents those activities which are responsible for the attainment of results. The activities outside the pyramid are in no way responsible for results—they assist the planning process by providing information and audit the results. The only ingredient which may cause some controversy is finance especially in relation to the management of funds. This can be easily explained: the management of funds, namely the obtaining and allocation of financial resources, is essentially a strategic task and is therefore included in the duties and responsibilities of the average strategic level.

The description of the pyramid as outlined above is illustrated in Figure 2.

This briefly is a conceptual structure for a typical firm. The situation becomes more complicated where the firm is operating as a cluster of separate companies or in different parts of the world. The whole question of

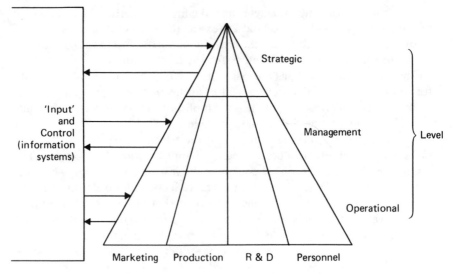

Fig. 2   The firm—a conceptual framework

centralisation and decentralisation rears its ugly head and must be grappled with in a logical and in a conceptually-sound way.

Organisational Options in International Business

Three distinct types of structure can be identified among companies operating on an international scale:

1 The *macropyramid* structure
2 The *'umbrella'* structure
3 The *interglomerate* (a convenient abbreviation of the better known term international conglomerate)

Let us explore each in turn and enumerate the characteristics of each.

1 The Macropyramid Structure

This is the type of firm that possesses a well-defined strategic focal point and conducts its affairs in a centralised fashion. The strategic level is located in a clearly-defined 'nerve-centre' and hence most of the strategic planning is undertaken at that location. The flow of information is multi-directional but nonetheless the central strategic organ is the unequivocal chief executive ensemble of the total corporation. It decides such basic questions as 'What business are we in?' or the level of returns on capital, profits and growth. The firm's foreign activities, whether they include production or marketing or both, are structured from levels below the strategic level; they look like pyramids that have had their pinnacles chopped off. In practice, the foreign activities are based on the management control and the operational levels only, regardless of the impressive titles that might have been bestowed on the managers throughout the world. Figure 3 illustrates the relationship that exists between the strategists at home and the operational outposts.

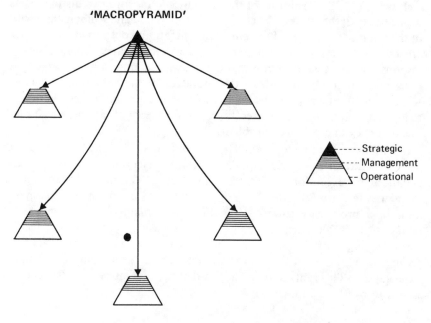

Fig. 3   The macropyramid model

The main characteristics of the macropyramid structure are:

(a) Strategic planning, as pointed out before, tends to be carried out in a centralised fashion.
(b) Local managers have to operate within rigid standards of performance.
(c) The firm on the whole tends to be results oriented. It is not uncommon to meet a 'Theory X' style of management.
(d) The marketing effort is directed frequently towards a maximum standardisation of its mix.
(e) In human/social terms the firm can be inflexible; it often lacks the empathy and sensitivity for dealing effectively with local/national pressures.
(f) Other functions such as production and R & D etc. also tend to be centrally planned, although as one would expect, locally executed. In this connection one normally encounters strong control procedures from the centre and obvious instances of interference in policy matters.

The 'bosses' are in the centre and there is little doubt in most cases as to who are the decision makers of the parent organisation. The situation can be somewhat confused where a senior person from an operational unit abroad is invited to join the main board, namely the strategic level of the macropyramid. In organisational terms such an appointment may tend to confuse the logic of the structure in so far as it gives the inevitable semblance of a hierarchical elevation to the unit managed by the promoted man. In fact what happens in such situations is the splitting of the appointee's role into two distinct parts: membership of the strategic level of the macropyramid and senior membership of the management level of an important operational outpost abroad. These are two distinct jobs and in organisational terms carry separate sets of responsibilities. It is important that the manager in question possesses a job description that clearly reflects the subtleties of the situation. Otherwise what normally stems from the firm's desire to show a sign of recognition to a loyal servant can inadvertently carry the seed of an organisational inconsistency and eventual problems.

In summary, the macropyramid approach implies that the firm has opted for a structure in which strategic decisions are vested in an identified centre and the actual execution is delegated to local levels. This inevitably stimulates a tendency towards centralised planning and control and this in turn manifests itself in a propensity towards standardisation mainly in relation to the marketing task. The macropyramid approach is usually efficient and effective for managing international operations. On the other hand it often lacks the feeling and responsiveness to national, albeit geographically distant, expectations. This is of course an aspect that the wise internationalist cannot afford to overlook in our changing world.

2 The 'Umbrella' Structure

This organisational pattern is based on the recognition that markets and countries differ and as such must be treated with local independence and hierarchical freedom. The structure differs from the previous one in the amount of strategic freedom which is permitted to foreign activities. Whilst a definite nerve centre still exists—invariably at the location of the firm's major unit and probably likely also to be the same spot where the firm first entered its period of dynamic growth—such a nerve centre has voluntarily curbed its strategic jurisdiction over the outposts. The centre exercises two major roles: the formulation of broad objectives for the total corporation and the provision of assistance, advice and support to the various branches of the organisation. These are expressed in terms of financial support and professional expertise. The centre develops a series of service departments of high professional quality. These departments are available to all the units wherever they may be located round the world. Hence the term the 'umbrella' structure.

Figure 4 illustrates the approach in a diagrammatic form and shows the relationship between the centre and the branches.

'UMBRELLA'

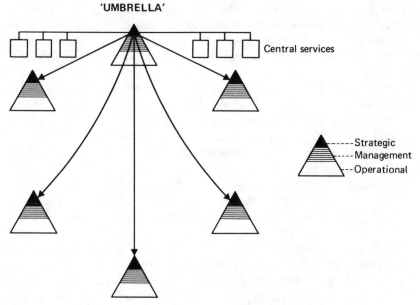

Central services

Strategic
Management
Operational

Fig. 4   The umbrella model

The rationale behind the 'umbrella' structure is the notion that each member of the international family is capable of looking after its own destiny within a set of performance goals broadly consistent with the corporate objectives. At the same time it would be grossly uneconomic for each unit to develop the whole armoury of skills and expertise which the management of a modern firm calls for. The parent organisation normally undertakes this task at the centre on behalf of the total corporation. Thus it would develop a series of service departments of the highest professional quality and these would be available to every company in the group. In fact it represents a kind of *synergy* in staff activities. Typical departments are management development, legal and patents, technology and research, transport and distribution, marketing services, etc. If each member of the 'family' attempted to set up the whole gamut of services as listed above, the aggregate cost to the total firm would be out of all proportion with the actual needs. Furthermore it is unlikely that each individual unit could achieve the professional quality that a central department with broader experience and scope should be able to attain.

The main characteristics of the 'umbrella' structure can be summarised thus:

(a) The centre normally lays down a broad set of objectives in terms of growth, profits and return on investment. Local management enjoys a considerable amount of freedom in the way they interpret corporate objectives and in adapting them to local needs and conditions. This can sometimes go as far as changing the nature of the business.

(b) Each unit in the group tends to become fairly autonomous and reasonably self-supporting. In spite of the availability of central services, local bosses often press for the development of local functional services. This can lead to conflict between central services and the managers of the outposts.

(c) Marketing, R & D, personnel policies and technology tend to become diffused. In product development one discerns a trend towards differentiation. The same applies to other ingredients of the marketing effort, for example pricing policy, promotional strategies, etc.

(d) Communication problems between the centre and the outposts are rife.

(e) The line of demarcation between loyalty to the corporation and loyalty to the local subsidiary becomes blurred.

(f) The firm is able, on the other hand, to react to parochial susceptibilities with greater alacrity and sensitivity than the macropyramid type firm.

In hierarchical terms each member of the 'umbrella' type group possesses its own strategic level as well as the two lower levels of management. It is evident that the strategic level of a subsidiary unit is ultimately subject to the overriding authority of the strategic level of the central board, but the latter functions more as a benevolent mentor or a 'watch dog' representing the stakeholders interests. Having the chief executive of a subsidiary unit on the main board does not carry the same dichotomy as in the case of the macropyramid model. Here it simply means a sign of recognition that the unit and its boss have performed so well that they deserve to be represented on the top strategic planning organ of the firm. In practice the manager who has been thus honoured sits on the main board as the representative (either expressly or by implication) of the many operating units sheltering under the corporate 'umbrella'. It is simply felt that either through outstanding performance or the relative size of the operation under his control such a manager deserves to be invited to join the 'top table'.

Many international firms have opted for the 'umbrella' structure because it is flexible, it offers scope for autonomy and hence managerial motivation. It also lends itself to rapid expansion and growth. On the other hand it is not always the most cost-effective structure. Individual units are normally limited to operations within certain regional markets and they would tend to become parochially orientated within such geographical constraints. This in turn generates communication problems among units and between each unit and the centre.

An area in which the 'umbrella' structure tolerates over-fragmentation is the marketing function. This is almost inevitable in an organisation based on a market structure, viz. where each unit has to satisfy the needs of a specific market or cluster of markets. Thus a large firm that has opted for an 'umbrella' approach has discovered that its aggregate range of wireless sets throughout the world exceeds 500 models! This could not happen in a firm based on a macropyramid structure. On the other hand, the latter is less likely to achieve the same level of sales as the former. But in terms of margins and returns on capital employed the macropyramid firm is likely to be more effective.

The fragmentation of the marketing effort associated with the 'umbrella' type firm is often characterised by distribution problems emanating from one unit 'dumping' illicitly its surpluses in another sister-unit's territory. An American chemical manufacturer with a number of international off-shoots located in the main industrial centres of the free world, and operating on the 'umbrella' model, discovered that large surpluses were being shipped from the US plant, via nominee brokers, into the European market in spite of the fact that the firm owned large manufacturing plants specifically established to cater for that market. Many months elapsed before the European management discovered that their own price structure had been undermined by their sister-company! This is of course an extreme example, but it illustrates the kind of weakness which excessive freedom within the 'umbrella' structure can generate. This is the type of situation which calls for a fundamental reappraisal of the organisation and the relationships among operating units. The point to remember, however, is that once a firm has opted, either knowingly or by accident, for the 'umbrella' approach, it is not easy to introduce the far-reaching changes which the introduction of a macropyramid structure would entail. In practical terms it would mean that the boss of an operating unit who had hitherto represented the strategic level of such a unit would cease to hold strategic authority; he would be down-graded to the management level in spite of the fact that his title might have remained the same. This could have a serious effect on his personal motivation.

Another important weakness of the 'umbrella' structure is the fact that operating companies often tend to lose confidence in the effectiveness of the central services set up by the centre. 'There is no prophet in his own land', often applies to such situations. The reasons probably are: (a) having a captive 'clientèle', these departments can easily become complacent and allow the quality of their service to deteriorate; (b) these services are often organised without adequate internal marketing 'input' in the sense that they are set up without having evaluated fully and systematically the real needs of the firm and its affiliated companies. The trouble is that central services do not have to fight for their existence in competition with other external professional firms. They do not have to seek clients or sell their services in a competitive environment. Undoubtedly fighting for one's existence is a salutary way in which to attain quality.

In summary, the 'umbrella' structure envisages a measure of de-centralisation within a family of operating units based on a multi-national, multi-market or multi-product division. Each unit is relatively free to determine its strategic direction. The main constraint on this freedom is 'big brother' who controls the purse strings and the appointment of key personnel. 'Big brother' also provides the organisation with a number of professional services which could not be mounted economically by each unit on its own. On the positive side it must be emphasised that an 'umbrella' structure is better equipped for dealing with local needs and sensitivities. The very nature of the structure means that the responsiveness to local idiosyncrasies is brought nearer to the market place. It may not be the most efficient way for operating internationally, but in the age of mounting awareness of social responsibility it has its attractions.

3 The Interglomerate

The word *conglomerate* has lost its lustre; *international conglomerate* is cumbersome; *family of companies* smacks of self-righteousness. Let us call this type of structure *interglomerate*—this term is fairly descriptive and is less of a mouthful.

Here we have a complex international operation embracing multi-national, multi-market, multi-product, multi-technology activities. The diversity is such that the only meaningful scope for synergy hinges around the financial dimension of the firm. All that the centre expects from the various units (whether they are in turn organised as macropyramids or as 'umbrellas') is profits and cash flow. The boss at the centre—and the location of the centre depends once again on financial considerations—wants each member of the organisation to generate a given amount of profits and cash flow in accordance with pre-set criteria.

If the chief executive of a Peruvian subsidiary feels that there is more profit in fish paste than in explosives, nobody will stand in his way provided the change in the nature of the business generates the expected results in terms of profits and/or cash. The interglomerate encourages entrepreneurship of this kind. The strategic level at the centre manages money; the strategic levels of the various international subsidiaries manage businesses which in turn will produce money.

International Telegraph and Telephone Corporation (ITT) is an interglomerate. The activities of the firm are diverse; any attempt at justifying the nexus between electronics and car hire in terms of a synergistic common denominator other than a financial one is a futile exercise. Each company in the group is a business in its own right and inevitably it has its own strategic level responsible for defining its objectives and determining the way these objectives should be achieved. The strategic level of the parent board will presumably be quite satisfied if each unit belonging to the group generates the profits and cash which the overall objectives of the group demand.

Figure 5 shows how such a firm is structured. The strategic level of the centre is a pinnacle without a body: it represents a small unit of thinkers/planners/deciders/controllers. In practice, they do not manage anything; they direct and control a large number of semi-independent pyramids each with its own strategic level. A few of these pyramids will be structured on the macropyramid approach; others may be structured as 'umbrella' organisations. Both these organisational patterns can live quite comfortably together within the framework of the interglomerate. It must be remembered that the interglomerate, by its very nature, is a federation of enterprises with a common parent who is mainly concerned with maximum return on the total investment of the whole group of companies.

The interglomerate structure is normally characterised by:

(a) Obsession with financial controls; money is the main concern of the organisation and it is not surprising that funds are being manipulated on a trans-national basis with the view of capitalising on exchange disparities.

(b) A very small central staff—mostly advisers to the top strategic level and troubleshooters.

(c) Strong communication between the centre and the subsidiaries. Very poor communication between the various units *inter se*.

(d) Social/moral issues pertaining to demography/geography are only tackled when omission to do so may affect profitability.

(e) Very few interglomerates develop a range of central services other than those required for effective planning and control purposes.

(f) The total organisation is controlled by a handful of people operating from a conveniently located centre. Convenience in this connection relates to tax, financial or logistics considerations.

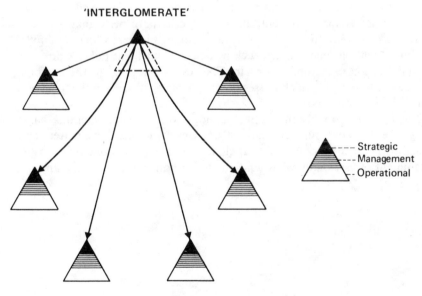

Fig. 5   The interglomerate model

In terms of the marketing function the interglomerate normally delegates the full responsibility to its constituent parts. The senior board takes very little interest in the way the marketing function (or indeed any other function) is

28   *International Marketing*

organised. To the interglomerate board the acid test of excellence is profits and/or return on capital employed. If the Chief Executive of Avis can achieve such results without a marketing function—well and good. The parent board is neither geared to nor interested in usurping the duties of the junior board. In other words the interglomerate allows each of its units to organise the marketing function in accordance with each unit's needs, style and objectives. If the unit is large enough to sustain its own macropyramid structure it will probably develop a strong centralised marketing organisation for planning, directing and controlling the international marketing effort of the unit. If, on the other hand, the unit has opted for an 'umbrella' approach it will delegate the main marketing activity to its own sub-units but will develop a central marketing services department to act as a co-ordinator, communication organ, adviser and educator for all the sub-units. The hard core of the marketing effort will be undertaken at the outposts.

The subtleties of the three concepts outlined above are important. They will be referred to frequently in the following chapters and will form the basis for comparison and analysis. The implications of the three structures described can be perhaps better appreciated by drawing a parallel from the world of political economy and the way governments have opted to organise the management of countries. The UK is organised as a macropyramid—objectives and strategies are evolved by the Government at Whitehall; the implementation of policies takes place at regional and/or local levels but always in accordance with centrally-evolved criteria of performance.

Switzerland with its cantonal system comes closer to the 'umbrella' structure. Only in major areas such as defence and fiscal policies does the central Federal Government step in. The rest is delegated to the cantonal governments, each of which possesses its own strategic level in the form of a fairly autonomous body.

The EEC is probably the nearest analogy to our interglomerate. It is a conglomeration of a number of diverse units, each organised in a pattern best suited to its members and political climate, but they all work towards the attainment of essentially what amounts to economic and financial aims.

Chapter 3

Marketing Ecology in International Business

Every textbook and every dissertation on marketing starts with a fresh attempt at a definition. Such definitions vary from the naive to the incomprehensible. A few are laconic, others long-winded; witty aphorisms are contrasted with tedious descriptions. By the time the practically-minded reader has digested the written message as to the meaning of marketing he gives up in despair. He is no wiser than when he started; he may be highly stimulated but he is certainly no wiser.

'Marketing is the process for reducing uncertainties', declared a wise professor of marketing.

'Marketing is the creation of a standard of living', pronounced another.

'Marketing is the creation of a consumer', said yet another.

'Marketing is the process of matching segments of supply and demand', mused another highly stimulating academic.

Scores of similar pronouncements are scattered through the literature. At the other extreme, we have the definition developed by the Institute of Marketing that suggests that: *'marketing is the management process responsible for identifying, anticipating and satisfying customer requirements profitably'.*

The practitioner is bewildered. He has probably been holding various positions of importance all connected with the marketing function. He suddenly discovers a new world which seems totally unrelated to his perception of the marketing task. He picked up a book or books with the intention of improving his knowledge or skills and hopefully his performance at work. How can he hope to achieve his objective if no apparent unanimity exists as to the exact meaning of marketing, its role and its scope? Why is it so difficult to attain a single, clear, all-embracing definition of the subject?

The Special Flavour of Marketing

Over two decades have passed since the dawn of the marketing concept era and we are still fumbling and groping in an inexplicable mist of verbiage, tautology and sophism. The sad part about it all is the fact that some of the most capable, creative and innovative marketers in modern business have never heard of the marketing concept; never set eyes on Levitt's *Marketing*

Myopia; never opened a textbook on marketing and never attended a marketing course. On the other hand it is very rare to meet excellence in the production or personnel functions among managers who have not been exposed to training and development programmes. In other words marketing, whether called by that name or not, appears more susceptible to entrepreneurial talent than other functions of the firm. Without derogating from the value of training and development in the marketing area experience seems to show that flair, intuition and entrepreneurial qualities can enrich the marketing effort much more than other functions of the firm. Management development can of course help to harness these innate qualities or compensate for their absence, but the value of these intangible attributes is vital for a successful marketing career. Here probably lies the secret as to why it is so difficult to define marketing. One can define the managerial aspects of marketing; the institutions that the process calls for; the techniques and methodologies that facilitate the workings of this function. What one is unable to convey in a succinct statement is the less tangible aspect of marketing—the dynamic interrelationships between products, consumers and the environment. The ability to plan and develop these interrelationships among the entire assemblage of *marketing mix* ingredients is the essence of good marketing. The term—the marketing mix—was first propounded by Neil Borden. Since then it got chewed, mutilated, reconstituted endless times. Being the corner-stone of modern marketing the concept deserves a re-visit.

The Marketing Mix Re-visited

Marketing defies definition, so does the term the marketing mix. For the purpose of this book the term will be taken to mean *the assemblage of ingredients developed to satisfy perceived needs of an identified market or target group (a segment) within a given environment (consisting of political, cultural, economic and institutional dimensions).*

Diagrammatically the concept described is shown in Figure 6. The return arrows shown on the chart indicate the feedback/control procedures—the process for measuring effectiveness. The person responsible for developing the marketing mix assemblage must find out whether the needs that he has attempted to satisfy have been correctly identified. Needs are normally dynamic by nature and might have changed since they were first identified. Alternatively they might have been wrongly understood by the marketer or totally misjudged. The feedback would also help the planner to judge whether the marketing mix selected was effective and correctly geared towards satisfying the consumer's needs. All this has to be done of course within the framework of given environments. The assemblage of 'satisfiers', if we can refer to the ingredients of the mix by that term, will probably be totally different in France than in the Fiji Islands. Variations in the political, cultural, economic and institutional dimensions are significant factors of the kind of mix that must be developed if the consumer's needs will be fully satisfied. It is right to say therefore that in an international marketing effort the environmental dimensions become very important, in fact even more so than in domestic marketing, and we shall treat them as an integral part of the marketing mix.

THE ENVIRONMENT

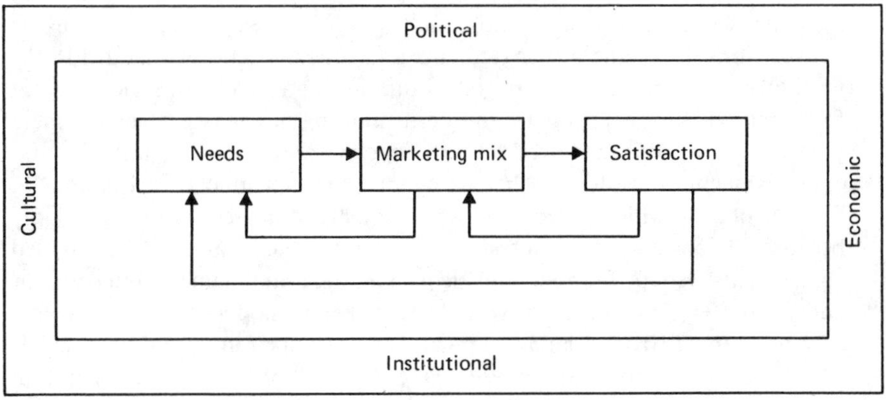

Fig. 6   The marketing mix within an environmental framework

In other words the marketing mix can be said to consist of two sets of ingredients: *external—uncontrollable elements*; *internal—controllable elements*. More specifically the concept can be summarised thus:

1 External—Uncontrollable Elements

The elements that fall under this heading can be divided into four major parts:

> Environment
> Competition
> Institutions
> Legal system

These elements are referred to as uncontrollable because with very few exceptions little can be done to alter them or change their influence. They exist and the marketer must take full cognisance of their existence. Trying to fly in the face of these external dimensions is asking for trouble.

2 Internal—Controllable Elements

In this book we shall include the following elements under this heading:

> Product
> Price
> Promotion (including advertising, sales promotion, publicity)
> Personal selling
> Distribution

For those marketers whose grass-roots belong to a different school of thought the writer wishes to offer his apology and reassurance. No real difference exists between this list of the mix ingredients and others often put forward in the literature or in practice. Packaging, branding and product service are not forgotten. However, product in modern thinking has ceased to be the mere physical form of the product. It incorporates all the utilities and embellishments and addenda that go to make up the product with a capital 'P'. The bar of soap which we buy and which satisfies our needs is a product only because it consists of a cluster of well-designed and well-assembled components—soap, wrapper, outside packaging, brand name, printed matter and so on. Very few consumers would be satisfied in modern conditions with a slice of soap cut from a large soap-cake and wrapped in an old newspaper! This broader concept of the product is reminiscent of the amusing definition of an aeroplane which is said to be 'A collection of spare parts flying in formation'. By the same token the product is a collection of utilities in a common assemblage. In his book *The Marketing Mode,** Theodore Levitt refers to the notion of 'The augmented product concept'. He gives the example of the airline that provides a service from point X to point Y. On the face of it the product that the airline offers is no different from the one offered by a competitive airline. Nonetheless in the eyes of many passengers one airline is alleged to be a better one than the other. Many hidden and unquantifiable attributes can be attached to a product that makes it a better and a more satisfying one in the eyes of the consumer. Indeed the product can be augmented through tangible and non-tangible utilities which add to the overall attractiveness of the totality thus enhancing consumer satisfaction.

Similarly, the supporting software reservation service of the airline in question is a feature which acts as a 'product augmenting' element. Also the punctuality of the airline, the colour scheme of the cabin, the general courtesy of the cabin staff and even such a minor item as the cage-type closure of the luggage rack which allows the passengers to rid themselves of their parcels during the journey all constitute significant 'product augmentation' elements.

Computer companies have come to realise that their product consists not

* Theodore Levitt, *The Marketing Mode—Pathways to Corporate Growth*, McGraw-Hill, New York, 1969.

only of a heap of well-designed hardware but also of augmenting services such as well-structured and well-supported software competence.

Hence when the modern marketer talks about a product he automatically includes all those product augmenting elements which are required if the consumer is to attain maximum satisfaction—which is the main objective of the marketing function.

Any reader who feels that the marketing mix as described above omits other ingredients that his training and early orientation have instilled in him could, on close rationalisation, find a suitable 'home' for the seemingly neglected ingredient among those which have been listed. As many as sixteen ingredients and as few as four can be placed at the two extremities mentioned in the literature—one more eloquent proof of the unfortunate haze that surrounds the theory of marketing.

The marketing mix as stated above can now be summarised in a simple diagram:

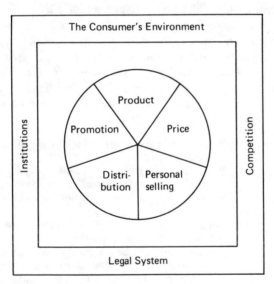

Fig. 7   The controllable and uncontrollable elements of the marketing mix

The marketing mix is a fundamental concept which is fairly well understood by most experienced marketers. It is normally appreciated that no marketing effort is complete until full cognisance is taken of the interrelationships between the internal ingredients and the external ingredients. However, in practice the process often suffers from a lack of harmony, inadequate symbiosis, between the various ingredients. To attain the perfect mix would imply that *each one of the internal ingredients* must in turn be fully congruent with *every one* of the external/environmental parameters. The task is further complicated through the fact that the internal ingredients must be in a state of equilibrium *inter se*. Achieving this kind of harmony in a dynamic environment is certainly not an easy job!

To amplify the point further let us explore an example: a domestic appliance manufacturer markets a high quality washing machine through the most exclusive retail outlets. He matches the price to the quality of the product and the image of the channels thus selected. In other words the price is high in relation to other products available in less prestigious outlets. To complete the mix he promotes the product in question through the kind of media that are read by the patrons of the exclusive stores chosen. The selling effort to the stores will have to be consistent too with the whole assemblage. Now for various reasons the manufacturer decides to add a direct selling approach viz. selling direct to the housewife through door-to-door salesmen. The whole mix has to change: the product may have to be down-traded, especially if the manufacturer wishes to maintain a foothold in the existing and more exclusive market; the price will have to be adjusted to become more attractive to the housewife; the promotion will have to change not only in relation to the media used but also to the copy of the advertising effort. So far so good, but we must not forget that all this has to be done within important environmental pressures. Thus each ingredient of the mix must be fully consistent with each one of the uncontrollable dimensions. If we take just one ingredient, the *price*, and try to match it to the external elements of the mix, we must try to identify a large number of possible pressures which will affect the final policy:

	Price
Environment	What is the purchasing power of the consumer within the selected segment?
	What are the consumer's attitudes to pricing policies, for example reaction to incentives or special discounts?
	What is the consumer's reaction to psychological pricing policy?
Competition	What are the prices of competitors for similar products?
	Do they have any special offers
Institutions	Are there any marketing institutions that may make our proposed strategy difficult? or easier? (For example in Switzerland the Migros Group of supermarkets always aims to undercut the price of well-known brands. Such an institution may have a tremendous impact on any marketing decision and pricing policy and consequently on the manufacturer's future mix.)
Legal system	How far does the law impose restrictions on the freedom to compete?
	Does retail price maintenance exist?
	Can we discuss and agree prices with our competitors?

In brief the determination of the price for a given product is subject to a thorough understanding and assessment of the external ingredients of the mix as well as a fine tuning of the price in relation to the *controllable* elements of the. mix. This is a delicate operation and calls for considerable information 'input' coupled with a flair for *marketing empathy*. One must always remember: the paramount task of the marketer is to satisfy the consumer and in that respect empathy is a vital attribute—it means in this context the ability to gauge what mix will create real satisfaction and in the final analysis this is the determinant factor as to whether the marketing effort will be successful or not.

The ability to 'mix the perfect *mix*' is fundamental to good marketing. Some people achieve perfection through intuitive judgement; others seek to attain effectiveness through systematic and analytical research and planning. The ideal is of course the judicious combination of both. Whilst methodologies and research can be acquired, unfortunately intuition and flair cannot be learnt.

Ecology in Nature

Ecology is a popular word nowadays. It is the science that deals with the interrelations between organisms and their environments. The basis of ecology lies in the notion that organisms vary with environment; in fact life and environment are inseparable parts of a greater whole. Plants, animals and men are intimately associated with the environment and live in a finely-balanced equilibrium. It is often that a man-made catastrophe originates from an unconscious interference with this ecological state of equilibrium. Examples of such man-made interferences are pollution, overgrazing, overcultivation or large-scale diversions of rivers.

In the natural environment, says the ecologist, the arrival of a new species on the scene places the environment in a turmoil. The new species must adjust itself to the physical influences that are in operation and to the biological factors already established. Under such conditions the new population may do one of the following:

1 Adjust to the total environment
2 Emigrate to another environment
3 Die

If the organisms adjust this implies that they can compete or co-operate with other species for food and shelter.

In other words nature has struck a state of harmony between men, animals, plants and their environments. Provided external interferences do not upset this balance all is well with the world.

Marketing Ecology

By now the perceptive reader may detect a parallel between the concept of ecology in nature and the concept of the marketing mix.

Marketing ecology is analogous to the way ecology operates in nature. Its basis lies in the notion that the marketing mix is intimately associated with the environment and has to exist in a finely balanced equilibrium. The wrong mix or failure to tune the mix in relation to the environment will in most cases lead to failure. The marketing ecology can be easily disturbed through a host of external interferences; failure to adjust to the new environment may cause decline in performance and possibly the death of the product. If the mix is adjusted to the changed environment the product and its supportive marketing assemblage can continue to compete in the marketplace and maintain its proper posture on the local scene.

In nature ecological catastrophes can take place through the unconscious application of unsound human practices. Similarly in marketing and especially in international marketing, total failures occur only too frequently through a failure to gauge the impact that the marketing mix assemblage may have on the environment and vice-versa.

In order to be able to develop a well-balanced mix which blends harmoniously with the ecology of an international market it is essential for the marketer to gain thorough knowledge of the environment to which he plans to direct his attention. No one person can ever hope to possess detailed knowledge of more than two or three markets. The most seasoned international operators have probably worked in as many as half a dozen markets. However, they will be the first to admit that a few years' absence from the scene is sufficient to obliterate their intimate appreciation of the forces that make the market function. This dynamism is particularly noticeable in those countries where the economic and industrial development is accelerating at a rapid rate.

A considerable amount of research is normally required in order to collate the data which is needed to be able to develop the right mix. Where a number of markets are involved it is important that such research is conducted in accordance with a systematic and well-planned pattern. Otherwise any attempt at comparing similarities or variances between the ecologies of these markets may be abortive. After all, the international marketer treats the world as one vast market with a large number of segments therein. The ability to spot similarities between markets or identify major environmental variations is a vital objective. It is normally acknowledged that a fully standardised marketing mix for the whole world is an elusive goal. At the same time one should always strive towards avoiding a situation whereby one hundred different mixes are developed for one hundred countries! The objective that the international marketer must aim to achieve is the classification of world markets into clusters of countries which are characterised by similar marketing ecologies. Having identified such clusters of markets the marketing mix can be relatively standard for each such cluster.

Thus as a first step towards the task of getting fully familiarised with world markets the international marketer must undertake a systematic analysis of these markets in accordance with a standard procedure. The tool available to him is the *marketing profile analysis*. This is a procedure for collating comprehensive information about the forces which operate in each market. The aim is to assess the interaction between each one of the controllable and each external ingredient in turn. In other words it is a tool for obtaining a full understanding of the marketing ecology that prevails at any given market.

Figure 8 shows the matrix which is recommended for such a study. Of course each rubic will be supported by relevant information and/or figures which should be attached to the profile analysis as supportive schedules.

The process of filling each rubric of the matrix is a demanding job. However, when the task is completed one possesses a most valuable instrument of planning both for international marketing strategies and for specific markets. The interrelationships between marketing instruments and the environment and its pressures become fully understood. It is only when such information is available that a truly international marketing effort can commence.

The important point to remember is that marketing ecology, like ecology in nature, is dynamic and can change in a mysterious and unpredictable manner. With hindsight the change that has occurred can be explained in logical terms and predictability ascribed to it. However, the real art is to spot such imminent changes before they actually occur. This is once more the entrepreneurial angle upon which marketing gains its special flavour expressed earlier. A recent development in the American market illustrates the point:

Example 1. Reports from the USA indicate that the sale of bicycles has soared suddenly to a peak of seven and a half million bicycles per annum. Most bicycle manufacturers in the world know only too well that the bicycle as a product has reached the decline stage of the product life cycle especially in high-standard-of-living countries like the USA. Any marketer attempting to penetrate the American market would approach it with very modest objectives and equally modest resources. Suddenly the marketing ecology has changed. Why? A number of factors have contributed to this upsurge. First, the choking traffic of big cities has created some disenchantment with the automobile as an instrument of comfort and convenience—this was of course predictable. Secondly, the ease with which the average citizen can acquire a car has reduced its attraction as a status symbol. This would affect the sale of cars in favour of any other instrument of transportation which is convenient and cheap. This again was predictable. What was not predictable was a sagacious statement made by an eminent doctor who had suggested that the bike was the best weapon against heart attacks! Since physical fitness has become the fad of American society the bicycle as a product has 'cheated old age' and returned to the market with renewed vigour. The new marketing ecology for bicycles may be short lived. It may prove to be a passing fad like the hula hoop. However, the real reason for the resuscitation of the bicycle is a combination of environmental reasons with a propensity toward hypochondria which characterises some nations but not others. The marketer who was smart

MARKETING PROFILE ANALYSIS

Country: ABC Product:	Product	Price	Distribution	Promotion	Selling
Environment *including:* The Consumer Cultural aspects Economic Development Industrial Development Political climate Others					
Competition					
Legal system					
Institutions					
Other factors					
General remarks					

Fig. 8 Marketing profile analysis

enough to anticipate this dimension and its impact on consumer behaviour would deserve the reward resulting from this predictive prowess.

At the same time it would be wrong to assume that what has happened in the USA will happen in other markets. Bicycles still sell in many countries as a means of transportation. In the USA a totally new marketing ecology has developed: the bicycle is bought for quasi-medical reasons. It is in practical terms a new market for an old product and as such it presents a new planning opportunity. The alert marketer should endeavour to spot all those environments that are characterised by similar forces to those applicable to the USA—similar marketing opportunities may be found there. The important point to remember is that the marketing ecology of one market encapsulates a host of environmental factors and not just the level of national hypochondria prevailing in that market. So many marketers have burnt their fingers in the past by assuming that what is right for the USA is *ipso facto* right for other economically or culturally similar markets.

Example 2. A manufacturer of plastic products in the UK got into the habit of making a yearly pilgrimage to the USA. His philosophy was that any product which gained consumer acceptance in America was bound to succeed in Europe. He treated the USA as his source of product ideas and inspiration. Whenever he detected a successful new product on the market he traced the firm that had developed it and sought to obtain a licence to manufacture and sell the product in question in the UK. Success in the USA, he felt, was a guaranteed formula for success in the UK. It worked extremely well on a number of occasions but a few major failures followed in quick succession. The products were based on a marketing ecology which favoured disposability—at that point the UK had not yet accepted the concept on a large scale. The price of the product limited its use in the UK to the AB segment—the comparable segment in the USA was much more broadly based. The two ecologies were different although superficially one could logically expect similar levels of consumption.

Example 3. A detergent manufacturer in Sweden decided to place an advertisement in the national press comparing the quality of his detergent to a competitive product. Instead of the traditional message that suggests that 'Brand X of ours washes whiter than Brand Y of another manufacturer', the advertisement claimed that 'Our brand X generates less pollution in the national waters than the competitive product Y'. Whilst the UK consumer is only vaguely interested in pollution problems, the Swedish counterpart is very interested and very concerned with the effect of pollution on the quality of life. Hence the message that links the product with the basic expectations of the consumer. In the UK we are still being exposed to the 'whiter than white' style advertising. No doubt in time we shall encounter the non-pollution type message as well but at the present moment the UK marketing ecology is not yet ready for such a communication message; such an effort would be wasted.

Example 4. A well-known manufacturer of sewing machines discovered that in different environments his product satisfied totally different consumer needs: in a few markets the sewing machine served to satisfy the need to enjoy a hobby; in other markets the machine helped to satisfy physiological needs, namely to clothe oneself and one's family; yet in other markets the sewing machine represented a family heirloom—a status symbol.

It needs no imagination to see that a standardised marketing mix throughout the world could not possibly be effective. The housewife in Nigeria is unlikely to be impressed by a promotional effort that suggests to her that she ought to invest in a sewing machine because it is an enjoyable leisure device. By the same token the American housewife will probably shy off the sewing machine if the message seeks to persuade her that the machine would satisfy her need to clothe the family. The marketing ecologies are totally different and hence the marketing mix must be differentiated if the manufacturer wishes to satisfy both housewives.

Like the alchemist the international marketer has to mix his ingredients with skill and creativity. Ideally he would like to develop one single, standardised, marketing mix for all his markets. This is seldom possible because international realities and the diversity of marketing ecologies make it extremely difficult. Nonetheless every international marketer must at least investigate how far a standardised marketing effort could achieve desired results. Life would be very pleasant if we could sit in London or New York and plan a mix which would operate successfully in all countries. Examples of successful standardisations do exist in the annals of marketing history. Standardisation is attractive because it is more economic—it uses resources in a more cost effective way. On the other hand, standardisation inevitably means that a certain rigidity is allowed to develop in the firm's approach to different marketing ecologies and that may mean a diminution in the total market for the firm's product. Thus standardisation entails reduction in potential volume coupled with increased cost-effectiveness; differentiation means enlarged consumption and sales volume coupled with increased costs and possibly some waste.

In subsequent chapters we shall explore the effect of standardisation policies on each of the ingredients of the mix and consider the extent to which such a policy can be successfully adopted in international marketing. Suffice it to stress at this point that the degree of standardisation depends on the similarity of the marketing ecologies of the various target markets. Where the ecologies are drastically different non-standardisation is inevitable. Where the ecologies bear similar characteristics standardisation policies are worth considering. Between these two extremes a large number of options exists— the identification of these options and the selection of marketing strategies for attaining maximum consumer satisfaction in each of the target markets/countries, whilst achieving at the same time the firm's objectives in a cost-effective way, is the real art of modern marketing management especially in an international context.

Summary

Many attempts have been made to define marketing. Unfortunately no single definition has so far managed to convey the full import of the marketing concept to a modern enterprise.

The essence of the marketing process rests in the identification of market *needs* and the development of a *marketing mix* capable of satisfying the consumers in a given market. The marketing mix is a finely balanced interrelationship between a cluster of controllable ingredients (product, price, promotion, distribution and selling) within an uncontrollable environment consisting of a number of dimensions (the environment itself, competition, institutions and legal system).

In international markets one has to perceive the fine differences that characterise individual markets before one can determine whether one mix will satisfy all markets (*standardisation* policy) or whether adjustments have to be made in the mix so as to match it to local needs and nuances (*non-standardisation* or *differentiation*). Before such a decision can be taken the marketer must collect comprehensive data about his markets. The tool available to him is the marketing profile analysis. It is a method for understanding and recording the way the marketing ecology of each market operates—such information is fundamental to a successful international marketing effort.

Chapter 4

Market Segmentation on a Global Scale

The Meaning of Market Segmentation

The concept of market segmentation has triggered the imagination of many marketers during the last decade. It is a strategy which enables the firm to maximise the results of a given marketing effort by exploiting clearly identified strengths in relation to a submarket which is either inadequately satisfied by other manufacturers or where the firm is particularly well placed to do an effective job.

Every marketer recognises that it is not possible to satisfy the specific needs and requirements of every consumer. It is necessary to deal with groups of consumers or clusters of individuals who manifest similarities in consumption habits, social behaviour, economic characteristics or in some other distinguishable criterion. The extreme logical choices for the marketer are either to focus his attention on a wisely selected subgroup or submarket *or* to aim to differentiate the marketing programme so as to satisfy the largest number of heterogeneous members of the total market. The former option is economical and if well planned highly effective; the latter can be costly but in terms of sale volume probably much more substantial. At the same time one must not forget that concentration on specific submarkets can be fraught with vulnerability; differentiation, on the other hand, whilst more costly as an approach, avoids the risk of 'placing all one's eggs in one basket'. It is not possible to determine which is the more appropriate policy for a specific situation without knowing all the pertinent facts surrounding the firm's circumstances and the characteristics of the marketplace in question. However, one of the basic decisions that a company must take in its marketing planning activity is whether it proposes to adopt a *market segmentation* policy or a *market aggregation* approach. A decision taken in this connection can have a significant impact on the long-term success of the firm's marketing effort and must not be taken lightly.

Market segmentation can be defined as the strategy whereby the firm partitions the market into *submarkets (segments)* likely to manifest similar responses to marketing inputs; the aim is to maximise the penetration of such segments rather than spread the effort thinly over the total market.

Market aggregation is where the firm treats the total market as one undifferentiated mass and whilst acknowledging that many social, cultural

and economic differences exist it chooses to ignore such differences and standardise the marketing effort.

It is the objective of the first part of this chapter to discuss market segmentation in general terms. The second part of this chapter will explore how this concept can be usefully applied to international marketing activities.

Alternative Bases for Segmenting Markets

Few areas of planning have evoked as much scope for creative thinking as the exploration of methods of market segmentation. The marketer who is able to identify a novel way for segmenting markets for his product or service may often escape the rigours of pernicious competition. Indeed segmentation can be an extremely effective way of rejuvenating declining products or giving them a new lease of life. Furthermore, it may enable a relatively small firm to hold its own in an industry in which it has to compete against giant firms.

There are many conventional ways for segmenting markets. The aim here is to concentrate on those bases of segmentation which have international relevance and applicability. To enumerate a few important ones:

1 Socioeconomic and Demographic Variables

Age, sex, family size, income, occupation, education, family life cycle; race, religion; social class, etc.

In the UK the IPA system for segmenting markets has endeavoured to encapsulate a number of socioeconomic parameters into one package. Thus when we talk about segments expressed on a scale of six grades: A, B, C1, C2, D and E we know that members of each segment possess certain income, occupation and social status characteristics. Although the system comes under severe criticism from time to time owing to its lack of dynamism and failure to recognise important social changes in the marketplace it has fulfilled a vital role in the marketing world of the UK. It enables the average marketer to divide the market into categories which are well understood and well monitored. Thus he can easily establish not only who consumes what but also who reads a specific magazine, who is the audience for a certain TV programme—and all this in accordance with a classification which is standard amongst all marketers and their supportive services. With all the weaknesses of the system it is reliable, well understood and universally applied in those situations where a socioeconomic stratification of the British market is needed.

The international marketer is less fortunate—he does not have access to a similar system on a global scale. He may find various types of segmentation systems in a number of countries but unfortunately they seldom lend themselves to comparability analysis. Furthermore in many countries no formal segmentation system exists. That means that the only way the market can be segmented in such situations would be for the marketer to develop his own breakdown of each market, measure the size of each segment and analyse the opportunities—this is no mean task when a large number of countries is involved.

To take an example: a car manufacturer (France based) has identified that his main product, Model X, is popular among consumers who satisfy the following description: age group 35–49; family size—2/3 children; occupation—professional, executive and business; income—at least 15000 francs per month; social class—middle/lower-upper. Research has indicated that 68 per cent of the buyers over a period have fallen into the segment described. This is very useful in so far as the company now knows which socioeconomic group it should try to satisfy and in which direction its marketing strategy should be concentrated. The fact 32 per cent of the buyers do not fall into the same segment is not very important. It is the 'greatest happiness of the greatest number' that should matter; this is the underlying principle of the segmentation approach. The company will now advertise its product in media which are read by the target group described; the price will be geared to this segment's expectations; the distribution system will be selected in accordance with the buying habits and social behaviour of the submarket thus identified. However, so far all this has been done in relation to one domestic market. Can the firm's marketing personnel extrapolate this micro-approach to world markets? Ideally the answer must be yes; but this must depend on the availability of data about each market in which the firm wants to sell its car. If one is able to identify a socioeconomic grouping in each country, which is identical in most respects to the one that has been selected in France, life could be relatively easy—a standardised approach would be applied all round. If, on the other hand, it transpires that the variables change too drastically to make a homogeneous grouping possible one must resort to a differentiation strategy. This is one of the major decision areas of international marketing and no effort should be spared in ensuring that the correct 'input' is assembled. Decisions taken with inadequate information may prove costly and in certain circumstances a source of serious problems.

Similarly the Volkswagen Beetle during its heyday used to satisfy two distinct segments: in some countries it was the main family car bought by middle class, reasonably high-earning, medium size families. In other countries it served as the second family car bought for the wife's use. These represented two different segments and as such called for different marketing approaches. It would have been ideal for VW if they could have identified a standard segment throughout the world. In their case it was not possible. In certain situations this is possible and it is the job of the marketer to spot these rare opportunities.

2 Cultural Groupings

This method for segmenting markets is particularly important in international marketing. Cultural influences are to a great extent determinant of the way the consumer behaves and the kind of consumption pattern which he develops. Cultural factors determine the kind of food that people eat, the type of homes they aspire to have, the style of design they favour and so on. Fashion is thus linked to culture and so are general attitudes.

Cultural attitudes, for instance, will determine whether a sewing machine in the household is a status symbol, a 'do-it-yourself' type tool or a 'necessity'. Similarly, in some countries the role of the mother in the home is such that she represents the ultimate authority when important issues are involved such as the purchase of expensive items. Another example is the cultural difference in relation to the treatment of children.

Grouping markets in accordance with their cultural differentiation can be very helpful to the international marketer. It may in certain circumstances be more useful than dividing markets in accordance with political or geographical borders. To take a simple example: in cultural terms the French part of Switzerland has probably more in common with France than with the German speaking part of Switzerland. In terms of market segmentation one is fully justified to cluster the French speaking part of Switzerland with France. This may be totally unworkable on political grounds or in monetary/fiscal terms but it is certainly logical on a cultural basis. Most international marketers accept political borders much too readily in their marketing planning; in fact there are many situations where such borders are quite meaningless in terms of marketing logic and potential synergy. The fact that a market is shown on a political map as a separate entity does not automatically make it into a separate marketing entity. Lichtenstein is a political unit of reasonable independence, nonetheless to separate it from the marketing scene of Switzerland could hardly be justified. The same would apply to Monaco and France. This point gains significant proportions where one deals with large blocs of markets which from a distance look homogeneous but in cultural terms are extremely varied. One often tends to bulk all the Latin American countries as one geographic submarket because a glance at the map indicates that they all belong to the same subcontinent. A partitioning on a cultural basis may yield a different segmentation decision by paying attention to the Spanish and Portuguese backgrounds of countries like the Argentine and Brazil. Similarly the Soviet Bloc seems a logical geographic/political segment for the international marketer. In cultural terms Czechoslovakia probably has more in common with Austria than with Bulgaria. Many firms opt for the political segmentation approach and probably not always for a rational reason. The fact that marketing in the Soviet Bloc calls for a different kind of negotiating skill than in free economies is not always a good reason for suggesting that the man responsible for selling to Bulgaria or Rumania should *ipso facto* be responsible for selling in East Germany or in Czechoslovakia.

3 Geographic Variables

Most marketers recognise geographic variations within their market. On the domestic marketing scene one encounters firms who distinguish in their marketing strategy between city customers and rural customers. Other firms may distinguish between various parts of the country and choose to devote more time and effort to those customers who happen to be located within easy access to the firm's main office and installations. In fact firms that organise their selling activity on a geographic basis have tacitly segmented the market by this variable.

It is easy to see that in international marketing the segmentation concept is similar except that it assumes a very much larger dimension. A firm that has decided to concentrate its marketing effort in Europe alone has in fact selected to satisfy one large segment in the overall context of the global scene. The world, in other words, can be partitioned into conveniently divisible segments provided one can identify similarities among the various submarkets. These similarities may be cultural or linguistic or expressed in standard of living terms. By taking this approach one actually endeavours to identify segments based on more than one dimension. Like the IPA system in the UK such segments can be based on the crossing of a number of parameters. The concept that markets can be segmented by a geographic, or any other variable, in conjunction with some other dimension can be illustrated very simply in a diagrammatic form—Figure 9.

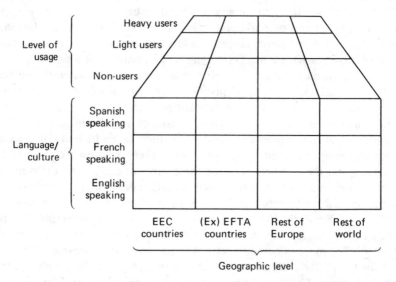

Fig. 9   Segmentation of world markets by geography, language, culture and usage rate

In this illustration, which is highly simplified, world markets are segmented by geography, by language (and culture) and by usage rate. Altogether in this illustration there are 4 × 3 × 3 = 36 segments. Each segment represents a possible opportunity area and has to be appraised and measured with the view of assessing whether it offers a worthwhile submarket area for commercial exploitation. Other parameters can be chosen or added thus increasing the number of permutations. Where the number of dimensions exceeds three it is not possible to illustrate the various combinations in a graphical form; it is still possible, however, to list them in a non-pictorial way. By using this approach to segmentation it is possible not only to identify a profitable geographic segment but also combine it with another dimension of significance to the firm's marketing strategy. One may finish in this illustration with a certain part of the world which is specifically, say, *French speaking* and where the population tend to be *high users* of the firm's product. This may represent a small portion of the world but in commercial terms may mean the best use of the company's resources and strengths as identified by the planning process.

4 Segmentation by Behavioural Patterns

Under this heading a large number of variables can be considered as suitable bases for segmenting markets. It must be emphasised that no attempt is being made here to list all the available alternatives; the aim is purely to list a number of useful ways in which markets and consumers can be segmented.

(a) USAGE RATE

Heavy users of any product class, whether it is a consumer type product or an industrial product, represent a significant segment. The Pareto law normally applies to most cases, namely 15–20 per cent of all buyers ordinarily are expected to consume over half of the total purchases. The light users consume relatively little. The non-users may appear a useless segment but in practice they may prove a very profitable segment to a firm that manages to identify the real reason as to why the non-user is avoiding the product in question. A non-user of Coca-Cola type drink may shun the product because he feels that the calory content is too high. Such a person will become a user as soon as a Cola appears on the market which is sugar-free and hence non-fattening. In other words if the information indicates that this is the cause for non-use of Colas the choice of the 'slimming' segment may prove a highly profitable one. A few companies in the UK have launched a whole series of dietetic foods such as sugar-free biscuits and chocolate—this is an interesting way to segment the market especially for companies that wish to escape from the rigours of competition which prevail in the branded biscuit and chocolate business.

Figure 10 illustrates the relative importance of the *non-user, light user* and *heavy user* segments in the US in relation to a number of product categories purchased by American households. The details show the significance of the heavy user segment. These details only relate to consumption pattern in the USA. Similar analysis in other markets may show important differences especially in relation to the non user group. Such data must be carefully studied and understood because they may yield useful ideas as to the marketing strategy that the firm should adopt in its international operations.

The marketing profile analysis can provide a lot of the information that the marketer will require in this connection. If the marketing manager of a wallpaper manufacturing firm discovers that 95 per cent of the consumers in Turkey do not use wallpaper he must try to understand the underlying reasons for such a high non-user pattern before he decides to abandon Turkey as a bad job. The reasons may be such that a good marketing effort could overcome them to the supplier's great benefit. If, on the other hand, the main reason is the lack of purchasing power coupled with the disastrous housing shortage, no marketing dexterity will overcome such a constraint.

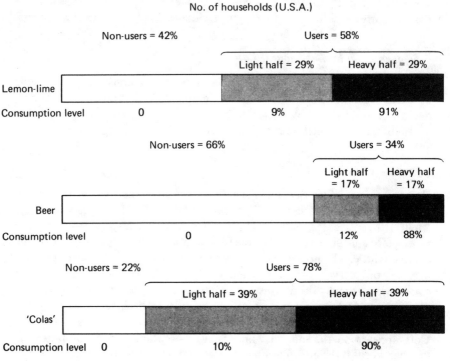

Fig. 10   Usage pattern of a few products in the USA
(Adapted from Dik Warren Twedt, 'How Important to Marketing Strategy
is the Heavy User?' *Journal of Marketing*, XXVII, January 1964, p. 72)

In the case of industrial products data about past purchases are a useful indication of the customers' buying habits and predisposition to buy in the future. The usage rate is an important basis upon which to segment one's marketing programme. In industrial marketing, a firm's dependence on a small number of customers can be even more critical than in the case of consumer products, in so far as the market is usually narrower, in the sense that a far smaller number of customers exist in the marketplace. It is therefore possible for a firm to list its customers in a 'usage' ranking as illustrated in the following table:

Group	Annual consumption in units	Number of Customers	% of Total Customers	% of total no. units sold
Heavy Users—A	exceeding 2000	8	5	38
Medium Users—B	1000–1999	22	13	28
Light Users—C	100–999	102	60	30
Occasional Users—D	Under 100	38	22	4
		170	100	100

Fig. 11   Segmentation by usage ranking

In practice each group shown on the list is a segment based on usage rate. The firm can then analyse each market separately and decide to direct its product to the heavy users in the ten largest markets. It is a risky strategy but if handled with care may bring forth quick results and probably high cost-effectiveness.

(b) CONSUMERS' MOTIVE

A market can be segmented by the motives that propel the customers to the buying act. A host of motives operate in a person's buying decision process; these motives differ between one buyer and another, between one nation and another and between one culture and another. It is impossible to extrapolate motives from one market to another without an in-depth study.

Motives are extremely important in understanding the marketing ecology of different markets and hence in determining the segments available for the most profitable exploitation. We saw earlier that sewing machines are purchased in different parts of the world for either satisfaction of physiological needs as a motive, or as a hobby satisfaction motive, or as a status symbol—the latter being a purely emotive reason.

In a study of the watch market the researcher* was able to divide the market quantitatively on the basis of the following motivational options:

Approximately 23 per cent of the buyers bought for lowest price,
Another 46 per cent bought for durability and general product quality,
And 31 per cent bought watches as a symbol of some important occasion.

With such data a watch company can decide which segment is the most profitable within its specific physical and marketing resources. Rolex have opted for the 'leaders of the world' segment. It is not clear as to what Rolex mean by this expression but presumably this segment includes those who project characteristics of leadership, as well as those who fancy themselves as leaders—in other words the status seekers. Once such a segment has been

* Daniel Yankelovich, 'New Criteria for Market Segmentation', *Harvard Business Review*, March–April 1964.

selected as the firm's main target group every ingredient of marketing mix is influenced by such a decision: the price will reflect the prestigious nature of the product; the promotion will appear in suitable media and the message will also reflect the 'snobbish' flavour of the product; distribution will take place through equally 'high class' channels.

In contrast Timex have undoubtedly chosen a different segment for their marketing objectives—the cost conscious, rational consumers who buy a watch as a device for time-keeping purposes only.

The question now arises: should a firm opt for the same segment on a global scale or should it change its strategy in this respect from market to market? If Rolex have selected the status seekers should they market their watches to the same type of people wherever they may live? The answer is not simple; it may be obvious in the case of watches but it is certainly not so in relation to other products. One may be able to identify 'snobs' as a fairly homogeneous group throughout the world thus forming a useful segment for a standardised marketing strategy. On the other hand, it is much more difficult to identify thrift on a trans-national level. The important thing to remember is that a firm that aspires to market its product internationally must gauge buyers' motives in different countries, and if a common denominator can be found the choice of a standard approach is highly desirable. If, on the other hand, a great diffusion of motives is discovered a differentiation policy is inevitable. In this latter situation it will mean that the marketing effort in Germany may concentrate on appealing to the cost conscious individual whereas the same product may be aimed at the status seekers in France. This is of course the main explanation why the smallest and one of the cheapest cars in the UK— the BLMC Mini—sells in France as a quasi prestige car. Mini drivers in France regard this vehicle as a status symbol whereas the British counterparts consider it as an economical work horse! This means that the promotional strategy in the UK is totally inappropriate in France; the price elasticity is such that the French buyer would expect to pay a higher price for the same model— in other words the marketing ecologies are different and the segments chosen are different.

(c) THE ADOPTION PROCESS

The 'adoption process' can offer a highly creative basis for segmenting markets. People respond at a different rate to the stimulus of new products or concepts. Behaviourally a number of individual buyers tend to respond favourably to any kind of innovation—as soon as they perceive a new product they desire it. These are the kind of people who would purchase a digital watch the minute it is launched. At the other extreme one encounters the so-called 'laggards'—they are the kind of individuals who resist change and in marketing terms they only respond to a product when it has been on the market for a long time, sometimes when the product has in fact reached the end of its life cycle.

Between these two extremes one finds other adoption characteristics of varying intensity. Five adoption segments normally exist and can be summarised as:

Adoption category	Possible size %	Typical characteristics
Innovators	$2\frac{1}{2}$	Venturesome; prepared to experiment; higher social status; higher income group; urban
Early Adopters	$13\frac{1}{2}$	Same as the 'Innovators' but less venturesome
Early Majority	34	Display less leadership than previous two; avoid risk; rural rather than urban types; active in community life
Late Majority	34	Conservative; imitators; extra cautious; dislike change; older; lower income groups; less prestigious occupations; more oriented to local contacts
Laggards	16	'Isolates'; stubbornly resist change; unimaginative

Fig. 12   Adoption categories and segmentation

The significance of this type of segmentation can be of considerable international value. An example from the pharmaceutical industry can illustrate the point.

Doctors can be easily divided into the five adoption categories listed above. A well-known firm in the pharmaceutical business decided to examine the prescribing habits of the doctors visited by its sales representatives. The result of the study showed that doctors can be categorised more easily into four segmentable groups:

(i) *Innovators*—these are doctors who normally prescribe a pharmaceutical product as soon as it first appears on the market.
(ii) *Early adopters*—these are doctors who wait for a while before they venture to try the new drug. They want to read the results of clinical tests before prescribing.
(iii) *Late adopters*—this segment is slow to adopt modern drugs and reluctant to change from existing prescribing habits. They adopt a new product under some social and professional pressure.
(iv) *Laggards*—these are the extra cautious, professionally isolated doctors who stubbornly resist change. Their adoption of a drug may occur so late that the product may already have been replaced by another one.

For the purpose of the study the firm in question has divided the four categories into equal-size groups of 25 per cent each. A comprehensive study was conducted into the prescribing habits of doctors in a given sample and the impact of time on the volume of sales ascribed to each category monitored. The outcome of the study was most valuable—it showed that the top two segments namely the innovators and the early adopters (50 per cent of the total sample) accounted for 92 per cent of the firm's sales. In other words the firm, its products and general image appealed to the more modern-minded, more sophisticated and probably more venturesome doctors. These were the two segments which the firm decided to develop and maintain in its domestic market, and following a similar study in the main foreign markets, adopted as the target groups in its international marketing effort. In other words the company geared all its marketing effort, including its R & D, towards meeting the special requirements and expectations of the innovators and the early adopters among the world's doctors. The fact that in some countries the innovators are more conservative than in others did not matter in the firm's overall plan.

5 Other Bases for Segmentation

As stated earlier, with creativity one can consider a large number of novel segmentation possibilities. Examples:

(a) Segmentation by attitudes, taste or predispositions,
(b) Personality traits,
(c) Channels, patronage or store location, (Where do people buy?)
(d) Sensitivity to pricing or advertising policies,
(e) Original equipment or replacement equipment (e.g. tyres)
(f) Branded products or 'own label' merchandise. (Cadbury as against chocolate made specially for Sainsbury.)

Conditions for Successful Segmentation

It is normally suggested that before one can determine whether a segmentation strategy is worthwhile one must fulfil three fundamental conditions:

(a) *The size of each segment under consideration must be measurable.* The marketer must make sure that sufficient data are available about the segment in question or, alternatively, that an appropriate measurement methodology exists. To select a segmentation policy in circumstances which make measurement impossible or too costly may defeat the whole purpose of such a strategy viz. the optimisation of resources. This is one of the attractions of the IPA system in the UK. It is by no means ideal but it is a basis upon which one can obtain data from a large number of sources or research organisations.

In international marketing this condition is of paramount importance in so far as there is little point selecting a specific segmentation policy if the measurability of the segments under consideration is problematic. A manufacturer of drills tried to market his products to the 'do-it-yourself' segment in world markets. He knew the size of the segment in European markets but found it impossible to measure the size of this segment in most countries outside Europe. Measuring this segment would have cost a fortune—far in excess of the eventual hoped for rewards.

(b) *As a corollary of everything that was said hitherto the segment selected must be such that it can yield adequate returns.* In other words it must be *substantial* enough to be profitable. This is simply a basic question of common sense. The trouble is that marketers that have been bitten by the segmentation bug, often tend to indulge in excessive segmentation; this in turn may mean that segments selected, although creative to the extreme, are too small to earn an adequate return on the effort involved.

(c) *Finally the marketer must make sure that a segment chosen can be reached in an effective manner; it must be accessible.* The institutional bodies that facilitate the marketing process must be in existence. Channels of distribution must exist in the marketplace; promotional media must be available; the type of selling that one would propose to use must be acceptable. It would be senseless to select a segment which calls for an efficient retail distribution where such a system just does not exist. Similarly, the marketer who chooses a segment that depends entirely on television advertising for its success, will inevitably fail in areas where television as an advertising medium is not available or not likely to become available for some time.

Applying Market Segmentation to World Markets

In a domestic context most marketing men recognise that the choice of a marketing strategy depends to a great extent on whether a decision to segment has been taken. Broadly speaking three marketing strategies are available to the domestic marketer: undifferentiated marketing, differentiated marketing, and concentrated marketing.

In the case of *undifferentiated marketing* the firm places on the market one product and seeks to draw as many consumers as possible with one uniform, *standard,* marketing mix. It ignores the existence of specific segments with special needs and demands. In the case of *differentiated marketing* the company modifies the product and the supportive mix ingredients to appeal to a number of submarkets. Through such a differentiation the firm hopes to satisfy a larger number of segments and their specific needs and desires. In the third situation—*concentrated marketing*—the firm isolates one or more segments for special treatment and concentrates the total effort on these limited submarkets.

These three strategies apply with equal relevance to world markets. The only thing which is different is the dimension of the total market and each segment. At one end of the spectrum one encounters the firm that decides to derive most of its sales from the domestic markets and tends to regard sales abroad as 'grist to the mill' only. Such a firm adopts an undifferentiated or standardised approach. It realises full well that through differentiation it could achieve a greater penetration of its markets, but it opts for the more cost-effective strategy viz. standardisation.

At the other extreme one meets the company that choses to satisfy as many consumers in world markets as possible. This is achieved through a differentiated marketing strategy. The company has identified a host of needs and it has embarked on the gargantuan and costly task of attempting to gear the product, the promotion activity, the distribution policy, the price and the selling effort to each country or each submarket. This often leads to a gradual decentralisation of effort so as to bring the marketing activity closer to the market place. Sooner or later each submarket becomes a self-contained marketing entity. This is why one often associates differentiation in international marketing with decentralisation.

It is normally true to say that differentiated marketing, whether it is applied within a domestic market or is extended to world markets, tends to be sales orientated rather than profit orientated. If Coca-Cola decided to adjust all the ingredients of the marketing mix to every submarket, it would soon find itself producing scores of flavours in dozens of different bottles or packs; the advertising effort would differ enormously from country to country; the pricing policy would be in a state of anarchy and the distribution strategy would be a logistical maze. On the other hand Coca-Cola would probably sell more but at what extra cost? In fact the product would cease to be Coca-Cola; it would become a host of differentiated products—each market would have a specially designed, flavoured and bottled beverage produced and marketed by a company belonging to or associated with Coca-Cola.

The third strategy open to the international marketer, as mentioned earlier, is concentrated marketing. The first two strategies, differentiated and undifferentiated, imply that the marketer goes after the whole market. Whilst the undifferentiated strategy aims at maximum sales with one single mix, the differentiated strategy is based on the acceptance of changes in the product and the mix to satisfy different requirements. The concentrated marketing approach is based on a decision to achieve a maximum penetration of one or more segments to the exclusion of the rest of the market. Instead of spreading itself thinly in many parts of the world, it decides to concentrate its forces on a few clearly-defined areas. The company tries to reach a strong position in those countries or submarkets in which its strengths and competences have been clearly identified. It seeks to satisfy the local consumers of such selected markets with a limited cluster of highly standardised products and marketing mixes.

This brings us to one of the key decision areas of international marketing. How far should one differentiate in international markets? Every international marketer who has ever experienced the agonies of differentiation on a global scale would no doubt admit that standardisation of marketing strategies is his deeply-felt, albeit elusive, ambition. This does not mean that standardisation is *per se* the best strategy in all circumstances. There are situations where standardisation, with or without concentrated marketing, could mean a complete failure. The concept that the international marketer must appreciate is that before selecting a strategy it is necessary to gauge which approach is likely to help the firm to achieve its overall objectives. Obviously standardisation coupled with concentrated marketing is attractive in effectiveness terms but if it fails to attain corporate objectives it must be avoided. In other words one cannot be doctrinaire in this respect and state categorically that one strategy is to be preferred over another.

The first ingredient required in choosing the right strategy is *information*—quantified data about one's international markets. Inadequate knowledge of international markets usually leads to the abdication of marketing decisions to local management and this in turn means that the opportunity to standardise the marketing mix has been lost. Decentralisation has its place in international marketing and in certain situations it is highly desirable but it must not occur through an omission to plan the firm's strategies or by accident.

It was suggested with some emphasis that the essential 'input' that the international marketer requires is comprehensive knowledge of the various markets in which the firm hopes to operate. The marketing profile analysis which we discussed at some length earlier is an excellent starting point. It must be assembled with great care and with systematic thoroughness. It is a tedious process but should yield rich rewards. Each profile analysis represents, together with its supportive schedules, a 'thumbnail' sketch of each market. With such information it is possible to determine which markets lend themselves to a single, standardised approach and which do not. Alternatively, it should be possible to separate the many markets into a small cluster of territories capable of being handled in a homogeneous way, thus reducing the marketing mixes to a manageable number. By the end of such an exercise one should find oneself in the position of selecting one of two strategies: in the first place develop a concentrated strategy in relation to a 'hand-picked' cluster of markets and devote all one's energy and resources towards the full exploitation of this cluster of markets. In the second place one can adopt a limited differentiation policy with a small but manageable number of 'mixes'—each mix applied to a clearly defined cluster of markets, countries or regions. The development which the international marketer must avoid is the drifting towards a differentiated policy which is tantamount to a total fragmentation of effort and its abandonment to local personnel. If this is

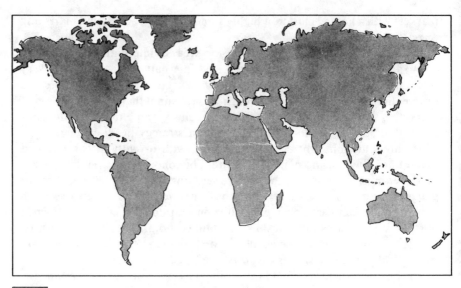

One standard 'mix' for all markets

Fig. 13   An undifferentiated marketing approach to world markets

allowed to happen the firm's marketing effort becomes a 'free-for-all' under the guise of international marketing.

Figures 13, 14 and 15 illustrate the concepts of undifferentiated marketing, differentiated marketing and concentrated marketing in relation to world

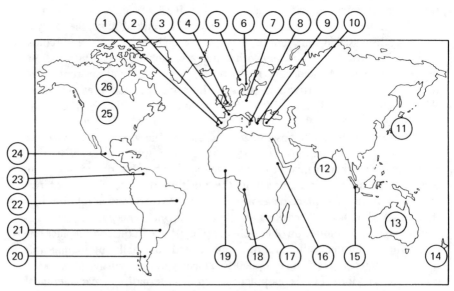

(N.B. Each circle represents a Marketing Mix)

Fig. 14   A differentiated marketing approach to world markets

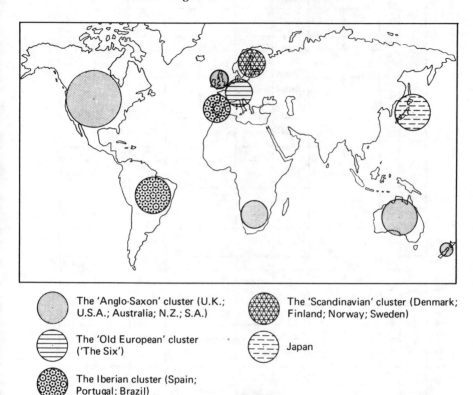

The 'Anglo-Saxon' cluster (U.K.; U.S.A.; Australia; N.Z.; S.A.)

The 'Old European' cluster ('The Six')

The Iberian cluster (Spain; Portugal; Brazil)

The 'Scandinavian' cluster (Denmark; Finland; Norway; Sweden)

Japan

Fig. 15   A concentrated marketing approach to world markets

markets. It will be readily noticed that concentrated marketing can easily drift into a differentiated strategy if allowed to develop into an excessive number of packages. The essence of concentrated marketing is the deliberate limitation of the marketing effort to what one considers the most profitable segment in world markets. The minute one broadens the number of segments, one inevitably tends to embark on a differentiation policy. In other words differentiation commences as soon as the firm decides to accommodate the special needs of its various markets. Furthermore, a firm may adopt a concentrated approach in one part of the world and differentiate lavishly in another part. In this book the term concentrated marketing is applied to situations where the firm has a small number of marketing assemblages in relation to rationally-linked clusters of markets.

A simple device for determing which markets lend themselves to the clustering process is described in Figure 16.

The idea behind this chart is that with adequate information one should be able to 'pair' markets that manifest similarities in their vital characteristics. Whilst one recognises that complete pairing is not likely to occur where foreign markets are concerned, one is prepared to accept minor differences.

Ingredients of the marketing mix

Bench-mark territory say	Product										Price										Promotion										Distribution										Selling									
	0	1	2	3	4	5	6	7	8	9	0	1	2	3	4	5	6	7	8	9	0	1	2	3	4	5	6	7	8	9	0	1	2	3	4	5	6	7	8	9	0	1	2	3	4	5	6	7	8	9
France																																																		
Germany																																																		
Italy																																																		
Holland																																																		
Belgium																																																		
U.K.																																																		
Switzerland																																																		
Spain																																																		
Portugal																																																		

0 = standardisation impossible; 9 = standardisation desirable

Fig. 16 A matrix for exploring the scope for clustering international markets

Thus, for instance, Norway and Denmark are different countries; in marketing terms there is a strong case for unifying the approach to both these markets. Finland has a language and a culture which differ from the other Scandinavian countries, nonetheless it has enough in common with the others to justify a clustering approach when applying a concentrated marketing strategy.

The clustering approach described here presupposes that every firm has one single market which can be treated as the basic 'bench mark' territory. The bench mark is selected either because it represents the firm's strongest marketing centre or because it is intended to turn it into the focal point for international marketing. In other words there is no point in selecting a bench mark which does not represent a marketing opportunity in its own right. Thus if, for tax reasons, the firm's headquarters are located at Lichtenstein, choosing that small country as a bench mark would be quite absurd. Similarly, there would be little point in choosing a large country like China as a bench mark in so far as in marketing terms it is yet a desert in the sense that it is neither measurable, nor fully accessible and probably in purchasing power terms not yet substantial.

The aim of the clustering method is to identify, in a somewhat qualitative way, how far other markets come close to the bench mark. The top row in Figure 16 shows once again the various elements of the mix; the left column lists the countries selected for observation. Each element of the mix has a scale and in relation to each country, ranging from 0 to 9. Different scales can of course be chosen if so desired as long as they provide sufficient scope for highlighting variations. '0' on our scale implies that there is no scope for standardisation in relation to the bench mark territory and the appropriate element of the mix. '9' means that standardisation is perfectly feasible, probably even desirable. In between these two extremes one can insert an X at the point which seems to the international analyst most appropriate after having studied carefully the implications contained in the various marketing profile analyses. Inevitably subjective judgement creeps into this methodology. This subjectivity is at least based on a thorough knowledge and understanding of the facts. Ideally this method should be tackled by a group of people who are close to the marketing function; this should reduce subjectivity. An average of the various opinions expressed on the grid will be tantamount to the outcome of a 'jury of informed opinion' methodology.

By its very nature the bench mark will be shown as '9' all round. Other markets are compared to the bench mark and an X inserted at a point on the scale which reflects the opinion of the analyst or the committee. Figure 17 illustrates the matrix completed in respect of the listed countries. One can discern at a glance those markets which enjoy some marketing similarity with the bench mark in relation to a specific product. At this point the international marketer must take an important decision: What is an acceptable variation from the bench mark beyond which differentiation is inevitable? If one decides that '7' is the limit of tolerable difference for

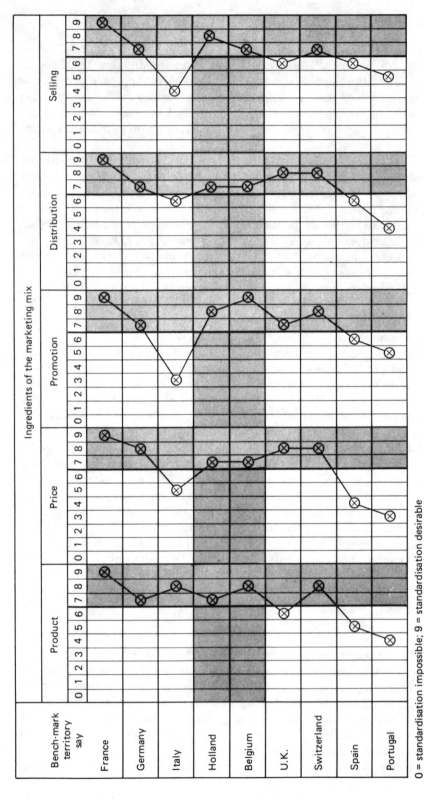

0 = standardisation impossible; 9 = standardisation desirable

Fig. 17   Analysing clustering possibilities

standardisation to be justified one can now cluster all those markets that represent this, or a higher, level of similarity.

Figure 17 shows that in relation to a specific product (a domestic appliance) all the ingredients of the mix have been marked '7' or over in Germany, the Netherlands, Belgium and Switzerland. In these four markets it is now logical to assume that one can operate, in relation to the product under study, with a standard product and marketing strategy. No doubt if one would decide to differentiate the marketing strategy, even among these four countries, one should be able to achieve still higher sales but it is doubtful whether the cost would be justified in the light of the findings described. One is in the position of obtaining maximum mileage from a standard mix.

The process can now be repeated a number of times in order to identify another cluster of markets which will respond to a second standardisation package and so on. The aim of this simple methodology is clearly established: to reduce the number of mixes into an economically manageable level. It can help the firm to overcome the wastefulness of over-differentiation and the constraining effect of non-differentiation. The method is not fool-proof in so far as it contains a considerable amount of qualitative 'input'. At the same time one must recognise that without such a disciplined approach one runs the risk of pursuing a strategy which is not necessarily the most economic nor the most effective in a given set of circumstances. The method described above should help international marketers to approach the whole problem with the kind of sensitivity which marketing on a global scale demands.

Chapter 5

Researching International Markets

The process of researching international markets is not fundamentally different from the way marketing research is conducted in a purely domestic firm. The objectives, tasks and methodologies of the process are similar; but the scope, coverage, intricacies and, inevitably, cost, of international marketing research make it a highly specialised and complicated activity. It is quite easy to spend vast amounts of cash on researching international markets with a minimal pay-off. Marketing research always calls for a very clear understanding of the underlying reasons for the study coupled with concise and logical terms of reference. International marketing research requires an even deeper appreciation as to why certain resources are being allocated to a multinational study and a better assessment of the results that may emanate from such an expenditure. This problem is particularly acute in those situations where the resources available for international studies are limited and the major decision becomes the choice of priority areas within those limited resources.

Whilst most readers would be familiar with the marketing research process it may be appropriate to review it briefly in order to have an agreed conceptual platform from which to develop the international dimension.

The traditional approach to marketing research is undergoing considerable change and in a number of companies some disenchantment with the process has emerged. It is therefore relevant to identify the reasons for these gyrations and at least for the purpose of this book take a clear posture as to what it is intended to discuss. On the other hand in a rapidly changing managerial environment it would be wrong not to emphasise the direction towards which the academic literature seems to be pointing.

The commonly accepted meaning of marketing research is adequately defined by the American Marketing Association as ' *the systematic gathering, recording and analysing of data about problems relating to the marketing of goods and services'*. This definition is fairly narrow but nonetheless for the purpose of this book we base our discussions thereon.

At the same time it is important to mention that a broader approach is developing among modern marketers. According to this concept marketing research is an integral part of the much broader concept of *marketing information system*, which in turn is a part of the total concept of *management information system*. The rationale underlying this broadening of the concept is:

A well-designed information system can ensure that managers obtain data which is relevant to their specific decision-making needs.

The system designers can ensure that information is communicated to all those managers who may have use of such data. In other words the information can be used more effectively and duplication of research can be avoided. Managers thus become aware of the major sources of information, of alternative methods of supplying data, and of the impact of the major changes of information technology.

MIS (management information system) by its very nature is dynamic, changing with the environment and the organisation.

The whole process encourages understanding of the critical areas of operations, identification of specific information requirements and also recognition of the technological, economic and personnel constraints which may make the collection of certain types of information impractical.

Firms that possess sophisticated EDP facilities may discover a new promise in these installations in the development of an all-embracing marketing information system.

A number of firms have undertaken highly imaginative projects to develop such information systems; a few of them have proved very successful, others have failed. The design of an efficient and dynamic system calls not only for considerable skills on the part of the designer but also a high level of conceptual awareness on the part of those managers who should benefit from the system. Undoubtedly, in time, many firms will invest considerable time and effort in developing comprehensive information systems encapsulating marketing systems. However for the purpose of this book we shall explore the application of the narrower meaning of marketing research to international markets.

The Marketing Research Process

The major steps in marketing research activities are:

> Problem definition
> Development of the research plan
> Data collection
> Data interpretation
> Summary of findings and report

Figure 18 sets out the process in a logical flow model identifying the tasks to be performed under each step and showing also specific points to be watched in international marketing research activities.

It is not proposed to elaborate here on the details of the marketing research process nor on the various methodologies that can be used. Many excellent

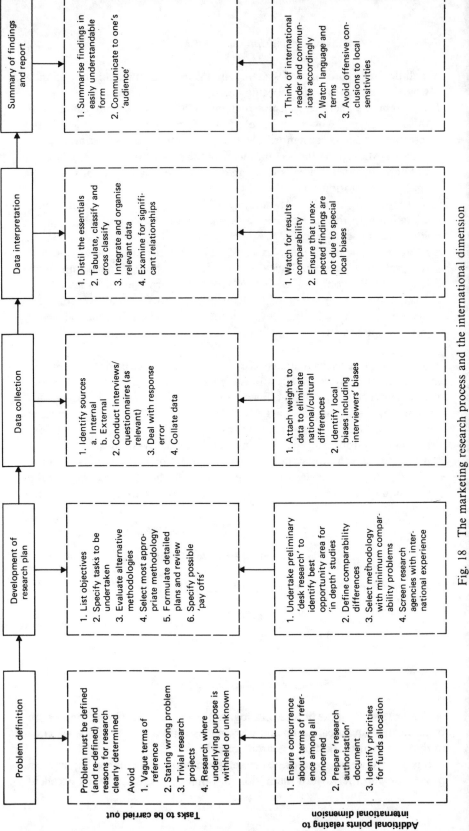

Fig. 18   The marketing research process and the international dimension

Problem definition

Problem must be defined (and re-defined) and reasons for research clearly determined

Avoid
1. Vague terms of reference
2. Stating wrong problem
3. Trivial research projects
4. Research where underlying purpose is withheld or unknown

1. Ensure concurrence about terms of reference among all concerned
2. Prepare 'research authorisation' document
3. Identify priorities for funds allocation

Development of research plan

1. List objectives
2. Specify tasks to be undertaken
3. Evaluate alternative methodologies
4. Select most appropriate methodology
5. Formulate detailed plans and review
6. Specify possible 'pay offs'

1. Undertake preliminary 'desk research' to identify best opportunity area for 'in depth' studies
2. Define comparability differences
3. Select methodology with minimum comparability problems
4. Screen research agencies with international experience

Data collection

1. Identify sources
   a. Internal
   b. External
2. Conduct interviews/questionnaires (as relevant)
3. Deal with response error
4. Collate data

1. Attach weights to data to eliminate national/cultural differences
2. Identify local biases including interviewers' biases

Data interpretation

1. Distil the essentials
2. Tabulate, classify and cross classify
3. Integrate and organise relevant data
4. Examine for significant relationships

1. Watch for results comparability
2. Ensure that unexpected findings are not due to special local biases

Summary of findings and report

1. Summarise findings in easily understandable form
2. Communicate to one's 'audience'

1. Think of international reader and communicate accordingly
2. Watch language and terms
3. Avoid offensive conclusions to local sensitivities

Tasks to be carried out

Additional points relating to international dimension

textbooks are available on the subject and every marketer must acquaint himself with the process and its tools. Marketing research is an indispensable instrument of effective marketing management—no marketer can claim to be an accomplished marketing virtuoso without possessing a thorough knowledge of its skills. Moreover, when a marketer has to face the extremely intricate problems of international marketing research, any personal gaps in experience or education in this area, at a domestic level, may prove to be a serious weakness in the quality of his work. It cannot be overemphasised therefore how important it is for every manager who embarks on an international marketing career to ensure that he is fully familiar with the fundamentals of marketing research and its supportive techniques before indulging on multinational problems.

The International Dimension of Marketing Research

Marketing research can be a daunting activity; the number of research areas that can be identified is enormous. Inevitably good management demands that only those areas that can yield the most promising 'pay-offs' should be researched. The situation is magnified into almost unmanageable proportions when the choice of projects is translated into multinational, multi-product, multi-market dimensions. At this point it is difficult not to waste the firm's money.

The major problems that should be borne in mind in international marketing research are the following three:

1 Selection of the most profitable research projects
2 Comparability of results
3 Organisation of the marketing research function on a global scale.

1 Selection of Projects

An international firm that operates in a large number of countries and markets a range of products, each of which has a number of consumption segments can be described in a three-dimensional diagram (Figure 19). Each box represents a measurable project and the total number of projects would amount to a $\times$ b $\times$ c. A fairly significant number of potential projects for research.

If we add other dimensions such as distribution patterns, advertising channels, socioeconomic variations, etc., we can generate an astronomical number of projects and in theory each one of those projects would be capable of research. Some selectivity must be worked out if the firm's financial and human resources are not to disappear on marketing research activities. Whether the firm is organised in a centralised fashion or is totally decentralised (as in the 'umbrella' style structure) it is still important that

PROJECTS FOR MARKET MEASUREMENT ACTIVITY OF AN ALUMINIUM COMPANY

Assuming 5 countries are to be researched; 3 products and 3 market segments—possible projects for research $5 \times 3 \times 3 = 45$

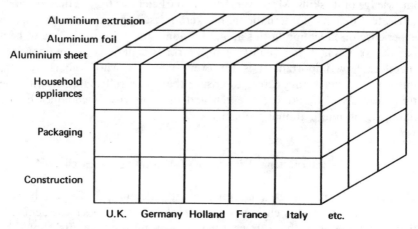

Assuming 70 countries are to be researched; 5 products, 6 market segments—possible number of projects: $70 \times 5 \times 6 = 2100$

Fig. 19   Possible projects for market measurement activities of an aluminium company

selectivity is applied to marketing research projects. It is of course much easier to lay down screening criteria in a centralised marketing situation where the decision for alloting funds is clearly located at the centre. It is much more difficult in a decentralised company where the researchers are responsible to a local manager and the unit may be operating thousands of miles away from the centre. Decentralisation bestows the kind of autonomy which entitles local managers to decide how to spend their research money, or indeed how much they should spend on marketing research. This latter case makes good sense for each individual unit in the total organisation but one often finds that when the total expenditure of all subsidiaries in the world is aggregated the final figure ceases to make sense. There is no easy solution to this problem. If the firm has opted for a decentralised 'umbrella' structure one has to accept the penalty of waste that emanates therefrom and marketing research is one more area where cost effectiveness often suffers. Paradoxically the waste is greatest in sophisticated companies, in so far as marketing research is a highly stimulating subject and researchers often allow themselves to be sidetracked by the intellectual fascination of research projects, and at the same time lose sight of the commercial relevance of the study undertaken.

Thus cutting waste out of the global budget for marketing research must be a prime task of those responsible for such activities. This can be achieved through a systematic educational process coupled with a screening discipline. This, in many companies, is one of the roles of the centrally located marketing services department. Of course such an arrangement is more relevant in the 'umbrella' type company; in the macropyramid firm the problem arises less frequently in so far as cost control is a central function in any event. By means of conferences, bulletins, published guidelines, etc. the central marketing services are able to communicate the message to all the far-flung marketing research departments that any research project undertaken must be capable of yielding maximum returns on the investment involved; where a number of projects are competing for authorisation the most promising ones in terms of such returns should receive priority. This is pure commonsense. Unfortunately as most experienced researchers know only too well this principle is not always adhered to.

A useful device for ensuring that research projects are screened carefully and their potential 'pay-off' fully appraised is the research project appraisal method. It is similar in approach and content to the type of appraisal that most firms use in relation to normal capital investment requirements. Figure 20 illustrates a simple form describing the type of information that should help to appraise and compare the value of each marketing research project. In those companies where the final decision is vested in a central marketing research department this appraisal form is a very useful device for comparing projects and identifying priority areas. In companies where the research programme is determined by the local research department, the form provides an excellent discipline for the managers responsible for taking a decision in this connection; they are forced to look at the merits of each project with a commercial orientation. They have to consider carefully the financial implications in relation to the commercial rewards that may be yielded by each project under scrutiny. This is a very important and sound procedure in international operations.

Coupled with the appraisal form one can use an algorithm type flow chart as described in Figure 21.

In selecting research projects as described earlier it is essential to establish the various criteria which must be met if the project and the eventual information resulting therefrom are to justify the expense and effort. Examples of such criteria are:

(a) Stable economies can better justify research resources as against territories suffering from economic or political instability through inflation, currency problems or political uncertainties.

(b) Economies which are sufficiently developed should have a priority over countries not developed enough to absorb large quantities of the firm's product.

(c) Financial considerations such as cost of research in relation to size of market must be examined.

(d) Legal and governmental constraints, for example patent anarchy, a hostile legal system, etc.

Reference No. _____

I Project Title _____

_____

II Project objectives _____

_____

_____

III Tasks required to achieve objectives, their duration and cost
(N.B. Cost of internal resources to be included)

Objectives (as defined in II)	Tasks	Resources*		Duration	Cost
		Internal	External		
	Total:				

Additional costs

Give details _____

_____ Total: _____

To be shown in man/days or other quantifiable standards

IV Pay off

(Explain how you feel that savings and/or added contribution could result from this project. Endeavour to quantify such 'pay off' in monetary terms. Attach supportive evidence.)

_____

_____

_____

_____ Estimated pay off: [   ]

Proposal submitted by_____ Authorised by_____

Date_____ Date_____

Fig. 20   International marketing research authorisation form

Screening projects for priority

1. Mark appropriate square
2. Place score in right-hand box
3. Add total

Highest score indicates priority

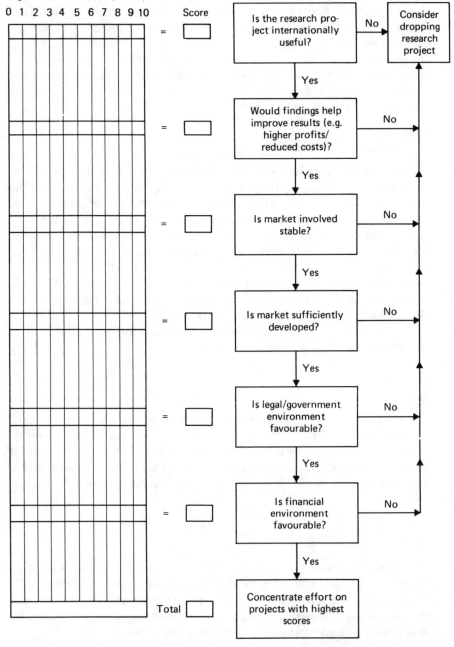

Fig. 21 Procedure for screening marketing research projects

The point to remember is that even after the main priorities have been established a further screening process must be undertaken to establish sub-priority areas. For example a centrally-controlled electronic firm decided after careful screening, to undertake a markets study in relation to two products only and in fifteen countries. It was only after thorough desk research had been completed that the firm was able to determine which of the fifteen markets would yield the best opportunity areas, and in relation to which one of the two products. At that point projects for further in-depth research could be formulated. In other words two stages of priority screening must take place: one at the total project level and the other one at the detailed research level. Once again failure to perform this double-pronged screening activity may lead to unnecessary research with resultant waste.

2 Comparability of Results

A major problem in international marketing research is the question of comparability of results. The various differences that exist among nations and their respective cultures and attitudes can defeat comparability. This becomes particularly acute where questionnaires are involved and the general reaction to questions differs from country to country. Whilst the responses can be quantified the results may be very misleading. When a Japanese consumer says that he 'likes' a product he may mean no more than the Dutch consumer means when he says that 'it is fairly good'. To analyse such responses and come to the conclusion that the product is more popular in Japan than in the Netherlands is of course quite absurd.

The following are the main differences that must be resolved before comparability of results can be attempted:

(a) LANGUAGES

Languages constitute a significant hurdle in international marketing research. Contact with the consumer must be in the language of his country. Nonetheless one must make sure that terms used in any research contact convey precisely the same meaning in all languages. The most subtle difference in meaning may nullify the objective of comparability thus reducing the overall value of the study.

(b) CULTURAL VALUES

This is particularly important where one tries to measure attitudes against a scale. It is important to identify such differences at any early date and if necessary ascribe weights to the respective markets under study with the view of adjusting responses in accordance with a basic bench mark. Overlooking this point can lead to serious misinterpretation of results.

(c) CONSUMPTION PATTERNS

Major differences in market data may occur as a result of consumption patterns originating from historical/cultural/economic developments. These must be identified and the underlying differences considered before the final analysis of data collected is undertaken. Research has shown that the per capita consumption of bananas in Germany is double that of the UK. On the face of it, it seems a puzzling bit of information which can easily lead to dangerous conclusions. However, on closer study, one discovers that whilst the consumption on a weight basis is double that of the UK, in terms of number of bananas per capita the consumption is virtually identical. The reason is simple: the bananas imported from the Caribbean into the UK tend to be much smaller than those imported into Germany, hence the disparity. This point must be resolved before comparability can become meaningful.

(d) TARGET GROUPS AND SEGMENTS

The international researcher must make sure that in conducting a project on a multinational scale, he has clearly defined the segments within which he seeks to measure the opportunities for a specific product or service. Thus a tyre manufacturer who wishes to measure the size of markets for tyres, and having established that he is particularly well placed for meeting the needs of the original equipment market, must spell out very clearly the segment he wishes to research in the various countries. This would of course immediately eliminate all those countries on his list which do not possess a car manufacturing industry.

(e) SOCIOECONOMIC CONDITIONS

Socioeconomic variables may create great problems at the point of comparing results. Failure, for instance, to identify at an early stage the differences in income patterns can be the cause of considerable inaccuracies. To take an absurd example: measuring the size of markets for razor blades in a number of countries, one of which is India. If one ignores the extremely low level of per capita income in India, one may come to the conclusion that for some unexplained reason the average Indian consumes only one hundredth of the quantity of blades as his Swedish counterpart. Great care must be taken in highlighting the various differences that exist in socioeconomic variables such as family size and family life cycle patterns, religion, race, social class, education and occupation, etc.

(f) MARKETING ENVIRONMENT

The marketing profile analysis is the tool that should help the international marketer to identify the environmental differences that may affect comparability of results. Competition, legal systems and the institutional structure of each market are the most important dimensions that may make comparability at the interpretation stage a real nightmare. These conditions must be detected and differences tabulated at a fairly early stage of the research work.

(g) INFORMATION SOURCES

Here one is often confronted by the problem that statistics gathered for a number of countries by a single source are not truly comparable inspite of the fact that the details are tabulated in the same report. It is most frustrating to discover after studying carefully published data that the conclusions shown must be read together with an endless number of footnotes that explain disparities and lack of comparability. The situation is even more frustrating where the footnotes are omitted in order to make the report more readable. In such instances the findings can be very misleading and should be treated with some suspicion.

It is relevant to mention in this connection that the various United Nations agencies have made considerable progress in grappling with this problem. By using standardised industrial classifications they have come very close to meeting the marketer's need for comparability of data. Thus international commodity trade statistics are fully comparable. Similarly an increasing number of countries have adopted the UN National Accounting System and as a result macro-economic studies are readily comparable.

(h) MONETARY PROBLEMS

Comparative analysis of data expressed in monetary units often presents major analytical complications. This is particularly difficult during an era of monetary uncertainties and when a number of currencies float in relation to other major currencies.

There is no easy solution to this problem but nonetheless the international researcher must endeavour to establish a fair basis for comparing data before attempting to enunciate conclusions in terms which can only mislead the recipients of such information.

3 The Organisation of the Marketing Research Function on a Global Scale

The organisation of marketing research activities within an internationally orientated firm can present considerable problems and often leads to conflicts between those responsible for research in the centre and those attached to foreign marketing organisations. These conflicts are of course typical of any organisation which has a large number of operational locations and where the relationship between the central organs and the decentralised units have not been clearly defined.

The whole question of how to organise the marketing function on a global scale is covered in a subsequent chapter. Obviously the way the marketing function is structured in a multinational firm will determine also the relationship of the marketing research department in the total structure.

A number of fundamental questions arise:

Should marketing research be organised in a centralised or a decentralised fashion?

In the former case how does one manage personnel located ten thousand miles away?

Furthermore, in a centralised structure what is the relationship between local researchers (who are responsible to the centre) and other marketing personnel who are in the local line hierarchy?

In a decentralised structure how does one communicate findings from one market to another and are such findings transferrable?

Who should be responsible for and where should marketing research plans be prepared?

Who should administer supervision of the work?

In a multi-product company who should determine the allocation of the necessary resources?

How does one ensure that results of the research offer comparability?

These are significant organisational problems in international marketing and they must be resolved at an early stage of the international organisation development process; failure to grapple with these questions may only mean that one day the firm will realise that the marketing research function has grown out of all proportion to the real needs, and that the resources absorbed have reached commercially unacceptable levels.

The main organisational options for the marketing research department are shown in Figure 22. The list describes the characteristics of each option and the implications in terms of effectiveness, communication and cost.

Planning an International Marketing Research Project—a Checklist

Once a research project has been selected and its objectives defined it is important that great care is invested in the detailed planning of the assignment irrespective of whether the company will undertake the work with its own resources or outside agencies.

A number of fundamental questions must be resolved. The following checklist has been designed to assist international marketers in asking a number of basic questions the answers to which may help them to plan fruitful projects:

ORGANISATIONAL OPTIONS FOR INTERNATIONAL MARKETING RESEARCH
(Based on a macropyramid and an 'umbrella' structure types)

Structure Style	Main Characteristics	Typical Problems and/or Strengths	
		Problems	Strengths
MACROPYRAMID	1 A central Marketing Research Department responsible to a central strategic person, e.g. Marketing Director.	—frequent conflict between the Central MR Management & local managers as to responsibilities.	—funds used in a planned fashion.
	2 Such a Department is responsible for total research effort throughout world. They prepare budgets and determine presentation.	—smaller markets often neglected.	—priorities identified in a systematic way.
	3 Marketing Research Officers located in major foreign units are still responsible to boss in Centre. Their relationship to managers in own market is purely functional.	—extensive & often superfluous travelling.	—communication of findings good.
	4 Heavy travelling and costs.		—comparability sought & achieved.
	5 Extensive use of outside agencies.		—the Strategic level has quick & frequent access to information.
			—useful opportunities to explore standardisation possibilities.

Structure Style	Main Characteristics	Typical Problems and/or Strengths: Problems	Typical Problems and/or Strengths: Strengths
'UMBRELLA'	1 A small Marketing Research Department forming part of Central Services. Its role is mainly advisory, educational & residual viz dealing with corporate matters. 2 Marketing Research activities undertaken at local levels & responsible to local Marketing management. Relationship to Central MR Department is purely functional. 3 Larger foreign subsidiaries have their own MR departments; smaller units will use outside agencies as required. As soon as expenditure rises to a certain level tendency to have own MR facilities. 4 Aggregate expenditure throughout world heavy.	—inadequate communication of information and findings. —poor comparability of data. —heavy total expenditure.	—adaptability to local needs. —local MR personnel understand fully market conditions. —can be a useful source of creative ideas.

Fig. 22 Organisational options for international marketing research—main characteristics, problems and strengths.

		Yes	No
1	Have we allowed sufficient time for the project?	☐	☐
2	Have we defined the objectives with enough clarity?	☐	☐
3	Have we defined all terms?	☐	☐
4	Have we eliminated ambiguities?	☐	☐
5	If we base our research project on a number of assumptions have we checked their accuracy?	☐	☐
6	Have we communicated with local researchers, and if so are we certain that they have understood all the assumptions and objectives of the project?	☐	☐
7	Have we discussed and agreed the most suitable methodology with local researchers?	☐	☐
8	Have we identified problems that may affect comparability of results?	☐	☐
9	Once methodology has been established have we designed our master questionnaire with care?	☐	☐
10	Have we re-checked translation of the master questionnaire to avoid ambiguities?	☐	☐
11	Have we identified and agreed weighing parameters?	☐	☐

This is a simple checklist; unfortunately researchers often ignore the complications that may arise from failure to obtain satisfactory answers. It is certainly worth spending the time and effort in seeking the answers to all these questions before committing company money to intricate international projects.

In major international studies it may be useful to arrange face-to-face meetings with the individuals who will be undertaking the detailed work. This method should help to eliminate any residual doubts as to what the project aims to achieve and also remove any ambiguities as to terminology. Such meetings could be arranged either at the centre of the company or at some 'neutral' ground, or alternatively the marketing research manager could travel to visit the researchers in their respective offices abroad. It must be appreciated that the cost of travel is often minimal in relation to the overall cost of the total project. Trying to economise on travel may easily lead to eventual difficulties or damage to the quality of the findings and these may far outweigh the cost of travel of a small number of individuals.

At the same time it must be emphasised that during the face-to-face contact every detail of the programme must be discussed and agreed upon including the format of the final report. Local biases that may distort the findings or the interpretation of data must be highlighted and corrected. Where the correction of biases cannot be achieved owing to cultural or attitudinal differences they should be discussed and the appropriate weights attached to them as aids to comparability.

Sources of Information

Sources of information are extensive but they often suffer from lack of reliability or failure to comply with the basic rules of comparability; and to the international researcher today comparability of data is the biggest single problem.

For general statistical data the United Nations with its various agencies is an excellent source of primary information. Although data obtained from these agencies are not always as detailed as information from national sources they tend to be uniform, comparable and objective. Furthermore UN statistics are available to everyone at a very reasonable expense.

It is therefore recommended that before one delves too deeply into local governmental statistics or data collected by semi-official organisations, such as chambers of commerce and trade associations, one should explore with some care the excellent material provided by the various international bodies, both those affiliated to the UN and those representing multinational trade associations.

The following publishing bodies provide excellent information on an international scale:

European Economic Community (EEC)
European Coal and Steel Community
Economic Commission for Africa (ECA)
Economic Commission for Asia and the Far East (ECAFE)
Economic Commission for Latin America (ECLA)
Organisation for Economic Co-Operation & Development (OECD)
General Agreement on Tariffs and Trade (GATT)
Food and Agriculture Organisation (FAO)
International Labor Organisation (ILO)
International Civil Aviation Organisation (ICAO)
International Bank for Reconstruction and Development (IBRD)
International Monetary Fund (IMF)
International Telecommunications Union (ITU)
International Union of Railways (UICF)
International Air Transport Association (IATA)
Universal Postal Union (UPU)
World Health Organisation (WHO)

Other useful sources of international information
Business International
Informations Internationales
World Trade Information Service—The US Department of Commerce

Chapter 6

Product Policies for World Markets

The 'product' is the heart of the marketing mix. If the product fails to satisfy the consumer and his needs, no additional expenditure and effort on any of the other ingredients of the mix will improve the product performance in the market place. A washing machine that fails to perform satisfactorily will not become more attractive to the buyer just because large sums have been spent on glossy advertisements extolling the virtue of the machine in question.

Similarly an airline whose planes are consistently late will not improve its 'product' as a result of a television campaign which attempts to suggest that the airline is so punctual that any passer-by can virtually tell the exact time the minute he hears the plane's engines droning overhead. No communication message can in the long term improve the level of satisfaction emanating from a poor product.

In this connection one must remember that the word 'product' encapsulates a host of components and attributes. They must add up to an assemblage that will provide the level of satisfaction that the firm seeks to attain within its marketing objectives. Thus 'product' includes such items as the functionality of the product, the ergonomics in use, the aesthetics of its design, the packaging, the longevity, the supportive literature, the instructions incorporated in the literature, the maker's warranty, after-sales service, etc. The perfect product is the one which manages to incorporate all the attributes and qualities which in-depth research of consumers' needs and expectations has identified. The toymaker who designs an admirable model aircraft but incorporates in the package assembly instructions which are beyond the comprehension of reasonably intelligent children (and often of intelligent parents) can be accused of poor product design, although the written instructions are not part of the physical design itself.

A motor car may be of such an excellent design that it would delight buyers and potential consumers. However, if the after-sales service proves to be of a most inferior standard, the car in question would soon lose its attractiveness in the market-place. In other words the product would be considered incomplete or unsatisfactory. The fact that the physical side of the design has been developed with extreme care and attention to detail will be offset by the lack of an acceptable level of service. A sound marketing effort presupposes that the firm has researched the market to such an extent that all the supportive attributes of the product have been clearly detected. This task must be undertaken within a number of important dimensions:

1 within a time scale
2 within the framework of the firm's resources and goals
3 within a specified market or segment environment.

The first of these points relates to the need to interpret research findings in a dynamic fashion and take cognisance of the changing tastes and demands of the consumer. The American Edsel car was a failure inspite of long and laborious research studies. The popular interpretation of the reasons for this failure was that by the time the car was designed and ready market conditions had changed sufficiently to make the product out-of-date before it was launched. This is one of the tricky aspects of modern marketing. One must endeavour to combine facts with a rapidly changing scene. It is almost like trying to hit a moving target in a fairground. The skilful marksman aims ahead of the moving target to allow for the inevitable changing position.

The second point seeks to emphasise the importance of designing a product within the economic realities, resources and goals of the firm. Whilst the aim is to attain the full satisfaction of the consumer and his specific needs and requirements, one must endeavour to undertake this task in such a way as to make a profit or attain the firm's other objectives. This of course is not always easy in so far as the marketing objectives may be out of step with the financial and commercial realities of the situation. Thus a firm distributing perishable food products chose to make daily deliveries to multiple stores located in the centre of all major conurbations—a highly commendable marketing objective. The firm soon discovered that the cost of such a service was totally unacceptable to the stores and to the customers. In other words the 'product' in this instance, though highly desirable, was totally inappropriate within the resources framework of the company in question and its corporate objectives.

The third dimension refers to the need to design a product for a well-defined target group. The target group can be a very narrow segment or a very wide market-place, like a whole country or a geographical region. What is important to remember when designing a product assemblage is that the job must be carried out with a definite buyer in mind. This point is particularly important in international marketing in so far as the product that has been designed for a domestic consumer may or may not be suitable for the international consumer. If it is suitable for the non-domestic buyer, so much the better, but this would be simply a stroke of good luck. Sound international marketing envisages a planned effort and not just lucky strikes. This is the essence of international marketing: if the firm seeks to satisfy the needs of the international consumer the product should be designed accordingly. The product that has been designed for a home market and for which one discerns foreign opportunities is essentially an export effort rather than a fully-fledged global marketing effort. We shall see later the implications of this distinction in connection with product policy and planning problems.

The Product Life Cycle in International Marketing

General Principles

The product life cycle concept is well known to most marketers. Its impact on the firm's marketing effort differs from company to company and from product to product. A manufacturer of pharmaceutical products has to pay very serious attention to this concept and plan in advance the various strategies that he proposes to adopt at each stage of the life cycle. On the other hand a house builder need not concern himself too much with the meaning of this theory because in practice each house he builds is a product and once erected and sold the transaction is finished (with the exception of the after-sales service commitment) and the ravages of the life cycle hardly apply; any change in taste or habits can be easily translated into the next product without substantial planning and investment. Nonetheless the concept is a useful one; it alerts the marketer to the fact that market dynamism affects not only the appearance and functionality of a product but also the effectiveness of the supportive marketing mix ingredients at each stage of the product's life. This is the aspect which is often overlooked by those who tend to describe the value of the product life concept as an impractical one.

Briefly the product life cycle concept can be summarised thus: every product has a life span of a limited duration. Some products live for many years, others have a short life. If the sales of the product are plotted over a period of time the result will be a curve as shown in Figure 23.

The curve, or life cycle is normally divided into five distinct periods—introduction, growth, maturity, saturation and decline. Whilst the shape of the curve will be more or less the same for most products, the time duration and the rapidity of change from stage to stage will vary enormously among products. The life cycle of the hula-hoop only lasted a few months; the life cycle of the ballpoint pen has lasted many years although during those years the product has undergone fundamental marketing changes.

The significant point to remember in this connection is the fact that in most instances the product's profits tend to follow a predictable pattern through the life cycle. Profits are either absent or substantially absent during the growth stage and reach a peak during the maturity stage. During the saturation stage they normally manifest signs of erosion and all but disappear during the decline stage. If we plot the profit performance on Figure 23 (the scale shown on the right-hand side) it would become apparent that in typical circumstances peak profitability is reached before peak sales. The marketer who is aware of this situation seeks to overcome the problem either by *differentiating* the product thus giving it a fresh lease of life or by introducing new products in order to safeguard the firm's overall profitability. When a car manufacturer introduces a 'face-lift' to a well-established model he seeks to 'cheat old age' through differentiation. When he launches a new model he

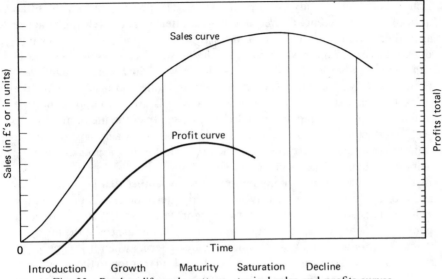

Fig. 23   Product life cycle pattern—typical sales and profits curves

introduces a totally new product with a distinct life cycle curve in order to
generate a new profit pattern which runs in parallel with the decaying product
and eventually takes over the task of sustaining the firm's profit performance.
This can be demonstrated in Figures 24 and 25. The first shows how an
endeavour is made through differentiation to give the product extra life where
in normal circumstances it would enter the saturation stage. Figure 25
illustrates how a succession of products with their distinct life cycles help the

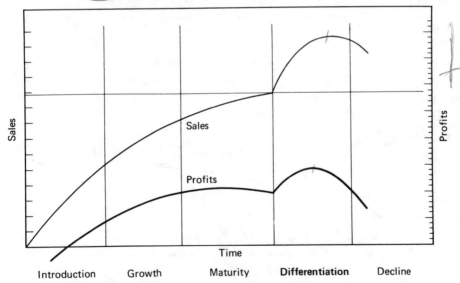

Fig. 24   The effect of differentiation on the product life cycle, sales and profits
curves

firm to maintain a steady profit performance. The point to remember is that quite often the difference between these two strategies is not as clear in practice as in theory. Is the Ford Cortina Mark II a new product or only a product differentiation from the Mark I range? If a brewer decides to market beer in cans instead of bottles does that constitute a new product policy or a differentiation strategy? In practice the distinction is subtle and need not give the marketer sleepless nights. On the other hand, it is useful to appreciate that differentiation often implies an endeavour to lengthen the life of an already 'sick' product and to that extent it must be looked at as a salvage operation rather than a total life cycle policy. The realisation of this aspect can be very helpful in planning the product strategy intelligently.

In this connection it is vitally important to remember that growth in sales and profitability is not necessarily a sign of long-term success. A product may well earn handsome profits for one, two or more years but may still represent a poor investment. A marketer must never overlook this aspect of the life cycle theory. A product is only successful in strategic terms when it is capable of earning sufficient returns during its total life cycle in relation to the investment made in it. In other words a product must be capable, first and foremost, to earn sufficient funds to recover the full investment that the firm has incurred in it. It is only at the point of investment recovery that the question of returns and/or profits arises. Furthermore, when we talk in terms of investment we must include not only the cost of design, manufacturing and inventory but also the full cost of pre-launch marketing projects such as market research, promotion, sampling, physical distribution, etc. It often happens that a firm needs to drop a product owing to poor performance but is reluctant to do so because the investment in that product has not yet been fully recovered.

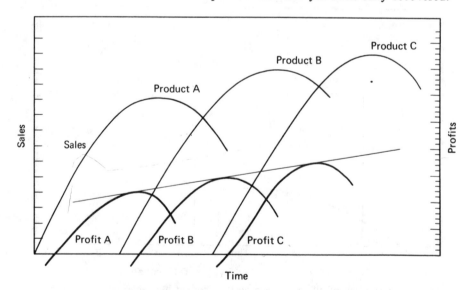

Fig. 25   New product policy and its effect on profit performance

Maintaining such a 'sick' product in the range is tantamount to throwing good money after bad. It is therefore essential for marketing managers to monitor not only sales and profits but also the investment recovery as the product life cycle progresses.

The position is shown in Figure 26. It shows the relationship between investment, sales and direct costs. The profit on this diagram is the gap between the sales curve and cost curve. As a generalisation one will normally find that if the investment in a product has not been recovered by the time the product has reached the saturation stage, it is unlikely to ever show a satisfactory return on investment over the life of the product. This is of course an angle which must not be overlooked when evaluating the future of ageing products.

International Implications

The product life cycle concept has a significant relevance to international marketing. Historically most firms tended to operate in their domestic

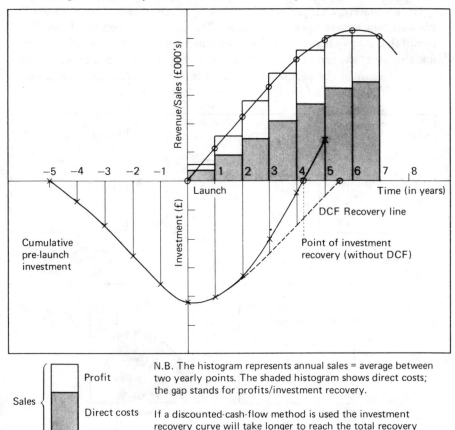

Fig. 26   The investment recovery process and the product life cycle

markets as long as such markets offered adequate commercial rewards. As soon as signs of sales and profit erosion started to manifest themselves the firm would seek to fill the growing gap through exports. This in turn meant that one could discern differing life cycle patterns in different parts of the world. Figure 27 illustrates this point. This diagram shows how a product that has reached the decline stage in the domestic market is at the growth stage in country A, at the introduction stage in country B, whilst in country C it is still unknown. The fifth chart in this diagram shows the gap that one would expect to detect between the two extreme situations (excluding of course those countries where the product has not been launched at all).

This represented a most comfortable routine. All a firm had to do was to classify world markets in accordance with their economic development and launch declining products in quick succession in these groups of countries in a descending scale of sophistication. One could always hope to find a number of markets which would absorb products which in one's domestic market had lost consumer interest.

Unfortunately, changes have been taking place in recent years in world markets which have upset this routine. The communication revolution has meant that the gap between the time when the home market reaches saturation and the last of the export markets reaches saturation has been narrowing. The total life span of the product over all its markets has become shorter and shorter. The trend, in fact, is for the pattern of the life cycle in a domestic

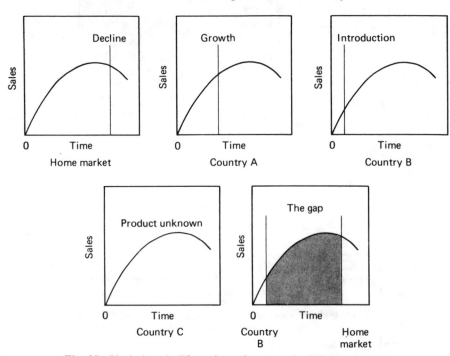

Fig. 27   Variations in life cycle performance in different countries

market to become identical to the pattern in other markets. This change, illustrated in Figure 28 is the underlying philosophy that has made international marketing so different from the previous process of 'selling abroad'. This is one of the main reasons why the marketer of today must gaze at international markets simultaneously, with the view of planning a global launch. Failure to do so may in many instances mean that good opportunities will be lost.

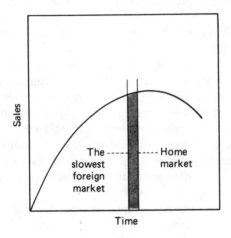

Fig. 28   The narrowing gap between product life cycle extremities

In summary, a full understanding of the product life cycle is an essential concept for the international marketer. It not only allows him to monitor the progression of his products through their various stages of development, thus determing marketing strategies, but it also enables him to plan for a rapid investment recovery effort. This latter point is becoming an elementary and important strategy in the kind of markets that one has to operate nowadays.

Standardisation or Differentiation

The international marketer cannot escape from the fundamental decision—should he design a product which is standard for all markets or should he match the product to the special needs and nuances of each market? This is a problem which we have explored in general terms in earlier chapters. However, it gains a very practical importance in relation to the product itself. A decision taken at the product design stage can determine the pattern of the firm's marketing effort for many years to come. A mistake at this early stage can make a major difference to the firm's fortunes. Whilst it is always very tempting to seek to standardise the product, as every international businessman knows, it is not always possible to do so. On the other hand, as a general rule, to differentiate where market conditions allow for total or partial standardisation is certainly a very extravagant policy. For Kodak to differentiate its range of 'instamatic' cameras in different parts of the world would be a policy of indescribable wastage. At the same time it is difficult to see how a typewriter manufacturer can afford not to differentiate, in order to accommodate the special needs of language and script variations in different countries. It is unlikely that a typewriter that contains Germanic letters only would gain popularity in the French market.

The advantages of product standardisation can be summarised thus:

1 Economy of scale in production, stock-control and servicing policies can be quite significant.
2 Product standardisation is an essential forerunner to the wider aim of developing a marketing mix standardisation. Without a standard product the other ingredients of the mix do not lend themselves to such a policy.
3 The chances of attaining a rapid investment recovery are greatly enhanced where a standard product exists throughout the world.
4 A firm that markets standard products internationally is invariably an easier company to manage both in terms of organisation and control procedures. This is of course quite an attractive attribute to aim for.

On the other hand it is relevant to mention a number of disadvantages that a standardisation strategy entails:

1 Marketing flexibility is often lost in foreign markets through the inability to match the product to detailed local requirements.
2 Standardisation often discourages creativity and innovation especially among personnel of local companies. As their main role is to sell effectively they gradually lose the motivation to contribute ideas to product improvement and innovation.
3 Linked with the above point one often finds that personnel in foreign subsidiaries tend to seek their fortunes in other companies where total marketing jurisdiction including product design is possible.

These points must not be overlooked when planning the product for international markets. The ultimate product decision may indeed, on occasions, be based on personnel and human considerations rather than purely marketing ones. If the quality of the organisation will suffer as a result of a radical standardisation policy the management at the decision point must be fully cognisant of the indirect implications before taking such a step.

Major Considerations Determining International Product Policy

It is thus apparent that product decisions relating to international markets must not be taken lightly. Errors can creep in without the firm realising the full implications. The difficulties that may occur can be very costly. To try to unravel a mess is much more expensive than taking one's time in planning a sound and systematic product policy at the initial stages of the firm's development as an international company.

The main considerations that must be borne in mind in determining a sound product policy can be summarised thus:

1 Corporate Objectives

This point is fundamental; a firm that seeks to maximise profits regardless of international market penetration goals is more likely to strive towards product standardisation. By the very nature of such a strategy it is likely to generate, certainly in the shorter term, a better profit performance. However, this consideration must be looked at in juxtaposition to other and often equally important aspects to be discussed hereunder.

2 The Markets and Their Needs

Here we are concerned with the nature of the product itself and the special requirements of the market-place. We come back to the question of information and the basic 'input'. needed in this connection is the marketing profile analysis which we discussed at some length in earlier chapters. A profile analysis relating to the product itself can be undertaken. Figure 29 shows an enlarged version of the kind of information that the marketer needs to assemble. The 'product' is dissected into its major components viz. functional attributes, design, packaging and branding. Depending on the individual circumstances one can determine the exact nature and number of elements that one wishes to research. The important point to remember is that this is the kind of 'input' which facilitates the decision as to whether a standardisation policy is on the cards or not. Attempting to take a decision of this nature without the information that the profile analysis can yield is asking for trouble.

In other words, one of the major considerations which the marketer must explore when determining his international product policy is the real needs of the markets. He must ask himself: Are the needs of the individual markets so different from each other that standardisation will limit the use of our product to uneconomic levels?

3 Company Resources

Differentiation is a fairly expensive exercise. A firm seeking to attain maximum satisfaction of foreign markets through a non-standardisation policy must be cognisant of the fact that such a policy will absorb considerable investment in production resources, inventory, and. of course, in the various

EXTERNAL/ UNCONTROLLABLE ELEMENTS	CONTROLLABLE INGREDIENTS			
	THE PRODUCT— FUNCTIONAL ASPECTS	AESTHETIC DESIGN	BRANDING	PACKAGING
ENVIRONMENT	– Local ergonomics requirements – Special needs for size, dimensions, standards – Attitudinal constraints – Climatic effect – Available supportive services	– Attitude of local consumers to colours, shapes, general appearance? – Consistency with local taste and traditions	– Is the proposed name acceptable in the market? – Is it pronounceable? – Does it convey the correct message? – Is it easily recallable?	– Available packaging materials in selected manufacturing countries
COMPETITION	– Competitive products and their relative effectiveness (if any) – Unique selling points of competitive products – Product Life Cycle Expectations	– Any design weaknesses identified in competitive products? – Any identifiable aesthetic strengths?	– Competitive practices re names of products – Brand image of competitive products	– Quality of packaging, sizes and special features of competitive products – Can we improve or depart from these standards?
INSTITUTIONS	– Bodies controlling standards – 'Which?' type body testing and comparing qualities – Other institutions that can support and recommend use of product	– Design 'award' possibilities? – Any other body monitoring design quality?	– Are there any institutions that can help us to choose an appropriate brand?	– Are there any packaging testing centres? – Any quasi-legal packaging standards? – Any standards laid down by trade associations?
LEGAL SYSTEM	– Laws affecting use of product (e.g. prohibition laws) – Safety rules – Anti-pollution laws – Patent protection	– Can design be registered? – Any constraints on specific shapes?	– Can the trademark be registered and protected? – Any legal constraints on name selected?	– Special regulations re weights, measures, contents to appear on packaging – Rules re prohibited materials – Trade description rules

Fig. 29 The "input"–product/market portion of the marketing profile analysis

ingredients of the marketing mix. It is quite easy to drift into a differentiation strategy without fully realising the financial consequences.

4 The Nature of the Product

Here the marketer must have a good look at the product itself and try to consider the following points:

(a) IS THE LIFE OF THE PRODUCT LIKELY TO BE SHORT?

If the answer is the affirmative differentiation is probably a risky policy owing to the investment recovery principle explained earlier.

In this respect past history of the firm's other products can be very helpful in providing a clue as to the kind of life cycle performance that one can expect to encounter in the future. Although as a generalisation one can observe that there is a tendency towards a shortening of life cycle characteristics many firms will discover, on careful monitoring, that products do tend to behave in a fairly consistent way within a given industry.

(b) IS THE PRODUCT OF UNIVERSAL APPEAL?

Some products, by their very nature, are capable of international acceptance without needing any differentiation. Japanese manufacturers of Hi-Fi equipment, for instance, have recognised that a well-designed piece of equipment is capable of attaining a substantial penetration of world markets. It would be a strategy of immense waste to endeavour to re-design the product for every market. The interesting point to remember is that even in the case of Japanese electronics, total standardisation is not possible, insofar as wiring standards, safety rules and regulations are laid down by the laws of individual countries and need to be fully satisfied. Nonetheless, if a firm starts from the basic strategy of wanting to standardise the product, it can ensure that deviations from a standard product are kept to the absolute minimum viz. those demanded by the legal system of individual countries.

(c) LEVEL OF SERVICE REQUIRED

Products requiring considerable technical service and attention—either before or after delivery to the customer—usually prescribe a higher level of standardisation. A computer manufacturer would find the technical justification for a standard product or range of products a decisive factor in his product planning and approach. An aircraft manufacturer will also strive towards avoiding any kind of differentiation—partly because of the importance of service and partly because of the universal appeal discussed earlier.

(d) BRANDING

Where a firm has managed to develop an internationally accepted brand or trademark for a specific product the pressure would weigh against differentiation. Coca-Cola is an example; Kodak is another. Which comes first—the chicken or the egg? Has the firm sought a single brand in order to be able to standardise? or, is it now seeking to attain maximum standardisation because such a powerful and well-established brand has been developed? In practice the likelihood is that a firm that has consciously gone for standardisation will start with international brands from an early stage of its internationalisation process. Once such brands have developed the firm would tend to continue to support a standardised product policy under the banner of these international trademarks. Thus the major oil distribution companies like Shell and Exxon will frown upon any attempts at product differentiation under any of their internationally recognised and accepted brands. These brands act as a constraint on differentiation.

(e) EASE OF PRODUCTION

It is not possible to dissociate product policy from production realities. A product which requires intricate manufacturing processes is less likely to support differentiation strategies than a product which can be manufactured with ease. This is of course an important consideration and in many cases production factors may outweigh the marketing benefits that differentiation may yield.

Detergent production is a relatively simple process; manufacturers often opt for local production to serve local markets. In such circumstances it is obviously simple and economic to think in terms of differentiation. At the other extreme, a sophisticated aero-engine is likely to be manufactured in one location and this will have a major influence on marketing decisions, especially where the questions of standardisation and non-standardisation are concerned.

(f) LEGAL CONSTRAINTS

Legal systems can have a major impact on the design of the product, its packaging and the printed messages incorporated thereon. Thus, a packet of cigarettes sold in the UK must contain a warning about the health hazard of smoking. The same packet sold in Canada must contain a warning in two languages—English and French and the actual wording is different from the one prescribed in the UK. In other words the legal systems of the two countries virtually impose a differentiation policy. The law is not interested in the inconvenience that such regulations may impose on marketing personnel. Such variations in legal requirements are particularly troublesome in relation to weights, measures and contents of food products. Such legal requirements must be adhered to most scrupulously. The only way that partial standardisation can be achieved in such situations is through the incorporation of multi-lingual messages, each complying with the rules and regulations of the country of destination. However it needs a very large label to be able to accommodate the legal requirements of eighty or more countries! This is where the clustering method described in Chapter 4 becomes a most valuable tool. It helps the marketer to reduce the number of assemblages offered to the absolute minimum, thus achieving partial standardisation.

Product Strategies for International Markets

In domestic marketing one recognises that sound product planning calls for the application of one or more of the following strategies:

1 Development of new products
2 Deletion of old or weak products
3 Modification of existing products (differentiation) with a view to:

  (a) improving the product performance,
  (b) adjusting the product for new markets (segmentation).

The process of modifying the product may include *up-trading,* where the modification seeks to raise the appeal of the product to more exclusive and discerning segments of the market, or *down-trading,* where the product is being modified to appeal to wider and possibly more popular parts of the consumer population.

  These strategies apply with equal validity to international markets. However, a number of important aspects pertaining more specifically to international decisions must be emphasised.

1 Development of New Products

This is an area in which marketers without international experience often make major errors. It is difficult to resist the temptation of assuming that a product that enjoys some popularity in a home market will be an automatic success abroad. There are many instances where a very successful product at home has proved to be an unqualified disaster in foreign markets. Obviously this can be avoided with adequate research and the systematic evaluation of the 'input' emanating therefrom.

  Screening procedures for new products are always important. In international marketing such procedures can make all the difference between success and failure. Moreover the cost of failure where a few markets are involved is inevitably much higher than where the product has been launched and subsequently failed in a single domestic market. A firm that wants to launch a product in a number of markets, either simultaneously or in quick succession, must ensure that the risk of failure has been minimised through a careful and systematic process of screening. The point to remember is that statistically experience has shown that for every product which is launched commercially one needs to look on average at as many as fifty-eight ideas! Moreover the chances that a new idea will result in a commercial success are less than one in a hundred. It has been suggested that in some industries, for certain types of products, the odds against an idea developing into a commercial proposition are even greater. Thus the Pharmaceutical Manufacturers' Association of the US has reported that the odds are more than 6000 to one that a newly discovered drug will ever reach the market. Plenty of examples exist to illustrate how tricky the screening process can be and how important it is for a company to identify the potential 'breadwinners' of the future.

The classical screening process for new products normally takes the following steps:

> idea generation
> initial screening
> business analysis
> development
> market testing
> commercialisation

The process can be described in a simple chart (Figure 30) which is reminiscent of the technique used for purifying liquids by passing them through a funnel. Starting with a large number of ideas, and gradually moving through a systematic process of distillation, one ends with a very small number of products likely to show fair returns at the commercialisation stage. This process is used of course also in domestic marketing; our purpose here is to highlight the special implications pertaining to sound product screening in a multinational environment.

IDEA GENERATION

Ideas are the life-blood of any business; a firm that has ceased to recognise the need for new ideas or failed to harness the creativity process that exists among its personnel is doomed to a rapidly declining future. A firm operating in an international scene has the great advantage of being able to assemble a wealth of ideas emanating from a variety of nations, cultures and attitudes. The ability to synthesise such ideas into a firm's marketing thinking is the kind of strength which international firms enjoy. A successful product strategy in one country may be a source of inspiration to other parts of the organisation. Admittedly such a success is not a guarantee that the same product will be

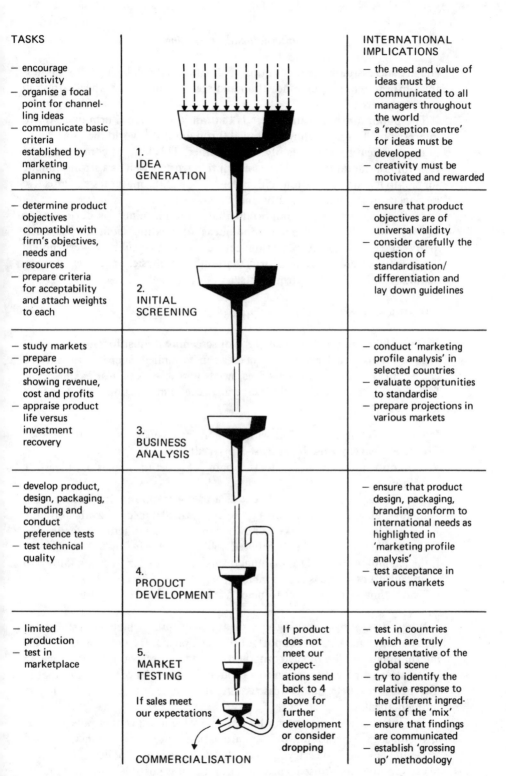

TASKS

- encourage creativity
- organise a focal point for channelling ideas
- communicate basic criteria established by marketing planning

1. IDEA GENERATION

- determine product objectives compatible with firm's objectives, needs and resources
- prepare criteria for acceptability and attach weights to each

2. INITIAL SCREENING

- study markets
- prepare projections showing revenue, cost and profits
- appraise product life versus investment recovery

3. BUSINESS ANALYSIS

- develop product, design, packaging, branding and conduct preference tests
- test technical quality

4. PRODUCT DEVELOPMENT

- limited production
- test in marketplace

5. MARKET TESTING

If sales meet our expectations

COMMERCIALISATION

If product does not meet our expectations send back to 4 above for further development or consider dropping

INTERNATIONAL IMPLICATIONS

- the need and value of ideas must be communicated to all managers throughout the world
- a 'reception centre' for ideas must be developed
- creativity must be motivated and rewarded

- ensure that product objectives are of universal validity
- consider carefully the question of standardisation/ differentiation and lay down guidelines

- conduct 'marketing profile analysis' in selected countries
- evaluate opportunities to standardise
- prepare projections in various markets

- ensure that product design, packaging, branding conform to international needs as highlighted in 'marketing profile analysis'
- test acceptance in various markets

- test in countries which are truly representative of the global scene
- try to identify the relative response to the different ingredients of the 'mix'
- ensure that findings are communicated
- establish 'grossing up' methodology

Fig. 30 New products—screening process

equally successful in other countries. Nonetheless it will be a great weakness for a firm to ignore such innovation and seek to 'invent the wheel' afresh in every market.

The important implication here is that an international firm must try to impress on all its marketing personnel throughout the world the importance of communicating ideas readily to each other. This kind of communication calls for considerable motivation and mutual trust as well as a strong climate for creativity and innovation. This indeed is one of the major tests of effective management in international business.

In this connection it is important that some machinery is developed to collate and communicate all good ideas originating from the far-flung parts of the world. A reception centre for ideas can be a very potent instrument of creativity in a firm that enjoys a physical presence in many national and cultural environments.

INITIAL SCREENING

Before a firm can undertake any type of screening it must formulate a list of criteria against which every product idea can be studied. Such criteria must be consistent with the firm's objectives, needs and resources. For example, the following represent fairly typical screening criteria in selection procedure for a new product:

Is the product idea consistent with the current business we are in?
The gross margin must be at least x per cent.
We are only interested in products capable of generating sales of at least £y million.
Is there a patent? We rank a patent as a useful feature in any new product policy and would favour such a product provided it meets the other criteria.
Is the product likely to make use of our existing manufacturing facilities?
Is the product likely to be distributed/sold through existing arrangements?
Is the technology needed for manufacturing the product in question known to us and if not is it easily available?
Do we estimate the product to be of a long or a short life cycle?

When determing screening criteria for a product which is destined for international markets it is important that one pays sufficient attention to the international validity of such criteria. It would be irrelevant, for instance, to try to attach a patent criterion to a product if the evidence points out that in the main markets under discussion the value of patents is highly problematical.

The international marketer who has to evolve new product policies must also consider the question of standardisation or differentiation within the screening guidelines he is trying to lay down. If the overall policy of the firm is to attempt to standardise its products as far as it is possible, this must find its way into screening criteria. A firm may prescribe in its product objectives such a directive: 'In order to be acceptable in our range a product must be capable of a certain amount of standardisation. In quantitative terms we would reject any product that calls for a greater variation in added value processing than 25 per cent'. A product which demands greater levels of modification in costs terms than 25 per cent will be trapped by the screening net. This is precise and measurable. If the information is not available to be able to measure such variations in costs, one has to go and obtain such information. It may be troublesome, but at the same time the discipline of obtaining data which help to screen products for international exploitation is in itself a very useful exercise. Defining criteria for international products is a very important task and it is difficult to see how a firm can safeguard itself against total or partial failure, without giving considerable thought to the basic guidelines which a new product ought to fulfil. Bearing in mind the cost of failure no marketer can be so foolhardy as to refuse to spend the time in defining the main criteria which an acceptable product should fulfil.

A useful tool in this connection is the flow diagram—the algorithm—in which the marketer tries to discipline himself towards setting out the various criteria in a logical sequence. If such a sequence is well prepared it can be a very potent tool in identifying at an early date those products which are not worth pursuing. (See Figure 31.)

BUSINESS ANALYSIS

Once the product has filtered through from the initial screening stage, a thorough study of the various markets must take place and data quantified with the view of preparing projections. The aim is to try to translate the data thus collected into financial terms. The data must be built into a profit and loss account and the various implications evaluated. The fundamental 'input' which is required for this task is a marketing profile analysis. As we have seen earlier this information should help the marketer to determine how far a clustering process is possible, and that in turn will reflect itself in the estimated revenue, costs and profits. The business analysis is an important stage in the new product development process. The marketer can still reject his earlier decisions in the light of the figures emanating from this analysis. However, he can be sure of one thing: he will not waste his time on analysing products which do not fit into the firm's corporate and marketing objectives. The earlier screening should take care of that.

The main aim of the business analysis stage in international marketing is to collect the information that will enable the marketer to determine:

(i) The commercial viability of the product.
(ii) The number of countries in which it is likely to be a success.
(iii) The level of standardisation which the product can sustain without incurring an adverse image and acceptability in the specific markets identified.

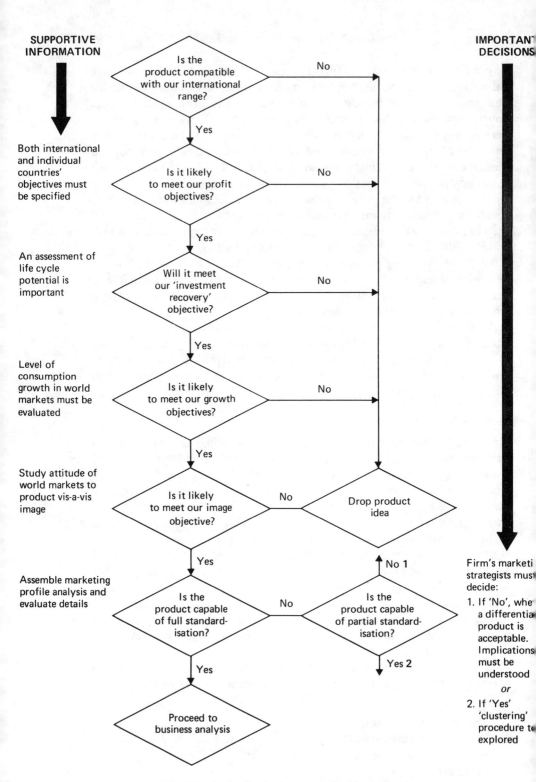

Fig. 31 A simple product screening flow diagram

PRODUCT DEVELOPMENT

This stage is essentially implemental. Here the marketing man needs to involve other functions such as production and R & D personnel. The details of the product are worked out; packaging and design objectives are laid down; internationally acceptable brands selected and preference tests conducted.

The quality of the work undertaken at this stage will depend to a great extent on the accuracy and thoroughness of the marketing profile analysis projects carried out during the business analysis stage. If these projects fail for instance to highlight major variations in consumer taste in various parts of the world errors of design will inevitably find their way into the product itself or into a few of its supportive accessories.

MARKET TESTING

It is not imperative to undertake test marketing activities in every set of circumstances. In fact there are occasions when test marketing is probably quite inappropriate. Examples exist where test marketing proved to be more harmful than useful, insofar as a competitor has gained considerable advantage from the wealth of information he managed to assemble from observing the way the test was progressing. Inevitably a marketer must assess very carefully the implications that a test marketing study may have on the market-place and the possible danger of valuable data leaking into the hands of competitors. Moreover, the writer has come across situations where a competitor was malicious enough to distort the results of a test marketing effort, by sending members of his staff to buy a product in fairly large quantities in order to lead the testing company up the garden path!

Nonetheless in many situations test marketing is a potent instrument for removing residual doubts about a new product or service or about one of its supportive ingredients such as the brand, the packaging, the design, colouring, etc. The aim of test marketing is to examine the performance of the product in a 'pilot' experiment and in a highly controlled market-place, and monitor results. Such an experiment may either prove that all the assumptions made at the product development stage were right or that the product has to undergo some modifications.

Test marketing can answer such questions as:

Is the new product labelled and packaged properly?
Is the new product liked by the consumer?
Is the firm justified in spending large sums on productive capacity?
Has the communication programme been right?

Positive answers to such questions will give reassurance and confidence to management and help to remove whatever doubts may still exist in the organisation about the new product.

Test marketing conducted in a domestic market normally calls for the following conditions:

(a) *The test area must be representative of the total market.* It is quite pointless to conduct a test in a city or a region which is not typical of the macro-market. Thus one-industry towns must be avoided. Similarly a city which is the frequent spot for test marketing may be so over-tested that it ceases to be a representative sample of the national market.

It is normally advisable to conduct tests in more than one town in order to 'smooth' regional differences. However, here the tester must gauge cost versus likely benefits and also the chance that a competitor will react to the whole programme. The wider the test the greater the risk of competitive interference.

(b) *The test must last as long as is necessary to obtain representative results.* To be useful the test must last long enough for the results to be indicative of success or failure. An initial spurt of purchases may stem from the innovators seeking to try a new product. In other words the test must last at least as long as it takes for repeat purchases to take place. The innovators will simply return to their old favourite brand following their first purchase. Other consumers, on the other hand, will re-purchase the new offering a second and third time. These are the hard-core buyers whose performance the test marketing exercise seeks to identify. Trying to jump to conclusions too early in the test nullifies the whole objective of the experiment and may lead the tester to unexpected surprises.

(c) *The test must be conducted during a period which is free of exceptional influences.* The test must be planned in such a way that sales performance is not distorted through unusual circumstances. Thus a test marketing exercise planned to start a short while before the Christmas shopping rush may well distort the results. Similarly a test planned to coincide with the re-opening of the schools after the summer holiday will create the wrong impression as to the real market potential of stationery products.

(d) *The area selected for testing must offer sufficient market data to make the results measurable.* This means that areas where accurate information about the consumer, his age profile, socioeconomic class, urban/rural domicile and employment must be preferred to areas where there is a shortage of such data. Furthermore some areas have better research institutions located in them than others. Such areas make better locations for controlled experimentation projects.

In international markets test marketing gains a very complex dimension. The world is the market-place and the test marketing area may be either a country or a cluster of countries. To attempt to conduct test marketing in one city in the UK and then, if successful, proceed to a test in the whole of the UK as a preamble to global marketing seems rather absurd.

As was suggested earlier over-indulgence in test marketing or in any other type of controlled experimentation carries some risks. It has been known for products to have reached the end of their life cycle whilst the firm was in the process of testing and re-testing. It is reminiscent of the saying that the operation was successful but the patient is dead! Time is often of the essence in successful marketing especially where some innovative strategy is applied. This is particularly true in situations where the firm has the multiple exposure which international marketing inevitably entails. In other words the international marketer has different dimensions of time and geography with which to contend.

The conditions listed earlier for a successful test marketing programme can now be adapted to the international scene. It must be first assumed that sufficient research has been conducted to be able to complete a marketing profile analysis of each market in which one intends to sell one's product. At this point it is possible to emphasise two major aspects which the planner of test marketing on the international scene must bear in mind:

The market selected for test marketing must portray a fairly representative 'marketing ecology' in relation to the main markets that one hopes to serve. If one refers to the clustering technique described in Chapter 4, one can select either the bench-mark market or any other market that fits into the zone which allows maximum standardisation. This means that the selected test market conforms to a greater or lesser extent to a batch of markets which enjoy a fairly similar marketing ecology. Needless to add that where the research has indicated that total differentiation is called for test marketing ceases to be a meaningful exercise.

Thus if the clustering technique has identified France, Germany, the Netherlands and Belgium as markets of similar marketing ecologies it is quite relevant to choose any one of these markets as the area for test marketing. The choice will depend on the market that satisfies best the next consideration.

The country selected for test marketing must possess professional institutions capable of collecting pertinent data about the market's response to the product under test. Conducting test marketing in a country in which information gathering facilities are poor is not to be recommended.

Market data is essential for a sound test marketing programme and that in turn requires monitoring and research capabilities in the country in which tests will be conducted. Thus countries in which store-audit facilties exist must be preferred to those which do not possess such a service. Moreover we have seen earlier that comparability of research data is an essential part of international information systems. Therefore the ideal test country is the one in the cluster which offers not only research facilities of high competence but also the one capable of presenting such data in a comparable fashion.

Grossing-up
The discussion on test marketing will not be complete without reference to the question of how to gross-up results. The whole purpose of test marketing is to gauge potential sales from the results of the pilot trial. The process of translating these results into estimated performance figures in the total market which one seeks to serve calls for some skill.

A number of methods for grossing-up can be used. In all the methods to be discussed it will be assumed that the ultimate aim is to market the product under test in a well-defined cluster of markets and that adequate data are available about the salient characteristics of such markets.

Direct share of market method. This is the simplest and crudest way for grossing-up test results. The assumption here is that the market share gained in the test country will repeat itself in the global scene.
This can be expressed in the simple formula:

If $T_s = 20\%$ therefore $G_s = 20\%$
where T_s means market share achieved in the Test country and G_s expected share of the Global market

The weakness is of course that one assumes that the marketing effort and the marketing institutions will be of comparable quality in all markets in the cluster. It also presupposes that we know the size of the present consumption in every market and can talk in terms of market shares on an international basis.

Population basis. This method is based on the idea that sales depend on the size of a country's population irrespective of socioeconomic or demographic variances. This may well be a reasonable assumption, within a cluster of countries identified as homogeneous markets, after comparing in detail their respective marketing profile analyses.

$$G = T \times \frac{G_p}{T_p}$$

where G = sales in international/cluster markets
T = sales in test country
G_p = population in international/cluster markets
T_p = population in test country

Buying Index basis. This relates to a product which is being launched into a well-established market where existing brands have an important position. Moreover current consumption levels of existing products or brands in the various markets are known and their percentage in each market in relation to the global consumption is also available. The formula that can be employed is:

$$G = \frac{T}{pc} \times 100$$

where G = sales in international/cluster markets

T = sales in test country

pc = sales in test country of all brands as percentage of total international/cluster consumption

Sales Ratio method. Here one tries to compare results in the test country versus the total market in parallel with another product or brand with which the product tested is assumed to have a logical relationship. An estimate can be made of the new product's international performance as follows:

$$G_x = \frac{G_y}{T_y} \times T_x$$

where G_x = sales of *new* product (x) in international markets

G_y = sales of *existing* product (y) in international markets

T_x = sales of product x in test country

T_y = sales of product y in test country

More complex grossing-up methods exist but they are outside the scope of this book. It is useful to illustrate the four methods described through a simple exercise:

A firm has developed a new type of razor blade (brand x) which it plans to market throughout the EEC (260 million population). Test marketing has been conducted in the Netherlands (population 13 million). Sales in the test country reached the sterling equivalent of £450,000 per annum representing a market share of 8 per cent. The Netherlands represent 6 per cent of the total EEC razor blade consumption. The total EEC sales at retail prices are £90 million. A well-known brand y sells £500,000 in the Netherlands and £9 million in the EEC as a whole. (N.B. these figures are put forward as an example only; they do not purport to offer data based on research.)

Let us now attempt to gross-up the results of this test:

(i) *Direct share of market method*

$T = 8\%$

Therefore $G = 8\%$ of £90 million viz. £7·2 million

(ii) *Population basis*

$$G = T \times \frac{G_p}{T_p}$$

$$G = £450,000 \times \frac{260}{13} = £9\ million$$

(iii) *Buying index basis*

$$G = \frac{T}{pc} \times 100$$

$$G = \frac{£450,000}{6} \times 100 = £7 \cdot 5 \text{ million}$$

(iv) *Sales ratio method*

$$G_x = \frac{G_y}{T_y} \times T_x$$

$$G_x = \frac{£9 \text{ million}}{£0 \cdot 5} \times £450,000 = £8 \cdot 1 \text{ million}$$

Thus, using four different methods for grossing-up the results in the test country, we obtain four different estimates of potential market sales in the total market: £7·2 million, £9 million, £7·5 million, £8·1 million. The average is about £7·95 with an error range of plus 13 per cent and minus 9·4 per cent. Maybe a disappointing range but nonetheless a most useful beacon in the process of steering a new product through the uncharted waters of multinational marketing. Test marketing may sound a formidable discipline in the task of reducing residual risks, but if handled skilfully it can yield considerable benefits and cut out considerable waste.

Where test marketing is conducted on behalf of an 'umbrella' type firm it is vitally important that the test, its objectives and methodology are fully communicated to all parts of the international marketing organisation. Failure to communicate the salient details of such tests to sister companies can nullify the whole value and purpose of controlled experimentation and can only weaken the enormous pay-off that an international presence can bestow on a company.

COMMERCIALISATION

Test marketing should pave the way towards finalising the plans for a successful launch. The purpose of the testing is to remove any doubts that may still surround the product, the packaging, the branding or some other feature associated with the product. Moreover, effective testing should highlight any defects or weaknesses which were not perceived during the product development stage. There is no better way for validating one's ideas and plans than through the dynamic exposure of a product to the rigours of the market-place and the consuming public.

Modifications may have to be incorporated in the product or in one of its ancillary features. Once these have been completed the plans to market the product internationally must proceed. This is a phase where one can tell the difference between a truly international marketer and the domestic marketer who wants to achieve extra sales abroad. The former has prepared global launching plans in advance. He is ready to proceed at short notice to commercialise the product in international markets or in a select cluster of countries. He is simply waiting for the 'all clear' sign before proceeding with the implementation of well-prepared plans. Furthermore the international marketer has developed contingency plans in the event that the test marketing results have proved surprisingly off beam. His plans encapsulate a total marketing strategy, including fundamental decisions on how far the product should be differentiated in world markets, and how far the supportive marketing mix should be adjusted to meet the specific needs of each market or cluster of markets.

At the other extreme the domestic marketer who proceeds to exploit world markets has to face contingencies as and when they arise. He suddenly discovers that the brand he had selected for the home market needs to be changed. That means of course that the packaging and supportive literature have to be changed. The promotional effort has to be adjusted accordingly. Production has to cope with a number of permutations based on these variations. Inventories have to be maintained at considerable additional costs. All these contingencies often occur in the non-internationally orientated company, and where no prior planning exists, all the financial assumptions are thrown out of gear. The difference between the two approaches may sound subtle but somehow its impact never fails to demonstrate the importance of planning international marketing strategies rather than let things happen.

In normal circumstances a test marketing experiment yields one of the following outcomes:

(a) *The test results meet fully the marketer's expectations.* Commercialisation here does not present any problems. The firm proceeds with the plans as laid down prior to the test having commenced. The main decision to be taken in these circumstances is the sequence at which the product will be commercialised in the various markets that have been identified as the main target areas for international marketing. The plans may seek to commercialise the product in all markets simultaneously. In many situations this approach is highly desirable in as much as a speedy exploitation of world markets may be the safest strategy for attaining maximum returns from a new product and quickest investment recovery.

(b) *The test results are only partially satisfactory.* The next step must be selected with care. Four options are open to the marketer:

   (i) To take an optimistic view of the results and proceed to full commercialisation.

   (ii) To arrange for a further test in a different country in order to validate or refute the first set of results.

   (iii) Identify the reasons for the partially satisfactory results and incorporate modifications in the product or its supportive mix.

   (iv) Drop the product altogether.

A decision as to which of these courses of action should be adopted depends of course on the firm's general circumstances, its financial resources and its urgent need for a new product. In this latter event a firm may be forced to adopt an entrepreneurial attitude and proceed to commercialisation, inspite of the fact that the evidence stemming from the test results is not overwhelmingly in favour of such a strategy.

(c) *The results of the test are poor.* Needless to say that the marketer must try to understand the reasons that contributed to this failure. Sometimes the results of a test are poor simply because the test itself was badly planned and executed. However, assuming that the test was properly designed three options are open:

    (i) Plan a new test marketing experiment in a different country. This is particularly appropriate where doubts exist as to whether the first test was properly conducted.

    (ii) Modify the product or the marketing mix in accordance with the results of the test and the interpretation of the reasons for the poor performance.

    (iii) Drop the product idea.

It is much more difficult to justify a commercialisation programme in a situation where the initial test results proved unsatisfactory. To take an entrepreneurial decision in the face of unfavourable indicators is asking for trouble.

It is important to emphasise at this point that a product is constantly 'on test'. The fact that it has performed well in a test marketing experimentation, and that the company has decided to commercialise it globally, or in a number of markets, does not mean that the product has graduated into total immunity from challenge and scrutiny. Indeed one of the main jobs of an effective marketer is to monitor the product and submit it to frequent 'check-ups.' Any weakness must be identified at an early date. In other words, a product is constantly undergoing a tacit test, and the comments made about test marketing, in general, apply to every product after it has been commercialised with equal vigour.

2 Deletion of Old or Weak Products

How to delete weak or decaying products from an international range can be quite a problem for the international marketer. What is a weak product? A product may perform well in a number of countries and very poorly in others. The marketing personnel in the former will want to keep this product in the range. The personnel of the latter will want it dropped or modified. These two points of view are inevitably in a state of conflict. Dropping the product may have serious repercussions in one set of markets. Refusing to do anything to satisfy the needs of other markets can generate equally unhappy reactions.

In an 'umbrella' type organisation, one would normally expect to see a large number of products and differentiations on the same theme. This is one of the inherent characteristics of such a structure and the freedom to innovate which it bestows on local management. The decision to delete products is essentially a local one, and whilst it may have some effect on the firm's global production performance, little or no interference normally takes place with local management's freedom to take such decisions. This can of course be a source of overall weakness in as much as the firm may fail to identify those products that have ceased to earn their keep within the firm's global objectives. After all, the fact that the product is still profitable in one or more countries is only relevant if in the total context of the international organisation, irrespective of the kind of structure it has, the effort invested in producing and marketing such a product can yield the expected results.

In most companies operating on an international scale, an examination of their products' performance will probably show a number of areas where the classic Pareto's law would apply. Pareto, a nineteenth century economist, propounded the theory that in most situations 80 per cent of total results could be attributed to 20 per cent of total activity. Thus an industrial chemicals firm has found that 80 per cent of its sales are handled by 20 per cent of its salesmen. An airline has discovered that 20 per cent of its routes generate 80 per cent of its revenue. This is a very useful tool when one tries to identify the real 'breadwinners' in any complex situation.

Before one can even consider dropping existing products one must attempt to quantify the total performance of each product in world markets. A focal point must be developed to collate information from all markets regarding the sales and contribution performance of the firm's various products. The aim is to identify the international value of products to the total firm rather than monitor individual markets' performance. Procedures must be laid down in order to evaluate the way a product is progressing in the various markets that the company is serving. Such procedures need not be complicated. However, they must specify clearly what is wanted from local managers, and where the marketing effort is conducted in a decentralised fashion it is important that local personnel are adequately motivated to respond to what appears as an additional bit of bureaucracy. In this connection an explanation of the underlying thinking is probably a useful aid to motivation. A full understanding of the product life cycle concept, and its implications to a multinational situation, should remove any residual doubt regarding the legitimacy of such procedures in the effort to identify dying products on a global scene.

Figure 32 illustrates a simple form that may help to collect the appropriate information that an international marketer may wish to obtain in his attempt to measure how a product is performing in world markets.

The important implication of everything that has been said in connection with product deletion is that some sort of product control must take place in a firm marketing its products internationally. Whilst this comes quite naturally to a centralised firm it is slightly inconsistent with the freedom that decentralised units enjoy. Nonetheless it is important that products are not

PRODUCT EVALUATION PROCEDURE

Product No. _____

Country _____

Form completed by _____ Position _____

Date _____

	1976	1977	1978	1979	1980	1981	1982
Sales in Units							
Sales value							
Contribution							
% Contribution to Total Turnover							

	Yes	No
1. Are there signs of weakening in consumer acceptance of the product _____	☐	☐
2. If 'Yes' would product modification help? _____	☐	☐
3. Are there other products in the pipeline which need the resources that are locked in this product? _____	☐	☐

4. *Assuming* that the product is dropped, try to:

    a. estimate the value of financial resources that might be released

        Direct ☐

        Indirect ☐

    b. managerial time that will be freed (in %)

        Direct ☐

        Indirect ☐

General remarks _____

_____

_____

_____

Fig. 32 Product evaluation procedure

allowed to drift on and on just because a few markets still want them. Somewhere along the line a method must be evolved to monitor the 'state of health' of ageing products. Through effective communication and creative motivation one can keep such products under constant supervision and without unduly interfering with managerial autonomy. This is certainly an area where the clarity of objectives in the first place helps enormously in taking deletion decisions. If, at the planning stage, the international marketer has laid down clear and quantitative objectives as to what a product must achieve to remain in the range, the ultimate decision as to whether to delete such a product or not becomes that much simpler. Thus if the product has ceased to contribute a predetermined level of gross margin or sales volume or profit, in relation to resources utilised, the decision becomes reasonably easy.

Modification of Existing Products

The process of modifying products with the view of either 'cheating old age' or penetrating new segments of the market is one of the strategies that marketers resort to when they perceive a weakening in product performance. A car manufacturer who introduces a 'face-lift' into a current model seeks to lengthen the life cycle of the product by giving it a slightly fresher look. In most instances he realises that such a strategy can only give him a limited breathing space during which time he must plan more drastic strategies such as the introduction of new models or the development of totally new products.

On the other hand the pharmaceutical manufacturer who modifies his Aspirin tablets by imparting to them a strawberry flavour aims to satisfy children thus serving a totally new segment of an existing market. In marketing terms such a modification is tantamount to the introduction of a new product, insofar as a different market is being served and the modified product will be enjoying the normal characteristics of life cycle pattern.

Whether a modification amounts to a mere product differentiation or to a new product often stirs considerable controversy. It is quite unimportant as to what posture one takes in this connection. What is important is that no modification is undertaken without clearly-defined objectives. Modifications which are not based on marketing 'input' are as likely to fail as new products which have been designed without undertaking the normal process of screening, development and testing described earlier.

Before carrying out any modifications to an existing product one must assemble the following information:

(a) *A general assessment of the product's performance over a period.* The aim of such an exercise is to identify weaknesses in the life cycle pattern of existing products.
(b) *The attitude of the consumer to the product.* If the average consumer is happy with the product and sales are still satisfactory there is very little reason to plan a modification.
(c) *Competitive practices.* Here the marketer must be alert to what his

competitors are doing and must try to keep himself up-to-date with trends in the market-place. A product modification based on a conscious attempt to pre-empt a competitive product strategy is the kind of situation which can only be carried out effectively if all relevant facts are available.

A product modification can be a potent strategy in many situations especially where the company's investment recovery programme has been slow to materialise. As stated earlier it is vitally important that sufficient information is assembled to indicate the direction that such a modification should take. Every marketer can recount many instances where a slight modification of the product or one of its associated components has helped to save the day. At the same time it must be emphasised that in international marketing the problem of modification is very complex and the marketer in such situations must be able to answer the following questions:

(i) Do we possess enough information to justify the idea that a product modification is necessary? [Yes]   [No]

(ii) Is the modification called for to satisfy local, regional or international needs?   Explain

Local	
Regional	
International	

(iii) If the answer to the previous question was *'Local'*: Can a modification be carried out in one market without affecting our international product policy?   [Investigate]

(iv) Can a modification be carried out without upsetting the following costs?

Production	[Yes]	[No]
Physical distribution	[Yes]	[No]
Marketing	[Yes]	[No]
Financing	[Yes]	[No]

quantify the implications

(v) Is the modification likely to 'down-trade' (or 'up-trade') the product in the eyes of the international consumer in whose countries the modification is not going to be introduced?   [Explore]

(vi) Have we up-dated our marketing profile analyses?   [Yes]   [No] → [Instruct]

(vii) If 'yes', is there any evidence to indicate that the modification can be standardised for all markets or for a cluster of markets?   [Yes]   [No]

Other questions can be added to the above checklist. The mere process of thinking around the implications of a modification policy is a useful formula for avoiding mistakes.

Chapter 7

Pricing in World Markets

Pricing the product is a tricky problem in a domestic market. In international marketing it can be a nightmare. The trouble is that the price is a quantitative and unequivocal figure. It is there to be compared and analysed by competitors, distributors and consumers alike. The mismanagement of a firm's pricing policy can easily lead to:

1 Substantial variations in the price of the same product in different countries.
2 Pressures for price reductions and/or bigger discounts resulting from such variations.
3 The development of a 'grey market' by unscrupulous traders. A grey market is created where the product is purchased in a cheap market with the view of being sold in markets enjoying higher prices.

In extreme situations these pressures can undermine the marketer's profit expectations.

A sound international marketing strategy demands therefore that a framework for decision-making in the pricing area is evolved. In the absence of such a framework or a series of guidelines the firm runs the risk of allowing its international pricing to run out of control. The problem becomes even more acute in an era of exchange anarchy and floating currencies.

The structure of the firm and the level of decentralisation developed therein have a major influence on the pricing policies of such a company. A firm that has opted for an 'umbrella' structure is unlikely to attain a centrally-controlled price uniformity. In fact the underlying philosophy of the organisation may be quite unsympathetic to such a strategy. On the other hand a company structured as a macropyramid is much better attuned to a policy of relatively homogeneous international pricing. In the extreme case one encounters the firm that seeks to impose a single price for its product throughout world markets. Attractive as such a policy is one must not overlook the complications that may arise from the incidence of local taxes, such as sales tax or value added tax, custom duties, etc. To aim for a uniform price at the retail level throughout the world is indeed asking for trouble. A well-known manufacturer of photographic equipment sought to homogenise its price in respect of a major product on a global scale. Price parity was the motto of the marketing boss; it meant that the price that the ultimate consumer would pay would be identical irrespective of whether he bought it in Germany or in South Africa or in Mexico. To achieve this objective the firm had to manipulate its basic ex-works price in such a way that by the time the product reached the consumer a standard price was applied. Thus a standardised price was attained in all countries, certainly in the main industrialised markets that mattered, inspite of the great variations that existed in the various custom duties and sales taxes. It was a masterpiece of financial juggling and accountancy. In marketing terms it was excellent thinking in so far as the consumer knew where he stood in relation to the product in question and knew that there was little point in 'shopping around' in various countries for lower prices resulting from the different duties prevalent in such countries. The consumer likes to be relieved of the need to make enquiries about comparative prices in different markets. It gives him reassurance that the price he is paying is non-negotiable and firm. Nonetheless in our particular case a major complication struck: sharp middlemen discovered that it was possible to buy large quantities of the product 'under bond', and prior to any tax having been levied, and ship them back to the country of origin. The firm's pricing objective became a source of acute embarrassment all round. The initial desire to standardise world prices with the view of giving the international consumer maximum satisfaction misfired badly.

It is advisable to plan one's international pricing policies with great care. No effort should be spared in assembling all the relevant data which may affect the development of such policies. Mistakes usually occur through inadequate understanding of market attitudes and conditions. The cost of mistakes often outweighs the cost of research.

A motor-car manufacturer launched a new model at £4,000 with prices hovering above and below this figure depending on the incidence of taxes and duties. Unfortunately inadequate research was conducted on the price elasticity of that particular model. In fact the price was more or less determined by the production cost per unit at a given level of output and to which a predetermined margin was added. Once the car was launched, it was soon discovered that demand outstripped supply and that a 'black market' developed to such an extent that the consumer was prepared to pay £1,000 above the list price. In terms of lost profit the price selected cost the firm vast sums of money. In terms of consumer satisfaction facts speak for themselves: the consumer seemed quite happy to pay £5,000; surely creative research should have highlighted what the consumer was actually prepared to pay for the car in question. Such research might have cost the firm a fairly substantial amount but definitely far less than the margins they lost through an error of such a massive proportion.

Once again the marketing profile analysis is a valuable tool for pinpointing the factors which affect pricing policies and decisions both at home and in international markets. The kind of information which this methodology can yield is illustrated in Figure 33.

ENVIRONMENT	Are there any social or cultural taboos on the consumer that may affect the amount of money he is prepared to spend on our product? Is it customary to build 'special reductions' into the price structure to allow for traditional haggling? Are there any psychological Do's and Dont's pertaining to consumer attitudes to price?
COMPETITION	Who are our 'brand' competitors and also 'functional' competitors? Obtain a summary of their attitudes to pricing decisions How do competitors behave in the face of pressures on prices? Can competitors' prices be linked with specific market segments?
INSTITUTIONS	Are there bodies which must be consulted prior to determining the price? Is there a body (e.g. · *Consumers Association* or *Which?*–type publication) which compares the cost/benefit of products thus influencing prices?
LEGAL	Are there any limitations on the freedom to determine a price? Any legal constraints on price changes? Retail price maintenance? Legislation against restrictive trade practices. Legal limitations on margins. Need to print price details on product and/or packaging

Fig. 33   The 'price' portion of the marketing profile analysis

Pricing—International Considerations

A number of major considerations should be studied with care before laying down guidelines for pricing policies for a firm's international markets.

1 Corporate Objectives

This is of course always the starting point: until one knows what the firm wishes to achieve one cannot determine a sound price for the firm's products. A firm may achieve a volume of profit by catering for a small number of consumers with a high quality product and at a high price. A competitor may opt for a different approach: he may wish to attain a substantial penetration of the market with a lower quality product at a lower price and yet achieve virtually the same amount of profit. The net result of these two extremes may be the same in terms of profit but totally different in terms of turnover, production load, productivity and so on. The underlying considerations in each situation will be different, and it is essential for a person responsible for determining the price of a product to understand these considerations and the goals of the firm that result therefrom. It is the role of the strategic level of the firm to communicate such a fundamental 'input' to the marketing personnel wherever they may be located.

Pricing decisions would differ substantially in each one of the following situations:

Firm A: 'We wish to maximise profits in world markets whilst concentrating on the top segment in each one of the markets that we serve.'

Firm B: 'We aim to attain maximum penetration of our world markets with a minimum market share of 40 per cent in all industrialised countries. This must be consistent with our overall profit aim of 6 per cent on sales.'

Firm C: 'We seek to make maximum profit and as soon as possible in order to improve our cash flow.'

Inevitably each set of objectives would call for a different orientation to the firm's pricing policy. In the case of Firm A the price and margins will be high so as to match them to the needs and image of the top segment which the firm wishes to satisfy. It may well mean that the sales will be much smaller than they could have been if the objectives were more flexible and all-embracing. However, the company may have very good reasons for wishing to remain exclusive in its market coverage and penetration, and its pricing policy must take full-notice of the implications.

In the case of Firm B those responsible for pricing the products will have to strike a balance between having a low price which will enable the company to sell sufficient quantities to attain a 40 per cent market share and at the same time maintain a 6 per cent margin on sales.

In the case of Firm C and its corporate objectives the pricing policy will be motivated by one major factor: 'What price should we charge for our product which will motivate our channels of distribution to pay promptly? Our liquidity position is serious and we need a better cash flow.' This will no doubt stimulate the firm to give better discounts for quick settlement and probably also a lower price for larger purchases. Once again the pricing policy will stem directly from the corporate objectives of the firm at a given moment.

2 Competition

Assuming that the firm's corporate objectives are clear and that they have been communicated to all managers one must gauge the impact that competition may have on one's freedom to manipulate one's prices. Competition, whether it is of the brand type or of the functional type, can be so powerful that the marketer is virtually forced to follow the leadership of the major manufacturer in the market. This in turn can have a significant influence on the pricing policy of the firm in other markets in as much as the marketing objective may call for a reasonably standard price throughout the firm's markets. In other words, competitive pressures may have an overriding impact on a company's pricing decisions.

It is often suggested that where the level of innovation is high, a firm can escape from the rigours of competitive pricing. This is probably right where the competition is of the 'brand' type. However, where the competition is of the 'functional' type it is more difficult to ignore the cost-benefit value of other products that perform the same function. For example a new packaging designed to replace glass bottles for milk could not justify a higher price than the total cost, direct and indirect, of the existing bottles. In exceptional cases, the new pack could carry a small premium for aesthetic and novelty values, but these cannot be more than a very marginal addition to the comparable price of the more traditional offering. By indirect cost we include a reduction in the breakage rate of the new product as against glass bottles, the amount of space it takes in distribution, the weight and so on. In other words when determining the price in relation to competition one must bring into consideration the total inventory of benefits that the one product can offer when compared to other products that have been designed to fulfil the same function. A good example of this kind of cost-benefit analysis is illustrated in the KLM-air cargo case incorporated at the end of this book.

Whilst talking about the influence of competition on a firm's pricing policies it must not be forgotten that on occasions the company determines a price with the specific objective of discouraging competitors from entering into a given market.

3 Investment Recovery Expectations

'What is the expected life of the product?' and 'How much profit need we generate in order to recover the total investment in this product during its lifetime?' are crucial questions for helping the marketing planner to determine a sensible pricing policy. A firm that has experienced short life cycle problems coupled with a heavy investment programme will inevitably try to charge the highest price that the market would bear. This is a familiar occurrence in the pharmaceutical industry.

4 The Firm's International Structure

This point was touched upon in the earlier part of this chapter. A firm that has structured its international operations on a centralised pattern (the macropyramid) is more likely to develop strong pricing guidelines emanating from some central authority. It is much more difficult to exercise control procedures or guidelines in a decentralised enterprise. It is much more common to find price variations among markets organised on the 'umbrella' principle than on the macropyramid structure.

Anybody who seeks to lay down an international pricing policy should first consider whether such a strategy would be consistent with the style of structure that has been selected for the firm's international presence. In fact any attempt at introducing rigidity on pricing policies in an 'umbrella' type firm may well defeat the whole purpose and points of strength underlying such an organisation. Giving managerial freedom with the one hand and withdrawing it with the other does not add up to consistent logic. In brief, therefore, it must be accepted that the organisation selected for a firm's international business will have a major influence on its attitude to pricing decisions.

5 Legal Constraints

Over the years pricing policies have attracted the attention of lawyers and legislators of many countries. It has always been recognised that the economic welfare of a country could be manipulated through pricing practices to the advantage of powerful manufacturers and to the disadvantage of the consumer and the public at large. Each country has adopted its own style of curtailment of the freedom to compete. The main objective of such interference with the freedom to manipulate pricing decisions was to safeguard the interest of the consumer and the economy in general. Thus the US has adopted the radical view that small businesses must be protected from the unbridled dominance of big business. The various anti-trust legal instruments seek to punish firms that attempt, through pricing policies, to gain undue power in the market-place. Hence any horizontal price fixing (an agreement among competitors on the level of price to be charged to the consuming public) is an offence carrying heavy penalties.

At the other extreme one encounters countries like Switzerland which tolerate price manipulations provided no abuse of this freedom takes place.

No international marketer can afford to approach the problem of pricing on a global scale without trying to evaluate the legal instruments which may influence such decisions.

6 Other Considerations

(a) LEVEL OF SERVICE REQUIRED IN EACH MARKET

Variations in the specific needs of each market in relation to the installation and/or after-sales service has an important relevance to the price that could be charged.

(b) THE COST OF TRANSPORTATION

Assuming that a standardised pricing policy is adopted the obvious question arises as to who pays the extra cost of transportation to distant destinations? This is an important consideration even in domestic markets. A US manufacturer on the East Coast of the country who sends goods to the West Coast would feel entitled to charge for the freight across the Continent. However, he may easily cost himself out of the market if a competitor is located on the West Coast. This kind of consideration applies with equal force to international markets. The international marketer must resolve the question as to whether he proposes to equalise world prices regardless of distance and transportation costs.

(c) CURRENCY PROBLEMS

We live in an age of currency uncertainties and this aspect is fast developing into a major problem. Ideally one wants to apply a common currency in all markets but this is of course not always possible. Until a short while ago it was possible to decide to invoice in one currency throughout the world. Thus a British company might have chosen to invoice in sterling irrespective of the country of destination. A standard currency for international trade can be a great help in monitoring performance and controlling cash-flow and bank balances. However, with floating currencies and the uncertainties surrounding currency values many companies have opted for the practice of invoicing in the currency of the recipient country. This is of course fine as long as such countries enjoy reasonably hard currencies which can be converted in the open market. It makes sense to invoice the German market in D. marks and the French market in French francs. It does not make sense to invoice the USSR in roubles and the Brazilian market in cruzeiros.

Altogether the influence of currency instability on pricing policies is enormous. The choice of one basic currency is useful but it is important that such a currency is universally recognised as a desirable one. International airlines adhering to the IATA rules and price structure have adopted the US dollar as the basis upon which prices are calculated in the various countries. However, as most people in the air travel industry know this is not always a comfortable basis for determining the price of a journey and many anomalies do occur.

It is outside the scope of this book to lay down dynamic principles for dealing with currency problems. The problem is too intricate and solutions much too short-lived to justify in-depth discussion. What the international marketer must consider carefully are the implications of the problem and the need to develop a policy which has some validity in world markets. When currency problems exist marketing personnel and distributors throughout the world grope for help and the ability to offer such help is the test of sound pricing management. In this connection the writer has recently encountered a firm that has taken a 'basket' of seven major currencies as the basis for determining international prices. This is a particularly useful solution in situations involving a series of instalments spread over a long period as is the case in turnkey projects or large installations.

Pricing Objectives

It was emphasised earlier that pricing strategies stem directly from the firm's corporate and marketing objectives. In fact the price of the product is the instrument through which the firm's profit or other quantitative goals will be attained. Whilst each ingredient of the marketing mix is important in the process of attaining results, the price is the most quantitative element and is least adaptable to change.

If the corporate and marketing objectives have been clearly defined the formulation of pricing objectives should follow logically therefrom. Thus each one of the following marketing objectives would have a direct impact on the pricing objectives of a firm in relation to a product or a group of products:

Return on Investment

Such an objective can be simply reiterated as the basis for pricing decisions. The marketer determines a price which will satisfy the needs of the consumer on the one hand and which will at the same time enable the firm to attain a pre-set return on the capital or investment involved. A price which satisfies the consumer but fails to meet the return on investment goal has obviously failed to meet the underlying objective.

Market Stabilisation

Here the marketer wishes to operate in the market in such a way that little or no disturbance of competitors takes place. Adhering to a pricing policy whereby one follows the recognised leader of the market is a sound way for maintaining stability. The international implication is that one has to identify the leader in each country and aim to operate a pricing policy which upsets him least. This approach may be inconsistent with a desire to have a fairly standard price throughout one's international markets, but it is a case for deciding which objective is the most important in a given set of circumstances. The point to remember is that giant competitors seldom react to a marketer who behaves in a responsible way and does not undercut their prices with the intention of nibbling into the leader's market share.

Maintain and Improve Market Position

Price is a potent instrument for improving one's market share and where the firm is in a defensive position it helps to maintain its existing share.

The pricing implications are obvious. However, the international marketer, especially where he is in control of the global marketing scene, must translate this overall objective into clear pricing strategies for each market. Through price he may be able to improve his market position in less sensitive markets thus creating minimum upheaval in others. The essence of a successful implementation of such a strategy is the availability of information about each market and the behavioural pattern of competitive reaction to price changes. A well prepared marketing profile analysis should provide the marketer with the necessary details in this connection.

Meet or Follow Competition

This is a perfectly legitimate objective in situations where one enters markets for the first time or where one is operating in markets in which one or more competitors enjoy a dominant position. The assumption is that such competitors have been in the markets for some time and therefore they have had an opportunity of testing the validity and acceptability of their existing prices. Moreover, it is seldom a good policy to enter a new market with a flagrant price cutting strategy. The reaction to such a provocation may quickly defeat the marketing aims of the pricing strategy.

Pricing to Reflect Product Differentiation

A company that has a wide range of products serving the same market can choose to highlight the differentiation among these products through variations in prices. Such prices do not aim to reflect the actual difference in cost of production of the products in the range. They seek to attach a subjective 'price tag' to each product thus appealing to a range of segments. A watch manufacturer can offer two different models—one at a very high price and one at a low price. The former will appeal to one segment of the population; the latter will appeal to a totally different segment. However, the price variation need not fully reflect the cost of production. As long as the products are seen as different and the more expensive product offers a sufficient number of unique selling points to reflect the differentiation, everybody is happy. Such a strategy can have important international implications: if the firm is aiming at a pricing policy to reflect product differentiation, it must ensure that this game is played consistently throughout the world. The strategy is sure to fail if in one country the price differentiation is adhered to and in another market the underlying philosophy is ignored and the two products are sold at more or less the same price. With the speed at which international rumours are communicated nowadays it will not be long before the strategy is in shreds. The problem is of course less likely to occur where the price is determined at one centre. However, this problem can be quite acute in a decentralised firm where the price is fixed by the local management of each market.

Market Skimming Objective

The aim here is to set a price which is at the top end of the range of possible prices. The seller will continue with this price until he feels that he wishes to penetrate the market more deeply. At that point he would lower the price, especially where he has evidence that demand elasticity exists. Skimming objective is particularly useful where the product is new and the firm has production limitations and it is not fully aware of the market situation. Normally in the case of new products price is less important, in so far as the innovators who are the initial purchasers of the product are less price sensitive than the subsequent buyers. In any event market skimming can act as a hedge against a possible mistake in setting the price. It is always easier to correct a price downwards; it is very difficult to raise a price which proves to be too low to cover costs or which is lower than the market reaction warrants.

Market skimming is quite popular in international marketing. The size of the potential market is such that a small penetration of the global market can be sufficient to meet the immediate marketing objectives. The high initial prices can generate the level of revenues and profits which could justify a major market development. The difficulties arise where the international distributors, especially those who are independent of the firm, cannot derive sufficient sales because of the high price and become quite unhappy. It must be appreciated that a pricing policy which is good for the marketing company is not always good for its international distributors. This point must be borne in mind when selecting an approach to pricing.

Market Penetration Objective

This is almost the opposite of the previous approach. To attain this objective one sets a low initial price in order to reach the mass market immediately. It is a more aggressive marketing objective and it calls for a more decisive pricing policy. This strategy can be more satisfactory when the following conditions exist: first, evidence exists to show that demand is sensitive to price; second, the production process is such that substantial reductions in cost take place when a large-scale operation is established; third, there is an inadequate innovators market to sustain a market skimming policy; fourth, competition can be forestalled through an aggressively low price.

A full understanding of the relationship between the price and the product life cycle is an essential element in a successful penetration policy. Used in the right circumstances it can give the marketing firm a significant grip on the market by making it unattractive for competitors to enter in view of the high investment needed in the substantial production and marketing facilities and the anticipated low margins. On the other hand, a penetration policy can be disastrous if it is based on a product with a very short life cycle. However, a firm that has a good international distribution network is probably well placed to exploit the life cycle on a penetrative basis. The fact that the life cycle may be short can be offset by the rapidity at which international markets can be covered.

Early Cash Recovery

A firm that has identified liquidity problem as one of its weaknesses must inevitably aim at a pricing policy which is capable of generating a better cash flow through an early cash recovery process.

Improving liquidity calls for whole list of steps at all levels. Among others one has to control credit terms rigorously, one has to monitor costs, one has to obtain maximum credit terms from suppliers. At the same time one can improve one's liquid resources through an imaginative pricing policy. By offering special discounts for prompt payment one can motivate the buyer or the distributor to pay on time. One must not overlook the fact that an 'early cash recovery' objective is closely linked with the choice of channels of distribution. A firm often selects longer channels for the simple reason that marketing through middlemen often improves the cash flow of the firm. In other words this kind of objective does not only affect the pricing policy but also the other interdependent ingredients of the mix.

Preventing New Entry

A firm may wish, as part of its marketing objectives, to take all the tactical steps within its power to stop a competitor from entering the market or part thereof. As we saw earlier in connection with market penetration, price is a potent tool through which this objective can be achieved. Such a pricing policy must be handled with care, because it may be based on the fallacy that competitors are fully aware of the cost of production and distribution, and will be deterred from entering a market which is unlikely to offer fair rewards. This is of course a dangerous assumption, inasmuch as not every competitor is efficient and painstaking in the way he assembles data about markets and costs. Many competitors simply follow others blindly, and in such an event the marketer who seeks to prevent new entry through low prices may find himself faced with a price war in which nobody is likely to earn a living. This risk is particularly high in international marketing where one is likely to encounter competitors who are particularly ill-informed about the cost realities of marketing in foreign countries.

'Loss Leader' Policy

The underlying marketing objective here is that by pricing one product at a very low level the consumer will be attracted to the supplier's market-place and at that point he may purchase other commodities which are priced in the normal way. In other words the low price of the 'loss leader' product acts as a promotional bait to the consumer. This strategy is particularly attractive in the retail trade. Supermarkets often indulge in this kind of practice. They advertise a product and indicate a very low price for it. The consumer will probably buy other items in that store once he has gone to the trouble of visiting the supermarket in question. The margin lost through such a low price can be rightly attributed to the promotional effort of the firm.

Other examples where loss leadership can be a useful strategy can be found in situations where *derived demand* exists. Derived demand occurs where the demand for one product stems from the existence or availability of another product. The demand for razor blades occurs only when the consumer possesses a razor. The marketer may decide to sell cheap razors on the basis of loss leadership; once the razors have been purchased the demand for the blades will follow. The marketer will endeavour to achieve his profit objectives through the sale of the blades. This policy is often applied in international marketing but the pitfalls are numerous: first, loss leadership may contravene the law of certain countries where selling a product on this basis is considered an offence; second, in some markets it would become impossible to raise the price once a decision has been taken to sell the product very cheaply; third, psychologically it is a dangerous strategy vis-à-vis foreign distributors who may get the impression that the supplier can be pressurised to concede low prices in relation to other products.

We have tried to look at the influence that marketing objectives may have on pricing decisions. We listed a number of pricing objectives that stem from corporate and marketing aims and the international implications of such objectives. The list is by no means comprehensive and the point to remember is that a few of the pricing objectives listed are complementary rather than mutually exclusive. Return on investment and market penetration objectives are perfectly compatible. On the other hand market stabilisation and loss leadership may well be in a state of total contradiction. The marketer's job is to ensure that the price selected for a product in its international setting fulfils the various objectives envisaged by the marketing plan and at the same time meets the needs of the market-place. Performing such a task in an international environment calls for considerable skill.

The Mechanics of Pricing Decisions for International Marketing

It is important to review briefly the various methods that are available to the marketer in trying to select the most appropriate price for a product destined to be sold in world markets. Most of these methods are similar to those used by the domestic counterpart when choosing a price for his home market. The differences stem from size and geography rather than methodology.

The various methods and their international implications can be summarised thus:

1 Prices Based on Costs

This is the simplest approach and is normally based on the way the accountant would determine a price for a product. The firm calculates the total cost of the product, including production and marketing costs, plus an allocation of overheads and then adds a percentage to represent a margin of profit. The total yields a selling price.

The trouble with this method is that the cost calculation is based on a predetermined level of activity. It tends to disregard the fact that costs do not act alike as output increases or decreases. Moreover, it takes little cognisance of markets, their dynamism and elasticities. This is particularly true in international markets where minimal elasticity can translate itself into substantially increased volume, stemming from the fact that the global scene is so large.

2 Market Demand versus Break-Even Analysis

The aim here is to try to calculate the break-even point at several demand points based on different selling prices. This method tries to explore the effect that different prices may have on demand and the impact of both on the break-even point. This approach brings into consideration the effect of elasticity and tries to find the most profitable supply/demand relationship at a given price level. Having carried out such an exercise the marketer can decide which level of activity would best meet his profit and marketing objectives.

This approach can be best illustrated in a series of figures based on a simple case: a firm has discovered that a certain elasticity of demand exists when prices are changed in relation to a certain product. When the prices vary from £30 to £60 in steps of £10 the sales are likely to be 20, 16, 12 and 8 respectively. Now it wishes to find out which is the most attractive combination. The firm's objective is to maximise profits. Total fixed costs are £200. Total variable costs per unit sold are £12·50. The interrelationship between price, sales, total revenue, profit and break-even points is shown in Figure 34.

Price £	Demand level	Number of units likely to be sold	Total Revenue £	Fixed costs £	Variable costs £	Total costs £	Break-even point	Profit £
30	A	20	600	200	250	450	11·42	150
40	B	16	640	200	200	400	7·27	240
50	C	12	600	200	150	350	5·33	250
60	D	8	480	200	100	300	4·2	180

Fig. 34   Demand, costs, break-even points and profits at four different prices of a hypothetical product

The various calculations can be incorporated in a graphical form. Figure 35 illustrates the break-even chart on the basis of the price being £30. Figure 36 shows the break-even calculations at the four different price levels mentioned. Figure 37 shows the same chart with the four demand points (A, B, C, D) superimposed on the chart thus showing simultaneously all four profit

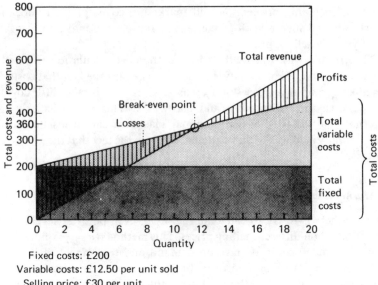

Fixed costs: £200
Variable costs: £12.50 per unit sold
Selling price: £30 per unit
Break-even point: 11.42 units

Fig. 35   Break-even chart

performances. It becomes quite clear that if the aim is to maximise profit demand point C at a price of £50 is the best course of action.

The merit of this approach is that one at least attempts to correlate accountancy calculations with demand realities. This is extremely important in an international situation where the slightest elasticity variation may have a significant impact on total demand and obviously on results. It is not always the highest sale that is the most attractive result. If the profit motive is high one must find the price and demand levels at which the best results can be attained.

The weakness of this approach stems from the fact that it is not always possible to estimate the effect that price variations may have on demand. The best way to establish elasticities is through test marketing a product at a number of different prices. This is of course not always practical. Trying to sell the same product at different prices is much too quantitative an experiment to justify the risk.

3 Following Competitors and Their Price Practices

The underlying notion here is that one or a few competitors are more experienced or knowledgeable than we are and therefore our best strategy is to take notice of what they are doing. This approach only applies where direct competitors exist or where one has sufficient confidence in their commercial and marketing sense. It is hardly wise to follow the practices of competitors who are known for their poor judgement and performance.

One can follow competitors in a number of ways:

(a) price one's product at the same level
(b) price the 'product below competitors' levels
(c) where one has distinct 'unique selling points' price the product above competitors so as to reflect such differentiation.

Whilst following competitors' pricing policies may sound quite crude it can be very effective in international marketing especially where such competitors are well established in the market-place. Problems arise when one tries to follow the practices of competitors who have no pricing policies of substance or where one misinterprets the underlying motives of such practices. If the competitor that one is trying to emulate slashes his price in an attempt to reduce slow-moving stocks at the end of his financial year, it is hardly wise to follow his strategy. For the international marketer the bigger problem is how to identify a competitor who is a suitable leader in a large number of markets. In the absence of such a competitor one is often forced to follow the practices of different competitors in different markets. They may have different attitudes to pricing policies with the result that their actual prices may vary enormously. This in turn may lead the marketer to a position where his

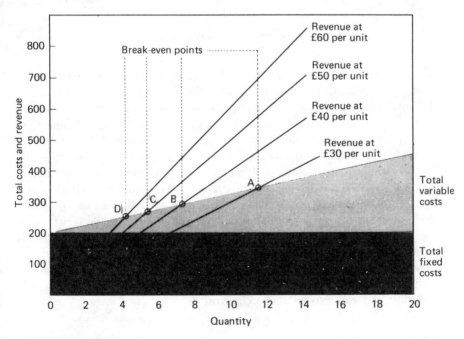

Fixed costs: £200
Variable costs: £12.50 per unit sold
Selling prices: a. £30 b. £40 c. £50 d. £60
        Break: A, B, C, D

Fig. 36 Break-even chart at four different selling prices

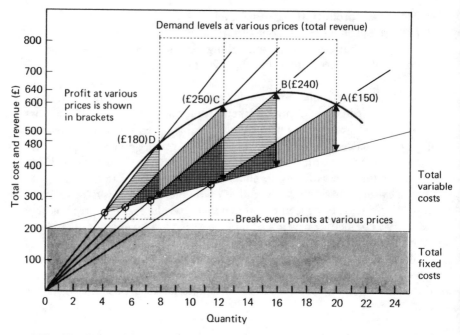

Fig. 37   Demand levels at four different prices superimposed on break-even
charts and the effect on profits

international prices for a given product cease to bear any semblance of strategy and drift into a total anarchy. On the other hand where one is fortunate enough to identify a responsible competitor, with a significant international presence, life can be reasonably easy in this connection. Following his pricing strategy can be extremely helpful provided one monitors carefully the way the competitor behaves when changes take place in the market and its environment. When following international competitors' pricing policies it is essential that one endeavours to scrutinise with great care not only the pricing structure but also the relative effect that the various prices have on competitors' performance. If competitors become the bench mark against which one is trying to gauge one's own performance it is important that one fully understands the structure of costs, marketing mix interrelationships and ratios of such organisations. If one follows a competitor without such data, the chances are that the smart competitor will one day lead you into an unexpected trap.

4 'What the Traffic will Bear'

The basis here is that the marketer seeks to price his product at as a high a level as he can without jeopardising sales. This method is consistent with a market skimming objective and its advantage is that it allows ample latitude for future reductions. Yet it needs a fair bit of research inasmuch as one cannot establish 'what the traffic will bear' until one had conducted some investigations.

This approach to pricing can be very suitable in situations where the product is expected to have a relatively short life cycle and the firm wishes to maximise the returns as quickly as possible with the view of obtaining a rapid investment recovery. High prices might appeal to the *innovators*. Once they are out of the market-place one would aim to peg the price in such a way as to satisfy the *early adopters* and so on. The important point to remember is that this kind of pricing policy must be synchronised on an international scale. A firm that feels that it can lower its price in the UK, because it is hoping to attract the *laggards*, will be asking for trouble if, in the German market, the target group is still the innovators. In other words 'what the traffic will bear' has to be dynamic so as to continue to satisfy the bulk of the international consumers.

5 'Barter' Techniques

These are a series of highly creative methods used for identifying products which are *perceived by the consumers* as comparable in value. One displays a large number of products, the majority of which are clearly priced. A panel of consumers is asked to *pair* those products which they feel are similar in value and which they would be prepared to swap or 'barter' for each other. The outcome of such an exercise gives the marketer a fairly good idea as to the price and value which the consumer himself ascribes to such new products under investigation.

Determining a price for a car for world markets can be a difficult task. A mistake can involve the firm in a substantial loss of revenue. The barter method can be extremely useful. One places a large number of cars, many clearly priced, others, including the car under investigation, unpriced, in a neutral showroom. A panel of typical consumers from the selected target group are invited and motivated to attend a panel discussion. The real purpose of the investigation must be concealed from the visitors in order to maintain full objectivity of response. It is not difficult to find an alternative story to tell the contributing panelists. The important point is that the visitors must not know that the price of Model X is the main topic of research. During the meeting the panelists will be requested, among many other stimulating exercises, to try to 'pair' models—some priced and some unpriced. The aim is to find out what the consumers feel that the new model is worth. If a large percentage of the panel place the new model as the 'pair' of a top Mercedes model it is fair to assume that this is the way they perceive its comparable value. This kind of technique can be developed into a very sophisticated instrument of pricing research. If carried out systematically in a number of large markets one can obtain considerable 'input' about what the consumers feel is the right level of pricing for a product. On the basis of such information one can explore the possibility of developing a price which is reasonably homogeneous for all countries or a cluster of countries. This is probably one of the most marketing orientated ways for determining the correct price of the product.

6 Pricing by Customer Before Purchase

This approach to pricing policy cannot be ignored by the international marketer. Many situations exist where the customer abroad specifies the price at which he is prepared to buy a certain product. This is particularly true with industrial products. The marketer may have no option but to accept the stipulated price or lose the business. In such a case all that is left for him to do is to investigate whether he can make profits at that price or some contribution towards production and marketing overheads. It becomes a simple case of economics as to whether orders should be accepted or not at that price level. Sometimes the firm may decide to accept orders at price levels which are unlikely to make any contribution to the firm's overheads; in other words where a net loss will be generated. The underlying reason for such a decision may be the desire to establish a commercial contact with important customers abroad. This is fine provided the marketing firm is aware of the cost involved and is able to quantify possible future awards. The thing to watch is the temptation of doing business with a foreign customer at any cost, with the illusory hope that matters will go right in the end.

7 Negotiating with Governments

This is rapidly becoming an important way in which the price of commodities and large installations is negotiated. More and more governments are taking active part in important international transactions and the likelihood is that such governmental participation in marketing decisions will increase in most countries. International marketing personnel are well advised to acquaint themselves with the intricacies of international barter and switch deals because in many situations the price of the product will be controlled by the incidence and details of such deals.

There is no one satisfactory way for calculating the *best* price for a product. A creative marketer may indeed try to calculate a price in many different ways and then compare the results. If all methods point to a single price this is of course excellent. On the other hand the likelihood is that different methods will yield a whole range of prices. One can explore an average price from the various results. Alternatively, one can resort to one useful residual tool which is relying on one's intuition. Experienced marketers with entrepreneurial flair often have an excellent eye for the right price in a given set of circumstances. Intuition, coupled with quantitative techniques, can be a formidable combination in the process of reducing the risk of errors in pricing one's products for international markets.

Restrictive Trade Practices

This is a very important topic for an international marketer. A knowledge of the comparative legislation on restrictive trade practices among the various industrial nations is essential for anybody responsible for taking pricing decisions. In fact the whole question as to how far one is free to compete in a given country stems from the legislation that has been introduced on the subject. A restrictive trade practice which may be taboo in one country may be acceptable in another. An American industrialist, who is accustomed to the uncompromising attitude of his country to price fixing and other types of restrictive trade practices, will be unwise if he carried the American antipathy to a country where such practices are tolerated.

The expression *restrictive trade practices* needs to be defined before we can proceed to a fuller discussion of the subject. Many definitions have been formulated over the years. A very clear definition is the one given in the *European Coal and Steel Community Treaty*:

'All agreements among enterprises, all decisions of associations of enterprises, and all concerted practices tending, directly or indirectly, to prevent, restrict or distort the normal operation of competition within the Common Market.'

Restrictive trade practices can take many forms and the list hereunder enumerates some of the more common types:

1 Horizontal price fixing—this is a price agreement between two or more competitors who are independent of each other.
2 Vertical price fixing—largely price fixing between suppliers, distributors and retailers, for example retail price maintenance.
3 Allocation or division of markets
4 Export and import cartels.
5 Boycotts.
6 Market-dominating enterprises.
7 Monopolies or monopolising practices.
8 Mergers or consolidations.
9 Price discrimination.
10 Discriminatory terms of sale.
11 Refusal to sell.
12 International cartels.

Restrictive trade practices have existed in ancient history and are by no means a phenomenon of the modern era. As far back as Roman days one can trace a law (*Lex Julia De Annona*) providing for the punishment of traders who committed acts or formed associations by which the price of provisions was raised. The *Lex de Monopoliis* passed by Emperor Zeno some fourteen hundred years before the Sherman Act of 1890 forbade monopolies of goods and fixing prices. Monopolies were punishable by deprivation of property and perpetual exile.

Over the years the whole question of how far competition should be allowed to act as the regulator of economic health has preoccupied politicians, economists and businessmen alike. The views of economists range from those who think that competition has ceased to be an effective weapon in preserving a dynamic economy, to those who think that competition is as indispensable as ever. In practice, some industrial economies have elected to preserve competition as the unequivocal prop of a well-regulated community; others have elected to leave market adjustments to the tug-of-war between supply and demand. In between these two extremes one finds a wide variety of shades of state interference to preserve and protect competition.

Moreover the laws on restrictive trade practices can be quite dynamic. Governments oscillate in their attitudes to the problem depending on the political flavour of the parties in power and the state of the national economies. Even the United States, the most ardent protagonist of free competition, with its very strict anti-trust laws found it necessary during the thirties to take steps to legislate for exemptions from the rigours of these laws. Similarly, in Britain during the same period, the government took active steps to restrict competition rather than stimulate it. Thus, one cannot be sure that the present fashion of hounding restrictive trade practices will prevail if economic conditions deteriorate to depression proportions.

The international marketer need not concern himself with the underlying philosophy that stimulates a government to tolerate restrictive trade practices or legislate vigorously against them. On the other hand, he must familiarise himself with the details of existing legislation, insofar as it may have a tremendous impact on his freedom to operate a pricing policy. It is of course not possible to list in a book on marketing the laws of every country on the matter. However, it is appropriate to describe briefly the kind of general patterns that one may expect to find.

Legislation against restrictive trade practices usually can take one of the following forms:

1 Complete Prohibition

Typical of this group is the United States of America. Under this heading any restrictive trade practice is illegal *per se* and the courts are not interested in motives, results and achievements. •

Obviously any businessman who ignores such rules may find himself in serious trouble and that can include the danger of imprisonment.

A number of landmarks from the USA describe the position in this connection:

The Sherman Act 1890—declared unlawful all contracts, combinations and conspiracies in restraint of trade. It also condemned any attempts at monopolising any part of trade or industry.

Clayton Act 1914—Certain restrictive practices: price discrimination, exclusive dealing and tying arrangements, and mergers by acquisition of stock, were held unlawful whenever their 'effect may be substantially to lessen competition or to tend to create a monopoly'.

Federal Trade commission Act 1914—created an administrative agency which was empowered after appropriate proceedings to issue *cease-and-desist* orders against what it found to be 'unfair methods of competition'.

Miller-Tydings Act 1930—created an exception to the illegality of vertical price fixing laid down in the Sherman Act, viz. contracts for resale price maintenance of *trade marked* goods and which are legal under the law of any state in which such resale is to be made—will be legal.

Robinson-Patman Act 1930—widened the provisions in the Clayton Act to give more extensive protection to small buyers who paid a seller higher prices than those charged to their larger competitors.

An important exception exists under the *Webb Pomerence Act 1918* which exempts from the anti-trust laws, subject to registration, associations entered into for the sole purpose of engaging in export trade provided that they do not restrain trade within the USA or restrain the export trade of any domestic competitor.

As can be seen from these few laws it does not pay to fool around with strategies that may smack of connivance with competitors. The penalties are heavy and the game is not worth the candle. Marketers who enter the American market for the first time must of course know these rules.

2 Registration and Investigation

Under this system all restrictive trade practices have to be registered and a special court or administrative body investigates whether the practices in question are in the public interest or not. In other words a distinction is drawn between good and bad practices.

The United Kingdom has opted for this approach. The main legislation on the subject is the *Restrictive Trade Practices Act 1955*. Its main provisions are:

(a) All agreements containing restrictive trade practices must be registered. This applies both to formal and informal agreements. Technically even the so-called *price leadership* situations have to be registered if they result from some furtive understanding reached informally.

(b) All registered agreements are being investigated by a Restrictive Practices Court which consists of judges and lay judges (industrialists, accountants, and a trade union official). If the Court finds the investigated practice to be contrary to *public policy* it will declare it void and the parties thereto will have to refrain from continuing with such an arrangement. In other words registered agreements are valid until the contrary is ordered by the Court.

The law is quite complex and it allows escapes in a number of circumstances:

(i) Where the promotion of the interest of the consumer is involved.

(ii) Where the offending agreement relates to exports.

(iii) Where it relates to the avoidance of regional unemployment.

(iv) Where it attempts to neutralise a dominant competitor or customer.

The spirit of this law is repeated in the Act that prohibits resale price maintenance in the UK. The *Resale Prices Act 1964* which prohibits such practices allows a few exceptions:

(i) The right to fix maximum prices is retained.

(ii) The Restrictive Practices Court may exempt various classes of goods if it feels that it is in the public interest to do so.

(iii) Any supplier can apply for exemption in respect of his goods. Once again the Court will adjudicate whether it is in the public interest or not. However, pending such adjudication the prohibition to apply retail price maintenance does not apply. It is difficult to see, at the present moment, in what circumstances the Court may consider retail price maintenance as a desirable practice in the public interest.

3 Non-Interference Until Abuse Committed

The theory here is that restrictive trade practices can be tolerated until some evidence of abuse comes to light. Where the abuse is a source of hardship, inequity or economic danger the State would step in and take the necessary action. Frequently some administrative body is set up as a 'watch-dog' to monitor existing practices and their likely effects. However, such bodies seldom act unless obvious dangers are brought to their notice.

Switzerland is an example of the latter system. The only serious attempt at reducing the impact of restrictive trade practices has been the *Federal Act on Cartels and Similar Organisations 1962*. The Act provides that the Federal Economic Department may ask the Cartels Commission to undertake special inquiries with a view to establishing whether certain agreements have a harmful effect, either economically or socially. The Federal Economic Department may, within a year from the date on which the report was submitted, institute proceedings before the Federal Court against a cartel which prevents competition or appreciably interferes with it, in a manner that is incompatible with the public interest especially one that is detrimental to consumers.

The description of the three approaches to legislation against restrictive trade practices has been simplified for the sake of brevity and clarity. However, the reader must appreciate that many hybrid legal approaches do exist. Nonetheless the three legislation approaches described form a useful starting point for trying to comprehend the legal scene of a country which one is trying to enter for the first time. Legal advice is still warranted but it is helpful to gain a general flavour of the legal climate of a marketing environment.

One further important point to remember: restrictive trade practices are not only controlled by national laws but also by laws prescribed in treaties and trans-national agreements. The prime example of course is the Treaty of Rome. The essence of the EEC's competition policy lies in Articles 85 and 86 of the Treaty. These regulations are so important that any marketer who enters the European scene for the first time must study them with considerable care.

In principle the rules forbid all restraints of competition between member states of which the *overall economic effects are not likely to be beneficial*. Their object is to ban restrictive practices which distort competition between Community members and prohibit the abuse of 'dominant positions' within the Market. The Treaty of Rome does not define what is meant by dominant position. In other words the Treaty applies to cases where the restraint on trade or the abuse of a dominant position are likely to have a perceptibly adverse effect on trade between member states. Otherwise the EEC rules of competition are inapplicable. Restrictions or abuse which affect the internal trade of a member state or trade with third countries are excluded. So, too, are agreements that do not appreciably affect the market. What matters is the likely effect, not the actual terms, of an agreement.

Firms which are in doubt as to whether the EEC rules of competition apply to their agreements, may notify their agreements to the Commission for the purpose of obtaining 'negative clearance', that is a declaration by the Commission that, on the basis of the facts at its disposal, there are no grounds for it to intervene under Article 85. Alternatively, if Article 85 is applicable, firms may notify the agreements and apply for exemption.

The rules of the Treaty of Rome and the laws of the UK run in parallel. Firms may find that agreements to which they are party and which are not subject to registration and examination under the UK legislation, fall nonetheless within the scope of the EEC rules of competition, if they restrict interstate trade. In other situations an agreement may fall within the national law of a member state as well as the rules of the Treaty of Rome. This can be quite onerous but no responsible marketer can afford to ignore the implications.

Chapter 8

Distribution Decisions in International Marketing

Distribution decisions are pretty difficult in domestic marketing; they are even more complicated in international marketing. The problem of selecting the right channels is simply multiplied by as many countries as one wishes to serve. Yet it is essential for companies which market their products internationally to be able to find their way through the maze of channels that are available or can be developed in each market.

The variations that exist in institutional availability are very extensive indeed and no one person can ever hope to become aware of the details of the channel options in every country. Furthermore, environmental and legal constaints play an enormous role in the choices that can be made and the distribution strategies that can be explored.

It is important to remember that the best product in the world may prove a commercial disaster if the channels of distribution selected are incapable or unwilling to provide the 'utility of place' and the 'utility of time' which the local consumer expects. The expectation of the consumer is ultimately the criterion of effectiveness and therefore failure to satisfy the consumer means a poor marketing effort.

This chapter deals with two interrelated aspects of the distribution process:

> Channels of distribution in world markets.
> Physical distribution (logistics) for the international manufacturer.

Channels of Distribution in World Markets

An international company can have a number of bases from which channel decisions originate. A manufacturing orientated company would have a number of plants located around the world and distribution decisions will probably stem from logistics rather than marketing considerations. On the other hand, a marketing orientated company will look at the problem differently: it will identify the best marketing opportunities, determine distribution patterns and then seek to recommend locations for manufacturing facilities which could best serve the marketing objectives.

The difference is fundamental insofar as the marketing orientated company may come to the conclusion that one manufacturing unit in one centrally-located place is perfectly adequate to be able to serve world markets. A production orientated company seldom wishes to recognise the validity of such an approach. To the production and technical personnel such an approach is much too parochial and they refuse to acknowledge that in certain circumstances it may be much more profitable to build a firm's international trade from one manufacturing base. There may, of course, exist very compelling legal and commercial reasons for establishing local manufacturing plants in various parts of the world. However, to the marketing orientated firm such decisions must be fully justified by marketing and commercial realities. In this connection the way the Japanese industry has developed its penetration of world markets is a good example of this approach.

It is useful to remember that a company that has proliferated its production facilities in many countries is gradually ceasing to perform an international marketing task. For all intents and purposes such a firm is approaching a situation where the company is becoming a collection of domestic units, operating under one corporate flag. In such an extreme situation each member of the group has a normal domestic marketing task to perform; knowledge of international marketing ceases to be an essential quality of an effective management. The channels of distribution selected in each market in such circumstances would be purely a domestic matter for the local management and in accordance with locally defined criteria of choice.

Our objective here is to deal with a situation where a marketer operating on an international scale has to lay down distribution policies in a number of countries. We are not concerned here with the problem of selecting channels in a single domestic market. Our aim is to assist the marketer who has to select, or help others to select, distribution channels in a number of international markets of differing marketing ecologies.

The Move Towards International Distribution

Most firms embarking on the path to internationalisation go through a classical pattern of evolution in relation to distribution policies. They commence their overseas development by means of an export effort. They appoint agents or distributors in foreign countries and motivate them towards hard and effective selling. At a certain point the firm comes to realise that the contribution from a certain market is sufficiently high to justify a wholly-owned subsidiary company. The agent or distributor in such a country has to be bought out or dismissed and a subsidiary compnay established to handle the selling on behalf of the parent company. The full contribution belongs now to the parent firm. Depending on the success of the subsidary and the size of the market, one starts considering the establishment of manufacturing or assembly plants. At this stage an intricate international structure comes into being and a fully-fledged multinational firm is born.

Some companies opt for licence agreements instead of building their own operating subsidiaries. With technologically advanced firms this approach can prove highly rewarding especially where the firm seeks to maximise profits rather than sales.

This description oversimplifies the real situation inasmuch as the modern multinational often operates through a myriad of arrangements. In a number of markets it will operate through subsidiaries. In other markets it will work through agents. Yet, in other countries it may opt for licence arrangements. A hybrid situation like this is fairly common and inevitably presents the international company with intricate management and control problems.

The internationalisation process is usually carried out in an evolutionary way. Thus, for example, the Cyanamid Corporation commenced its overseas activity almost entirely by direct exports. It has then followed by an increasing investment to cope with the growth in sales volume which finally led to the gradual establishment of overseas manufacturing facilities. This is a fairly normal pattern with most international companies.

Very few companies are able to boast about having planned the internationalisation of their marketing and distribution efforts in accordance with a pre-defined blueprint. Normally marketing success is the 'trigger point' for the development of local subsidiaries. One seldom encounters the situation where the internationalising company starts from a clear plan specifying the details of the various moves and, within a reasonable margin, the timing of each move. This is understandable but also regrettable. It is like a game of chess: the poor player waits for his opponent to make his move before he determines his next step; the experienced player plans a whole series of moves in advance based on a well-thought out strategy. The ideal situation in international marketing is to plan the whole process with clear objectives and systematic moves rather than allow events to overtake the growing firm and force its hand in the selection of tactical moves. This comment is particularly relevant to the process of choosing distribution policies in world markets.

Types of Channels in World Markets

Figure 38 shows the type of channel options that a marketer can expect to find in a typical industrialised market. The table is purely schematic and there is absolutely no guarantee that the various institutions shown always exist in every market. Moreover the terminology would obviously differ from market to market. Any good textbook on marketing would enumerate the kind of considerations that should be studied when trying to select the best channel for a company's distribution objectives in a domestic market. The table also describes the differences that exist between the channels available normally to the manufacturer of consumer goods as against the manufacturer of industrial goods.

It is quite difficult to describe in a schematic way all the permutations of channels of distribution that exist in world markets. However, as a general framework Figure 39 provides a useful starting point for exploring the kind of channels that one can expect to meet in world markets. Whilst the chart

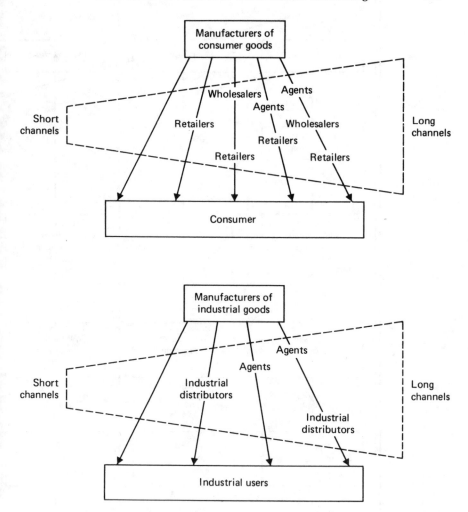

Fig. 38   Major channel options in each market

cannot be treated as comprehensive, any marketer who wants to study the distribution patterns of a country with which he is not familiar will find it a helpful checklist. On identifying the channels available to him, he can proceed to an evaluation of the advantages and disadvantages of each option and record his findings at the appropriate space provided.

The point to remember is that in most international distribution situations, goods cross borders and a machinery of sorts must be identified or developed for coping with physical movement of goods, including the transfer of title to intermediaries and/or consumers in foreign countries. This makes the selection of the right channel that much more complicated and mistakes pretty costly.

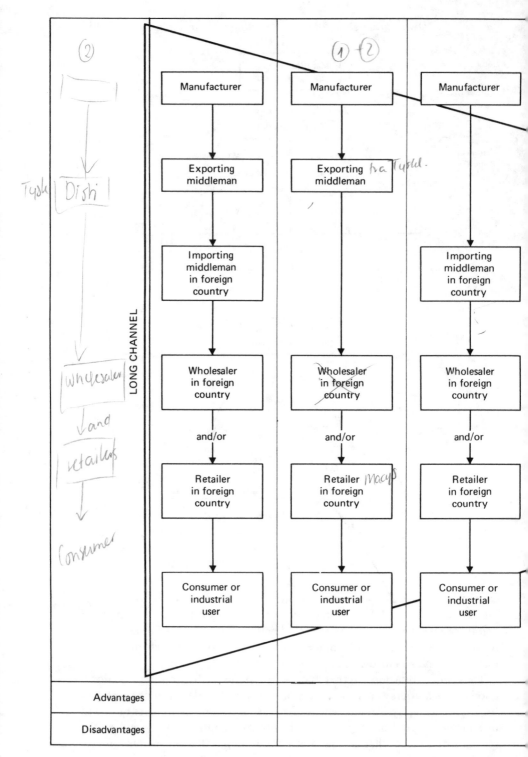

(2)

① + ②

Tysk — Dish

Wholesaler

and

retailers

Consumer

LONG CHANNEL

Manufacturer	Manufacturer	Manufacturer
Exporting middleman	Exporting *fra Tysld.* middleman	
Importing middleman in foreign country		Importing middleman in foreign country
Wholesaler in foreign country	Wholesaler in foreign country	Wholesaler in foreign country
and/or	and/or	and/or
Retailer in foreign country	Retailer *Macys* in foreign country	Retailer in foreign country
Consumer or industrial user	Consumer or industrial user	Consumer or industrial user

Advantages			
Disadvantages			

Fig. 39   Major types of distributi

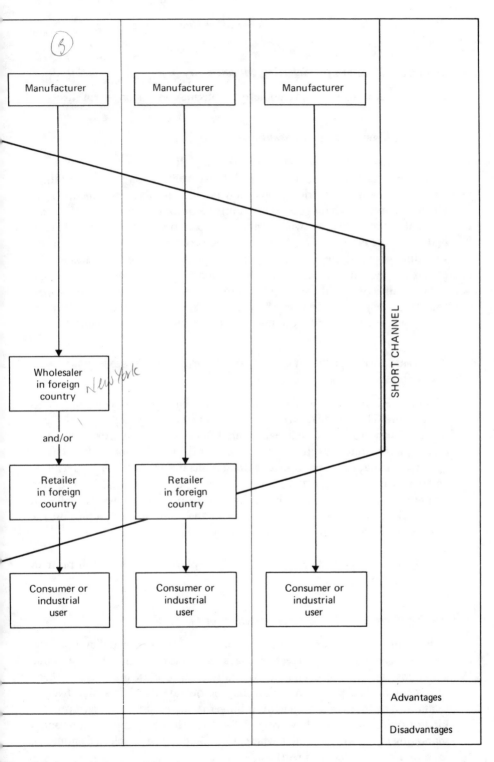

hannels in international marketing

Main Considerations for Selecting Channels

It must be borne in mind that channel decisions may have a long-term effect on:

1 EVERY INGREDIENT OF THE MARKETING MIX

An early, albeit well-intentioned, mistake may affect the company's position in a given market for many years. Alternatively, it may cost substantial amounts of money to extricate the firm from undesirable commitments. Thus a British company that chose to distribute its decorative products through a chain of supermarkets in Switzerland, on an exclusive basis, discovered that it had very little control over the price of the product. The distributor, in this situation, opted to use the product in question as part of his 'loss leadership' price strategy, with the result that the retail price eroded to levels that could not be justified within the supplying company's pricing objectives and policies. Inevitably the pressure on prices had to follow suit in other markets, where the supply was being made by the manufacturer's own marketing subsidiaries.

2 THE FREEDOM OF THE COMPANY TO CONTROL THE EFFECTIVE EXPLOITATION OF GIVEN MARKETS

Channel decisions normally involve the firm in legal commitments of a long-term nature. The cancellation of such arrangements can be highly problematic in certain instances. National legislation differs significantly from country to country as to what constitutes a just cause for the termination of distribution agreements, and as to the supplier's obligations in such cases. An agreement, entered at a stage when the firm is trying to introduce itself into foreign markets, may prove a serious obstacle at a future point when the firm will wish to launch a major penetrative strategy in the same market. Ignoring the pitfalls at the beginning can be very costly later on.

The following considerations should be explored in some depth prior to taking channel decisions:

(a) *The international marketing objectives of the firm*

This is fundamental; one cannot determine a distribution policy until the international marketing objectives have been clearly defined. In extreme situations, the selection of channels is totally inappropriate in certain markets, insofar as the markets in question may be outside the firm's objectives in relation to their size, development or longer term viability. Furthermore, the kind of objectives which have been defined for the company's international marketing effort will determine whether the channels to be selected should be long (indirect) or short (direct).

Examples of objectives that might affect channel decisions are:

Company A states: 'Our international marketing objectives are to supply our products in all those markets capable of absorbing a minimum of £1 million per annum within three years from commencement of the distribution effort.'

Company B: 'We wish to market our products in such a way that our cash commitment in each country would never exceed a total investment of £100,000.'

Company C says: 'Our international marketing goal is to achieve a 10 per cent market share in all those markets that fulfil a number of criteria (the statement goes on to describe the kind of market, size, growth potential, etc. that would be of interest to the company).' In other words all the smaller markets and the less stable countries will be excluded from this objective.

Company D adds: 'We do not wish to become directly involved in any way in the process of selling and distributing our products in foreign markets.'

At the other extreme Company E says: 'Having entered the pharmaceutical business in Europe we wish to develop a strong presence with our own distribution network. We are prepared to invest heavily in our own distribution and selling facilities, thus enabling us to exploit effectively and quickly new product opportunities emanating from our excellent R & D organisation which spends on average 10 per cent of the firm's turnover.'

(b)   Other corporate considerations

The choice of distribution in a multinational environment is often determined by the size of the company, the way it is organised and the managerial resources available to it. Given comparable market considerations, some companies are better equipped than others to have shorter channels or even opt for a direct distribution approach to the ultimate consumer or user.

In this connection the main considerations are:

(i) *Managerial resources and their experience.* The management of distribution channels depends to a great extent on the experience that vests in the firm's managers. A firm that is entering international operations for the first time, normally lacks the expertise that is required to be able to choose and control short channels or the firm's own local subsidiary. Obviously, companies with limited international marketing know-how would prefer to turn the job to middlemen. Even well-established firms often seek the help of middlemen in cases involving new products or new segments calling for the acquisition of a new type of experience. It is therefore essential that a firm identifies its strengths and weaknesses in this area; mistakes can be pretty costly.

(ii) *The firm's international organisation.* The way the international firm is organised is also very relevant. The firm that has opted for a macropyramid structure is likely to look at each market with a cold and factual approach with the view of maximising the opporunitues of each market. Such a firm will endeavour to identify the markets which are likely to yield 80 per cent of the company's revenue and sales, both in the short term and in the longer term, and pour its managerial and financial resources into the best opportunities thus identified. This is seldom the case with firms adhering to the 'umbrella' structure. The fact that strategic authority has been delegated to the local management means that channels of distribution, as well as other important decisions, will be taken at local level. In the 'umbrella' situation it is inevitable that the financial success of the local market will prevail over the international marketing considerations. In the extreme situation, as discussed earlier, the local firm becomes a purely domestic firm which just happens to belong to an international company. In such a case the meaning of international marketing and its value cease to apply.

(iii) *Company's image.* A firm must consider the effect that its distribution choice may have on its international image. This means, that among other factors, it must probe carefully into the question of middlemen's respectability and the way in which the world at large would view the arrangement reached with a given channel of distribution. Any arrangement which is made with a middleman, whose image is dubious, can have a long-lasting and far-reaching impact on the firm's image throughout the world. Competitors will be quick to capitalise on such an error of judgement.

Furthermore in reaching a distribution decision one must consider the effect on neighbouring countries. A decision to sever the firm's relationship with a local wholesaler, in order to set up one's own subsidiary, is bound to create a fear of repetition in neighbouring markets, and nothing is more harmful to the middleman's performance than the feeling that his security of tenure is limited.

(iv) *Existing distribution arrangements in each market.* A multi-product company may have existing distribution arrangements in many markets although the nature of the products is such that different channels are required for each product line. It is important that those responsible for selecting channels in a given country pay attention to other arrangements that already exist there. In other words, before one starts looking for totally new relationships, it would be wise to explore the usefulness of existing channels; they may prove better than one expects. They may be capable of further development. In any event a marketer must not generate unhappiness among existing channels, in spite of the fact that he himself may never have to work with them. The international marketer must be sensitive to any achievements and goodwill that other parts of the firm have attained in each market.

(v) *Timing.* The speed with which a firm has to penetrate each market is a vital consideration when one is choosing channels of distribution. The need to act fast and achieve results may force the hand of the marketer to select channels which in the longer term may not be ideal. However, such a decision must be taken with one's eyes wide open as to the longer-term implications.

(c) *Channels availability*

This is of course a major consideration. You cannot expect to select a specific type of channel in a given country if:

(i) such a channel does not exist,
(ii) it belongs to a competitor,
(iii) it is fully committed to other suppliers,
(iv) it does not wish to distribute your product.

It must be borne in mind that channels of distribution are independent and harnessing their help is not always an easy task. Furthermore, each country has developed over the years different patterns of distribution, coupled with supportive institutions, and it is hazardous to assume that because the Netherlands possesses a specific type of distribution method the same occurs in Belgium. This indeed is one of the difficulties and subtleties of international marketing and this is where the marketing profile analysis is an invaluable tool.

Once again this aspect is closely linked with the basic marketing objectives of the firm. Thus if the firm seeks to optimise its profits in world markets in the most cost effective way, it will perforce abdicate from those markets which do not offer a simple middlemen structure. On the other hand, if the objectives prescribe a penetration of all markets of a certain size, regardless of effort and expense, the company may find itself distributing its products through self-developed channels which in the short term may prove extremely costly. Nonetheless the firm may take a longer-term view of its aims in such markets. It is often true to say that overcoming channels' difficulties at an early stage may give the company a definite edge over its competitors. The important point to remember is that such decisions must be taken with the full facts at one's disposal. Trying to achieve results, without significant investment in markets that do not offer an efficient distribution infrastructure, is normally asking for trouble.

(d) *Financial considerations*

Two major ingredients must be studied here:

(i) The relative cost of distribution patterns,
(ii) The cash flow effectiveness of the channels under consideration.

(i) *Costs of different marketing channels.* Before selecting channels of distribution the international marketer must analyse in detail the relative costs of different channels. Such a study must bring into consideration the fact that in the initial stages costs are distorted by the start-up expenditure. These costs are in the main of a non-recurring nature. Furthermore, the cost evaluation must be geared to the expected market performance that one can forecast for the various channels. In other words, the fact that through direct marketing one could achieve a cost ratio of 6 per cent to sales can be meaningless if at 8 per cent ratio, based on indirect distribution (viz. using middlemen), one can expect to achieve three times the volume of sales. It is the total business coupled with the final pay-off to the firm that must be appraised.

In this connection the following elements must be investigated:

the cost of staffing and training local personnel,

the comparative administrative costs,

possible expenditure resulting from moving personnel from head office to the local subsidiary,

cost of cancelling current arrangement with a local distributor,

cost of incorporating a company and any additional costs involved in complying with the legal obligations of the market in question, having to have local directors, keeping books, etc.

the cost of promotion to be incurred in direct distribution as against indirect distribution,

cost of registering patents and/or trademarks,

the difference in cost of duty; in the case of a subsidiary importing there often exist complications,

tax differences based on the nature of the revenue received,

physical distribution costs including warehousing,

start-up costs and the length of time needed to break-even.

(ii) *The cash flow effectiveness.* For many international marketers it is often vital to ensure that the channels selected for distributing the firm's products are capable of generating a quick cash recovery. This in turn means that the company's cash resources must not be over-stretched through the inevitable level of credit that one has to grant to one's direct customers. In most instances middlemen provide the cash cushion that a firm with limited cash resources requires. Indeed, the provision of early cash recovery is one of the important tasks of a distribution channel. A company must balance its margin objective with the cash flow needs before deciding whether to choose 'short' or 'long' channel arrangements.

(e) *Capital factors*

Closely linked with the above consideration the marketer must explore the financial and capital implications of choosing a channel of distribution to the exclusion of another one.

Examples of this aspect are:

Can one raise local capital easily?
Is the local currency stable or convertible?
Can earnings be remitted out of the country and capital repatriated?
Are there borrowing restrictions on foreign companies?
Is the local government likely to offer substantial capital support to a
domestic firm in order to protect the country's balance of payment?

(f) *The market and its special characteristics*

The market itself, its state of development and special needs, constitute a very
important 'input' in determining the kind of distribution choice that should be
made. Once again the marketing profile analysis should prove a very valuable
tool in identifying the appropriate elements in this respect.
Relevant factors are:

the medium and longer-term economic health of the country,
the extent to which a channel selected may be vulnerable to political change,
the size of the market in terms of personal disposable income, income
distribution etc.,
the potential growth for the firm's products or similar ones,
special trade arrangements such as cartels or trade associations,
the market's receptiveness to new and sophisticated products,
specific habits of the consumer which preclude the possibility of by-passing
traditional channels,
marketing techniques which depend on third parties such as merchandising
agencies.

(g) *The Specific needs of the product*

The product itself may have a major influence on the type of channels that the
firm can choose for achieving distribution goals.
Points to remember are:

A product calling for extensive pre-sale or after-sale service is normally best
handled by the company's own distribution facilities provided of course it
can be achieved economically.
Bulky items can often justify direct marketing. Thus a firm distributing
tankers requires only one or two representatives in a whole region to
perform an effective distribution effort.
Sophisticated products such as computers or electronic equipment
installations are more likely to justify a direct distribution approach than
fast moving consumer goods. The client normally expects an intimate

knowledge of the intricacies of the product which is more likely to be available among the firm's own employees.

The unit value of a product also influences channel decisions. Obviously if the product has a high value more funds can be derived from each unit sold thus permitting the luxury of short channels.

Perishability is another significant factor in international distribution development. The fact that products subject to physical or fashion perishability must be speeded through channels to the ultimate consumer often forces the manufacturer to choose short channels. This is particularly common in the fruit and vegetable trade.

Products which are custom-made will probably be distributed direct to the ultimate consumer or user. Too much personal contact has to exist between the manufacturer and the buyer to allow for middlemen. Nonetheless, even in such situations, one often encounters active agents who collect an introductory commission for identifying and bringing opportunities to the notice of the manufacturer.

In the previous few sections we attempted to summarise a number of important considerations that ought to be explored in some depth before channel decisions can be taken in relation to international markets. Most of these points are based on simple commonsense. Unfortunately when a marketer is faced with a myriad of markets, with conflicting needs and conditions, he tends to lose sight of what is the best course of action in a given set of circumstances. One cannot overemphasise the value of a carefully assembled marketing profile analysis. Figure 40 illustrates a basic checklist that the technique seeks to answer. Other questions can be added in order to make the checklist more comprehensive and more relevant to a particular marketing project. This method is extremely useful not only in ensuring that all relevant facts are assembled but also in helping the marketer to look at all markets in a rational and systematic way. With these two ingredients he is more likely to take sound distribution decisions.

The Management of Middlemen

Middlemen must be managed with the same care as one normally applies to a firm's own sales force. Whether the intermediaries are the employees of the firm's subsidiary or whether they are totally independent there is a mutuality of interest between the supplying company and its channel's personnel and it is important that the best principles of man management are applied to the management of personnel working in the distribution process.

Assuming that the channels selected were right in the first place one has to manage them in such a way as to:

1 Create distributors loyalty,
2 Ensure that distributors are adequately remunerated,

The Distribution Portion of the Marketing Profile Analysis

A likely checklist

Distribution

	Channels of distribution	Physical distribution (Logistics)
ENVIRONMENT	—details of GNP, growth rate and their possible impact on demand —financial/capital climate —consumer buying habits and preferred location —local attitudes to foreign firms setting up own subsidiaries as against using local agents/distributors	—details of geography, distances to main consuming conurbations; distances to main rural areas —details of ports, airports, rail system and other logistics infrastructures —frequency and quantities likely to be expected by channels of distribution/other middlemen
COMPETITION	—do competitors use sales subsidiaries or local distributors? Appraise their respective performance —evaluate the relative effectiveness and productivity of agents versus 'own' subsidiaries of various competitors	—identify the physical distribution practices of competitors including: mode of transport used; inventory levels warehousing/depot facilities. Appraise their respective costs. Consider cheaper methods
INSTITUTIONS	—identify available channels for specific products —is there a suitable distributor that one can buy? —are there any government controlled channels (like monopoly channels e.g. in the USSR) —are there any cartel arrangements? —appraise financial reliability of available institutions	—study available logistics institutions and compare costs of using each one of them or combinations thereof —investigate reputation of each institution available for reliability, punctuality of service and geographical coverage
LEGAL	—identify legal 'red tape' in relation to channels, their selection and dismissal —government regulations on foreign-owned subsidiaries —corporate/legal structures and their respective advantages and disadvantages	—list special rules pertaining to safety, packaging markings, size of vehicles etc. —other legal constraints on transporting procedures —legal formalities and their cost

Fig. 40 The distribution portion of the marketing profile analysis

3 Train and develop distributors and their personnel,
4 Determine standards of performance,
5 Evaluate performance against standards,
6 Maintain an efficient communication system with every distributor.

1 CREATING DISTRIBUTOR LOYALTY

In order to achieve distributor loyalty it is important that he does not feel at any stage that his relationship with the supplying company is a temporary one. A firm that is able to demonstrate that throughout its international activities it has treated its distributors fairly and reasonably is more likely to earn the loyalty of its foreign agents and distributors.

The task of building distributor's loyalty should be shared with the public relations department; in the absence of such a department the marketer should employ some of the principles of the public relations function. In this connection one may find that house magazines have an important role to play. Similarly, organising visits to factories for the best performers and their families tends to develop a feeling of belonging. Such a sentiment is the foundation of a happy and fruitful relationship with people who are not directly under the firm's managerial jurisdiction.

Other ways that have been found useful in an attempt to build loyalty among the firm's foreign distributors can be summarised as follows:

Provide prizes, medals, plaques, cash bonuses to excellent performers and generate sufficient publicity among the international community of distributors so that others will strive to join those honoured in previous years.

Arrange for senior personnel of the parent board to visit periodically distributors in their own country and on their home ground. It is important that such visitors are alerted to the cultural idiosyncracies of each territory to be visited. Nothing is more harmful to a distributor relationship than a rumour that the chairman of the company visited a certain country and refrained from making contact with the local agent or distributor.

Organise a 'distributor consultative council'. The aim of such a body would be to provide:

  (a) a useful channel of communication,
  (b) a forum for ventilating distributors' grievances,
  (c) an excellent opportunity for comparing ideas from different countries/territories—the essence of international creativity.

It may in certain instances be very helpful to invite the son or daughter of the distributor to come to the firm's head office or regional headquarters for a period of training.

The point to remember is that although the distributor is trying to maximise his profit out of the firm's products, he is a vital link in the route to success and his monetary reward, however high, must not be looked at by the firm's own personnel with pusillanimous envy. It often happens that unnecessary friction develops between an agent and principal's staff for no better reason than the latter resent the level of success that the former has achieved. Good management in international marketing calls for the kind of generosity that enables a person to regard the personal success of a distributor as a pleasant evidence of the firm's achievement in the specific market. This approach does indeed help in most cases to develop a long-lasting and genuine loyalty.

2 REMUNERATION OF DISTRIBUTORS

Middlemen must be rewarded in such a way that they are motivated to do an effective job. In those countries where channel traditions exist the level of remuneration is probably well accepted by everybody concerned. The dificulties start in those markets where the product to be marketed is new and no precedents exist as to what constitutes an acceptable 'package'. The package normally consists of commission, contribution towards promotion, discounts for prompt payment, and other financial incentives. There is no hard and fast rule as to what constitutes a perfect level of remuneration in every situation. The point to remember is that a distributor can be as easily over-remunerated as under-remunerated. Those responsible for reaching a distribution arrangement with the foreign middleman must strike a happy medium between the two extremes, whilst maintaining at the same time equity vis-à-vis middlemen in other territories and the firm's own objectives. Over-remuneration can of course generate the right incentive among the distributors but is bound to affect the ultimate profit; under-remuneration may lead to minimal effort on the part of the middleman.

The biggest problem arises when a company entering the international marketing scene indulges in distribution/agency arrangements with different remuneration terms in each deal. Whilst this can work for a while, complications are sure to follow. Middlemen whose level of remuneration is lower than others will react strongly when they discover such deviations and the results can be quite unpleasant. Trying to keep special arrangements secret seldom work insofar as the slightest clerical error may bring the house down. It is sufficient for a commission statement to be inserted in error in the wrong envelope for the information to become public knowledge and a source of general aggravation.

Remuneration therefore must be worked out in detail and in accordance with a logical plan with the view of keeping all the middlemen happy. Ideally one should aim to develop a standardised remuneration package, in the same way as one is always trying to work in accordance with a salary grading system; anomalies must be capable of an explanation should the situation arise.

3 TRAINING AND DEVELOPING MIDDLEMEN AND THEIR STAFF

Distributors and their staff need training and development as much as any firm's personnel. It is very much in the interest of the supplying company to ensure that such training is actually undertaken, because in the final analysis competent personnel will perform a more effective job and that in turn will mean better sales in the market and hopefully better profits.

A well-planned programme of training held either at the centre or at some neutral venue can not only help distributors and their personnel to improve their effectiveness, but can contribute enormously to the feeling of loyalty that the firm wishes to foster. Furthermore, it may serve as a communication forum where distributors from different countries can exchange views and compare distribution methods and practices.

Training programmes could include:

Knowledge of the company and its products.
Knowledge of the specific products which the distributor handles should be developed in some depth.
The above should include specific details about servicing complicated products.
Selling skills—these must of course be adapted by the trainer to the specific needs of each market. To that extent a strong communication must exist between the trainer and local managemnt.
Communication skills including report writing, and effective presentations.
General management concepts including:
    budgetary control procedures,
    general understanding of marketing principles,
    managing people including organisation development.

4 DETERMINING STANDARDS OF PERFORMANCE

Once again distributors and agents have to be managed in the same way as one normally tries to manage one's own personnel, with the major exception that such middlemen do not actually work for the firm and should therefore be treated with considerable tact and diplomacy. At the same time there is a great merit, even from the middleman's point of view, to know what amounts in the eyes of his principal to a good performance and what constitutes a poor result. It is important, however, that standards of performance ascribed to each middleman are fair and based on a sound assessment of what is an attainable target in each market. Setting standards of performance which are neither realistic nor achievable can do more harm than good. A particularly useful approach is to have the supplying company and the distributor develop jointly standards for the latter's performance. Jointly agreed norms are always more palatable than are those imposed from above.

Standards of performance should include:

Sales volume objective
Market share in each market
Inventory turnover ratio
Number of accounts per area
Growth objective
Price stability objective
Quality of publicity
In the case of distributors who carry other lines the percentage of floor space
    allocated to the supplying company's products can be defined in standards
    terms.
General image of the middleman in the market place.

These are only a few standards that one normally encounters in international distribution. Others can be defined to meet the requirements of specific arrangements and locations. Standards must be meaningful in the sense that the middleman is able to understand what is expected of him. If they are too complicated or couched in jargon the likelihood is that the distributor will wash his hands of the whole matter and ignore the standards thus set for him.

5 EVALUATING PERFORMANCE

Where standards of performance have been defined and communicated to distributors it is relatively easy to monitor achievement. Such an evaluation should be carried out at periodic intervals and the results should be discussed with the distributors with the view of identifying weaknesses and dangerous trends. It must be made clear to distributors that such procedures are aimed at monitoring performance and if necessary form the basis of remedial help; they are not just an instrument of bureaucracy and red tape. Distributors abroad are normally happy to go along with the former, they deeply resent the latter.

Many firms operate evaluation forms especially where the firm has a large number of agents and distributors. Figure 41 illustrates a fairly typical form used for the purpose. It must be emphasised that in each marketing area one must identify the most important parameters to be evaluated. What is applicable in pharmaceuticals is not necessarily applicable in the produce trade. Furthermore there is no point including an evaluation dimension in the procedures unless it is relevant and measurable. Thus there is little point in including details of market share if neither the company nor the distributor possesses information about market share performance in a given market. Similarly, if the product is such that the price behaves in a commodity fashion and the distributor is unable to control price behaviour, it is futile to include price details in the evaluation procedures. The evaluation method must be based on standards which are directly relevant to what constitutes good or bad performance and very little else. The items measured must be such that consistently poor returns may cost the distributor his right to handle the firm's

Stanton Chemical Limited
DISTRIBUTOR/AGENT EVALUATION FORM
(Quarterly returns)

Name of distributor _____

Address _____

Region _____

Area _____

I. Sales volume

Quarter _____		Cumulative	
Actual	Budget	Actual	Budget

II. Market share

	%	Sales quarter	Market total (during quarter)	% share
Objective				

Explain differences from objective   _____
(attach separate report if necessary)   _____

III. No. of accounts

Beginning of year [   ]   Now [   ]

IV. General growth

Plot sales performance on a separate graph
based on moving annual average (MAA)

V. Inventory turnover ratio

$$\frac{\text{Turnover}}{\text{Inventory}} = \underline{\quad\quad} = \boxed{} \quad \text{Previous 4 qrs} \ \boxed{}\boxed{}\boxed{}\boxed{}$$

Fig. 41   Example of a distributor/agent evaluation form

VI. Price performance

	Average price during quarter		World median (net)
Product A	[ ]	——————	[ ]
Product B	[ ]	——————	[ ]
Product C	[ ]	——————	[ ]
Product D	[ ]	——————	[ ]

VII. Promotion

Expenditure _____ [   ]

Percentage (in ¢ per unit) _____ [   ]

Attach specimens of advertisements, sales aids and other
promotional material issued during quarter

VIII. Information

Appraise in general terms the quality of information
communicated by distributor/agent to regional office.
Attach supportive evidence

_____

_____

_____

_____

IX. Regional ranking

The following figures indicate how distributor's performance
ranks among all distributors in region

	Rank	Total No.
Sales growth	[ ]	[ ]
Price performance	[ ]	[ ]
Sales/per capita	[ ]	[ ]

X. Distributor's comments

Distributor should list here his observations regarding
quality of products, service and other elements that might
have affected his performance

_____

_____

_____

_____

products in the future. Anything else is quite irrelevant and must be avoided in such procedures.

6 MAINTAINING AN EFFICIENT COMMUNICATION SYSTEM

Good communication between the supplying company and its international distribution network is an essential condition for a successful marketing effort. With middlemen scattered all over the world and with major language and cultural differences, it is quite easy to let the international marketing task drift into a 'Tower of Babel' type anarchy. Developing a sound communication system with one's international distributors is certainly one of the major tasks of the international marketer. This is equally true whether the firm is small and is entering the international arena for the first time or whether the firm is a well-established multinational company with years of experience.

Communication can be effectively maintained through:

Ensuring that letters are promptly answered and such correspondence is carried out in very clear and sympathetic style.
Information sheets and/or house magazines.
Periodical visits to each distributor. Such visits must be well planned with clearly defined objectives.
Invitations to distributors to visit head office and/or regional headquarters.
Occasional conferences held in a central point or at some resort where all distributors can get together and discuss major issues of mutual interest.
The establishment of a 'distributor consultative council' as discussed earlier.

Changing Distribution Arrangements in Foreign Markets

We described earlier the classical transition from long to short channels of distribution in international marketing. Most firms commence their international distribution by using agents or other middlemen and then proceed towards developing their own subsidiaries. Progress means that channels which are right when a firm first tries to penetrate new markets cease to be appropriate when the firm is well established in such markets. This may sound very harsh on those hard-working middlemen who have pioneered the initial introduction of a firm's product into a new market. Although it may sound ironical, the more successful an agent is the more vulnerable he becomes when his principal decides that the time has come to own his own distribution channels.

Unfortunately this is a fact of life and one has to recognise that as a firm penetrates its markets more and more deeply it must consider the most appropriate and most economical institutional arrangements. Distribution patterns, like marketing in general, must be dynamic and their effectiveness must be commensurate with the actual needs of the markets they serve. Firms must monitor the effectiveness of their distribution at frequent intervals and examine whether it still meets their overall marketing objectives. Such a study often leads the marketing firm to the conclusion that changes are needed.

Two important principles must be borne in mind: having one's own selling subsidiary in a country is not necessarily more effective than continuing to use independent agents/distributors. In other words one must avoid making changes just for the sake of making changes. Secondly, if one decides to make changes in existing arrangements every care must be taken to plan and execute them in the most equitable and proper manner. In this connection equitable means not only that it must appear fair to the middleman himself, but it must also appear fair and honourable to the trade in general, and other middlemen in other countries. This is particularly relevant where the firm has assembled over the years a large number of international middlemen.

The first point was covered in some length in the section dealing with the 'Main considerations for selecting channels'. We explored the various factors which the marketer needs to consider before taking distribution decisions. A marketer who pays careful heed to these factors can reduce the need to make too many changes in the future. By being painstaking in the choice of middlemen in the first place, one can save a lot of trouble later. This is simple commonsense and indeed is similar to personnel selection procedures. If you select personnel with sufficient care you are less likely to go through the trauma of having to dismiss too often. The need for change in distribution arrangements is often inevitable owing to the dynamism of markets but at least let us make sure that such a need does not come about through careless decisions in the initial stages. Having to cope with the real needs of the marketing effort is difficult enough.

On the question of planning and executing changes in distribution arrangements in an equitable way it is worth remembering that the cancellation of contractual relationships with distributors can entail in certain situations serious repercussions:

(a) *It can provoke hostility in the trade.* A deal which sounds unfair or clumsy can create ill-feelings in the market with a resultant loss of goodwill to the marketing company. This in turn can damage the firm's prospect of maintaining its sales once the new arrangements come into being.

(b) *It can create insecurity among other distributors in other world markets.* A seemingly shabby termination of a distributor's arrangement is bound to worry other middlemen in other markets. They start wondering when their turn will come for dismissal. Such insecurity breeds defensive attitudes which lead to secretiveness vis-à-vis the principal and sometimes a drop in performance.

(c) *In many countries it can generate some governmental hostility.* This is particularly true in small and close-knit communities where the termination of an agreement with a well-known and well-respected distributor can damage the standing of the marketing company with the government or important public bodies. The distributor may be a relative or a friend of the country's president or prime minister and any clumsy cancellation of his contract can cause irreparable damage to the firm's distribution plans.

(d) *In some countries the legal implications may involve the firm in substantial compensation.* The legal systems of a number of countries have recognised that middlemen invest their own time and effort in developing their principal's business. It is unfair therefore to terminate their distribution contract without rewarding them for this investment. In a few countries if the problem reaches litigation courts tend to support the distributor. In assessing a fair basis for compensation the courts often include:

> the value of inventories and redundant stocks,
> records and customer lists,
> value of goodwill and know-how.

Litigation can be costly and can also create adverse publicity and international embarrassment.

Ideally one must try to plan developments in the international distribution area in such a way that most of these problems can be avoided. If one prepares plans which include the probability of future changes one should be able to avoid most of these pitfalls. After all every experienced international marketer must realise that distribution arrangements often are no more than a stepping-stone towards more permanent structures. Sound plans must try to specify how the marketers see the development of the distribution network and the type and timing of changes which they expect to take place, in order to develop more direct distribution systems. In other words, the plans seek to reduce the incidence of surprise, and that means that one should be able to programme in advance for a changeover from one distribution system to another. Litigation and trouble can be avoided if contingencies of this nature are foreseen and planned for.

The international marketer could take a number of prudent steps when entering into a distribution contract with a foreign middleman:

(a) List clearly in the contract the types of events which are likely to bring about a termination of the arrangement.
It is more difficult for a distributor to complain, either on legal or on moral grounds, if every contingency is listed.
(b) Specify the financial terms of termination.
Such terms must be at least as generous as one would expect the courts of the country in question to award in accordance with legal regulations and practices applicable to such situations. There is certainly no point in offering smaller levels of compensation than those prescribed by the legal system of the country. Where no legislation of any kind exists, the

contract should be of comparable generosity to an average compensation level prescribed by other countries that do have legislation. It does not have to match the highest compensation country, but at the same time it is wrong to expect to get away with derisory figures just because the law of the country does not provide for such contingencies. Fairness is the cardinal principle.

(c) If the acquisition of a successful distributor's business as a 'going concern' is a likely future event, the contract should spell out the formula upon which a purchase price will be calculated.

The distributor must be able to estimate, at any given moment, the probable value of his business. This can be a highly motivating element in a relationship of this nature and certainly eliminates in advance the risk of arguments. The formula for placing a value on the business can include qualitative elements as well as quantitative ones. The former would include such criteria as image, reputation, efficient facilities, quality of personnel, procedures, etc. The latter would of course cover items such as sales volume, profits, number of accounts, productivity, etc. It is normally difficult to argue about quantitative criteria. It is much more complicated to reach agreement on qualitative criteria and their fulfilment. It is useful therefore to lay down in the contract procedures for having these elements appraised and valued by an outside arbitrator such as the head of a firm of accountants, or president of the local chamber of commerce. The important point is that all this must be agreed in advance if trouble is to be avoided when one wishes to act.

On the whole this is a very tricky area of international marketing and one cannot overemphasise the importance of obtaining sound legal advice at an early stage of the negotiations, and certainly whenever a change in existing arrangements is sought. Some companies use standard forms for every situation. This can have its danger insofar as it may offend the local laws and prove a source of problems at the crucial moment when the contract's clauses have to be invoked. Once again legal advice by competent lawyers who know the local laws is always a useful precaution. Finally, in many markets, the use of a prominent local lawyer can be a safeguard against any danger that an ex-distributor would attempt to damage the marketing firm's reputation by exploiting his personal social and political status. The status of the retained lawyer can be a useful antidote against such a danger.

Physical Distribution for the International Manufacturer

The selection of channels of distribution is a vital step in the performance of the international marketing task. However, the integrated nature of marketing demands that the firm turns its attention also to the question of planning and organising an effective logistics or physical distribution system.

The best channels in the world may fail in achieving the firm's objectives if the right products are not available at the right place and at the right time.

Physical distribution is the process whereby the firm organises the physical flow of goods, to the right location and at the right time, so as to achieve maximum satisfaction of middlemen and ultimate consumers, and by doing so it achieves the firm's sales and profit objectives.

The process normally covers the following tasks:

1 Choosing inventory locations and warehousing system.
2 Determining materials-handling system.
3 Maintaining an inventory control system.
4 Laying down procedures for processing orders.
5 Selecting methods of transportation.

An effective physical distribution system will ensure that each one of these tasks is planned as an integral part of a well-balanced and logically structured total system. The elements of the system listed above are interrelated and as every marketer knows the failure of any one of these ingredients may lead to a poor marketing and distribution effort. Moreover the cost of these five elements (or fewer as the case may be) must be aggregated in order to establish the cost effectiveness of the total system. It is a well-known fact that the cost of shipping by sea is in most cases cheaper than sending goods by air-freight. This statement is based of course on the straight comparison of the freight rate per unit of weight or volume. Such a straight comparison is dangerous insofar as it ignores a large number of utilities and cost-savings that air-freight can offer in many circumstances. Obviously from a purely capacity point of view air transport is ruled out for some 90 per cent of goods transported. Such items as coal, iron, timber, liquid fuel and concrete are excluded in most instances. Exceptions may occur even in such commodities when speed is of the essence of the transportation objective in emergencies. On the other hand there are many situations where the economics of air-freight are much more attractive than appears at first glance. If one goes to the trouble of comparing total costs of transport including speed (total transit time) and the effect that it may have on cash flow; warehousing costs allowing for the fact that with faster transport one could cut back on the safety stock levels and that in turn saves money; cheaper packaging; handling costs; cheaper customs clearance; savings through lower theft at point of departure and at destination and many other small items that add up to significant cost variations, one may discover that air-freight is a better proposition than other modes of transportation. This kind of study must be undertaken in relation to each product and in relation to each market with the view of finding the optimum pattern of physical distribution in each case.

This kind of analysis is described very clearly in the KLM-air-cargo 'The true price of distribution' case which is incorporated in the last section of this book.

Physical distribution is a neglected area in many firms. It is often forgotten that it represents a significant cost area and any savings can amount to important amounts and profit improvement. In primary metals, chemicals and petroleum products physical distribution can amount to as much as 25 per cent of the sales revenue. In the food manufacturing industry it often amounts to as much as 30 per cent.

In spite of the enormity of these cost figures physical distribution is rarely managed with the same effectiveness as other functions such as production and the various aspects of the marketing process. The trouble probably stems from the fact that for many years physical distribution was 'no-man's land' in the firm's structure. In some firms it was attached to the production function because it appeared a convenient place. In other firms it fell within the jurisdiction of marketing personnel because no better 'home' could be found for it. Yet, in other firms it became a totally independent function responsible for global distribution. Each approach has its merits in a given situation but for the marketing man there is only one logical location for the physical distribution function, namely, within marketing. By definition, physical distribution is an integral part of the marketing mix. It is therefore vitally important that the management of such an activity falls within the jurisdiction of those responsible for the total marketing process, which includes of course the creation of the 'utilities of time and place'. Without being able to control these activities one cannot be held responsible for total results.

When planning physical distribution activities on an international scale one has to cope with a variety of possible situations which are described diagrammatically in Figure 42.

1 *A company manufactures in one country and supplies a number of consuming markets.* The management of the physical distribution process can be conducted centrally. This will probably be located close to the manufacturing plant but ideally should come under the direction of the marketing function.

The principal role of the distribution function is to ensure that goods reach the consuming countries in the most economical way and that inventories are kept at such levels that no risk of running out of stock ever occurs. Through size and central control one can secure the most advantageous rates and routes resulting in a bias towards a single mode of transportation. This latter point must be watched very carefully and implications analysed. Whilst it is very tempting to distribute goods through a single mode of transportation, it is quite possible that the interests of the company would be better served when a number of alternative transportation modes are used. The total economics has to be appraised and not only a component of the logistics cycle.

2 *The company has developed a series of self-contained units in various countries; each unit consists of both manufacturing and marketing activities.* This is the ultimate in decentralisation and inevitably international marketing hardly applies. The firm consists of a number of companies operating in domestic isolation and physical distribution is essentially a local matter. It is

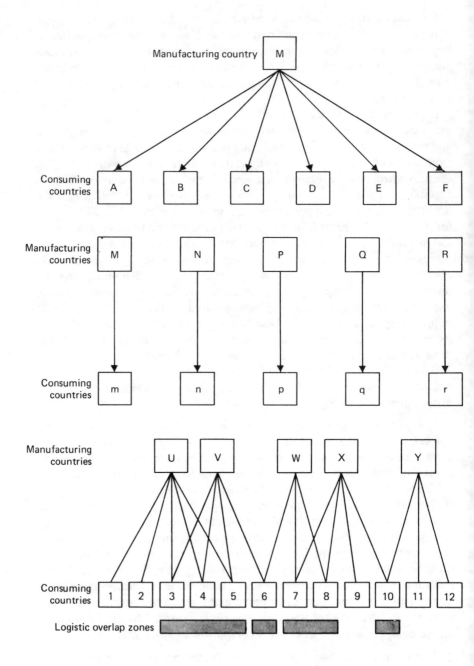

Fig. 42 Physical distribution pattern in world markets

difficult to see how a central organ can do more than offer general advice and assist in training personnel and the communication of good ideas. Each unit is responsible for conducting its physical distribution task in the most efficient and most cost-effective manner. At the same time one cannot visualise how such a distribution structure can hope to obtain any synergistic saving among the various units. If one unit is very slack and another unit is extremely busy, it is unlikely that they would be able to cushion their disparities, because by the nature of their independence one is bound to find that a high level of differentiation exist between the products they produce in their respective plants.

3 *The company has a few plants in the world which serve a large number of consuming markets.* This is a fairly common situation especially with companies that have been operating on the international scene for some time. It can develop into a most intricate distribution set-up and calls for good planning and allocation of responsibilities. As can be seen from Figure 42 a number of 'logistics overlap areas' arise because some markets can be supplied equally conveniently from a few manufacturing plants. This kind of situation calls for a consistent regard for the total economics of getting products to the customer from a corporate rather than a functional viewpoint. This is where the 'total logistics concept' becomes important and meaningful. The underlying aim of this concept is to organise the logistics systems of a firm in such a way as to:

(a) enable the company to use its working capital resources more effectively,
(b) plan plant and warehouse location in the most economical way from the total corporation's viewpoint,
(c) react to changing environments more rapidly.

This is a vast subject and it merits a careful and thorough study by every manager who aspires to become proficient in international marketing.

The main implications of what was said so far on the subject are:

(i) *Efficient and prompt information is needed about cost of each important segment of the distribution system.* With the advent of real time computer systems on an international basis the possibility of pertinent and timely data is becoming a reality. Of course the data needs and the frequency of reporting must be planned in accordance with the best principles of management information systems theory. The important point is that the right managers receive the appropriate information, and at the needed frequency, to be able to see distribution problems in the proper perspective, set the right priorities, identify potential savings and take the necessary action to improve performance.

(ii) *The level of knowledge and skills pertaining to the distribution task must be up-graded*. The talents and expertise needed to manage international distribution are of a very much higher level than those one would expect to meet in a domestic company. Top management must recognise that it takes managers of high calibre to deal successfully with the complex factors and techniques that typify international distribution and especially where logistics overlap areas exist. In this connection it is also vitally important that top management including senior marketing personnel acquire sufficient knowledge of the logistics process and its various techniques. They need to understand the dynamics of distribution economics in terms of the relative costs of the multiple impacts of alternative distribution configurations and strategies.

(iii) *A centralised body capable of planning and co-ordinating international physical distribution activities will emerge.* Irrespective of the kind of organisational structure that a firm might have opted for it is difficult to see how effective logistics could be attained without a central organ responsible either for managing this important function or co-ordinating the various international components that may exist. Whilst this statement smacks of a strong plea for centralisation it is not meant to be so. The central body envisaged can be in a staff role, as one would expect to find in an 'umbrella' type structure, or in the 'line' as would be the case in a macropyramid organisation. The important feature must be that every part of the international organisation must have access to the top-level capability and expertise that the firm will have to assemble. The level of sophistication of such expertise is likely to be so high that inevitably it will be a scarce resource and it is highly unlikely that such capability could be available in every operational unit.

Furthermore, irrespective of the level of decentralisation that the firm may have developed, it is important that certain logistics decisions are taken in an objective atmosphere and independently of operating subsidiaries. This can only mean at a central point. Thus for instance, decisions pertaining to plant location contain important distribution considerations; these must be collected and appraised by a top-level central authority. A central logistics management is as relevant as a central financial authority. However much one decentralises financial management there is always a residual authority capable of monitoring the way funds are managed and able to respond to changes affecting the supply, demand and cost of money in different countries. Similarly a central, competent and well-informed physical distribution authority is necessary in a firm marketing its products in a large number of markets. In a very cost-conscious world it appears an essential concept for the effective management of the flow of materials and products. The way such a central organ can be dovetailed into the total organisational scene may need considerable skill and imagination, especially in firms that have been accustomed to a measure of decentralisation. However, as a general principle, the writer believes that more and more firms operating in international markets will gradually develop a centrally located logistics capability for planning, integrating, co-ordinating and monitoring the flow of goods for world markets. This may appear contrary to the spirit of decentralisation that many international firms have chosen for their direction but at the same time it may prove a more effective way for using scarce managerial resources as well as ensuring that the international consumer will obtain products at the right time and at the right place in the most economical way.

Chapter 9

Communication Strategies in World Markets

Under this heading we include all the *promotional* activities of the firm as well as its *selling* effort. As we shall see later both aim at achieving similar objectives and it is, therefore, logical to bulk them under the title: *communication.*

The way a firm promotes or sells its products in international markets depends on a host of factors: the firm's total marketing philosophy, the level of centralisation or decentralisation, the type of products it offers and many others. It must be recalled that a firm which has opted for a complete decentralisation policy is of little interest to us here insofar as each country has to apply in practice the normal rules of domestic marketing. The intricacies of international communication become pertinent only when a firm operating in many markets seeks to co-ordinate these activities so as to achieve some sort of synergy among them.

Our attention will be focused on communication strategies that call for some international planning and control. It is not proposed to discuss in detail the way the communication process is managed in a purely national context except where it helps to explain the international dimension.

The Role of Communication in Marketing

As a first step it is important that nomenclature is defined and that the communication process is described. Most international marketers would know that terminology often creates considerable difficulties in the field of communication in world markets. What the Anglo-Saxons call 'advertising' is normally referred to in France as 'publicité' and inevitably this generates some confusion in discussions and correspondence. Surprisingly enough in Jugoslavia the word for 'advertising' is 'propaganda'.

The word *communication* in marketing simply means the transmission of a message, to the buyer or the consumer or the channel of distribution, in which the supplying company aims to tell each one of these receivers why they should buy or handle the product. In other words, in its least sophisticated form communication aims to make potential buyers (or middlemen) more favourably disposed towards the firm's offering. It seeks to achieve this objective by *informing* the recipient of the message of the existence of the product and its unique details or by *modifying his attitude* towards such a product or by enhancing his *preference* for one product against another.

The idea that communication's main objective is to increase sales or to increase market share is an over-simplification. It is only in rare cases that the communication effort leads directly to such results. Increasing sales or market share are the objectives of the total marketing process and communication is one more aid towards their attainment. If the results are poor owing to the product being unsatisfactory it would be grossly unfair to blame the communication effort. Similarly, if every ingredient of the marketing mix is right, with the exception of the price, once again it would not be fair to ascribe the failure to ineffective communication.

The objectives of the communication process can be varied and sometimes fairly intangible in the sense that they may aim to achieve objectives which are totally unrelated to the attainment of sales. An international firm, for instance, which seeks to develop a better corporate image throughout the world cannot, and certainly not in the short-term, express such an objective in terms of sales volume. The cause and effect relationship is much too tenuous.

Similarly an international engineering company that advertises in a number of international magazines, with the basic objective of attracting young graduates to apply for a job with that firm, cannot translate the communication objectives into sales terms. Whilst it is always easier to explain and illustrate the communication effort and its results in terms of sales volume; one must not lose sight of the fact that communication can be a very much more sophisticated and tortuous process.

An extreme example of an advertising objective which is not set in 'action' terms (e.g. to attain a sales figure), but in purely communication terms (e.g. to impart information or to change attitudes) is that of *alleviating cognitive dissonance*. Behind this jargon lies an important behavioural problem: the post-purchase anxiety or doubt which the buyer, especially of an expensive product, often develops *after* acquiring such a product. Dissonance is common among purchasers of homes, cars and major appliances. It is particularly prevalent among buyers in countries where the personal disposable income is relatively limited and the acquisition of such items involves a heavy financial commitment. The tension caused by dissonance leads the buyer to seek its reduction. He can attain such a reduction either by ridding himself of the offending product or its concealment in the attic or through persistent harrassment of the distributor who supplied it in the first place. He may, on the other hand, try to resolve the nagging doubt by searching for proof in the media that he had in fact made the right choice when he purchased the product in question. In this connection a well-designed advertisement, placed in the appropiate media, may attain the objective of reassuring the doubtful purchaser of the excellent properties of the product and the wisdom of the purchase. The consumer will be thankful for such an advertisement and his level of satisfaction will be greatly enhanced. This indeed is a very important communication task and its effectiveness cannot be measured in terms of quantifiable sales targets. What we are trying to do here is purely to safeguard the continued satisfaction of a customer whose future business we hope to maintain.

The last example helps to highlight the controversy that has been raging in the advertising world for many years. The controversy hinges around two extreme schools of thought: the first suggests that communication in its various forms must be geared towards the attainment of sales; the second believes that advertising with other forms of promotion must aim to fulfil clearly-defined communication objectives such as the provision of information, the creation of knowledge, the stimulation of favourable attitudes, etc. The exponents of the latter school of thought remind us that the achievement of a sale depends on an integrated marketing mix of which an effective communication effort is an essential component. Communication *per se* cannot achieve results in terms of sales volume. The first school of thought is *action orientated*; the second is known as the DAGMAR school (Defining Advertising Goals—Measuring Advertising Results).

The controversy is stimulating but probably not very useful insofar as both are right. Some communication programmes are action orientated. Others are of the DAGMAR type. The two philosophies are not mutually exclusive. Mail order advertising, for instance, is a case where the underlying objective is action. The advertisement aims to generate immediate response and indeed results can be measured in terms of orders received. On the other hand, an electronics company that advertises extensively, in order to develop an international corporate image so as to stimulate a favourable attitude towards its many products, is certainly indulging in a DAGMAR effort. The success of such a campaign cannot be measured in terms of sales: certainly not in the shorter term. The only way the effectiveness of such an effort can be measured is through having in the first place very clear advertising objectives. Thus, every communication campaign must be worked out on the merit of each case. Whether one follows the action school of thought or the DAGMAR philosophy, clearly defined objectives are always needed if one wishes to measure results in a systematic manner. The conceptual controversy as to what communication is all about does not change the basic fact that an effective communication strategy needs pre-set goals.

The Communication Process

It is useful at this point to review briefly the way the communication process works and highlight specific problems emanating from the international dimension.

Communication comes fron the Latin *communis*, common. When we communicate we seek to establish 'commonness' with someone. We endeavour to share information, knowledge, ideas or attitudes.

Figure 43 describes the process in a model form. This model has been

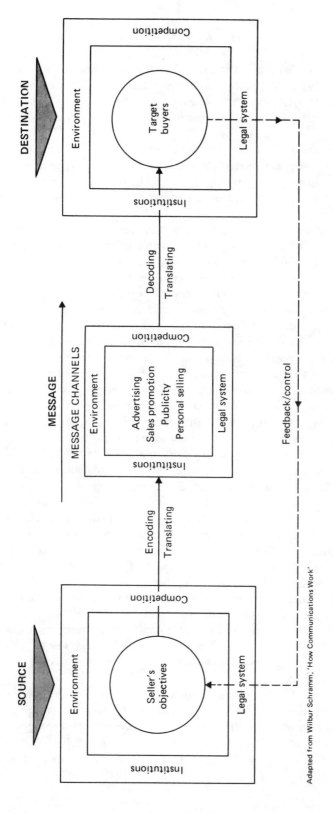

Fig. 43   Model of the communication process in international markets

Adapted from Wilbur Schramm, 'How Communications Work'

adapted from Wilbur Schramm's* classical description of how communication works. His writings on the subject, although published many years ago, are still most pertinent. The model has been adapted to incorporate the environmental elements that control an international communication activity.

Communication requires at least three elements: a *source*, a *message* and a *destination*. A *source* may be an individual (speaking, writing, gesticulating) or an organisation such as a government, a firm or an association of people. In the field of international marketing the source is normally a *seller* of a product or service.

The *message* may be in the form of a written note, radio waves, a gesture, a flag, a whistle or any other signal that can be interpreted meaningfully. In marketing, the message normally takes the form of a description of the product coupled with a eulogy of its unique selling points.

The *destination* of a communication effort may be a specific individual listening, reading or watching; or a member of a group such as an audience of a seminar or in the cinema; or an unspecified individual of a mass audience such as a person watching television. The destination in world markets may be a vast number of potential buyers who live in many different countries and probably belong to different cultures and speak a myriad of languages.

In order to attain commonness which is the ultimate objective of communication the source of a message must *encode* it into a form which he knows that the destination is capable of *decoding. The destination and the source must be in tune.* Failure occurs where the destination decodes the message in a manner which does not correspond to the intention or objective selected by the source. This in turn means that the source must have adequate or clear information as to how the destination behaves and his decoding capabilities. The source of the sender must possess a full understanding of how the destination will respond to a specific message. Will the message be decoded or interpreted in accordance with our objectives or will it be distorted? Will the 'picture in the head' of the receiver bear any resemblance to that in the head of the sender? This means that a sender must find out in some detail what the destination is able to decode or comprehend.

Thus a Hi-Fi manufacturer who uses such messages as '20Hz–25kHz $\pm$ 3dB and impedance and RMS power and wow and flutter and so on' must establish that the destination of such colourful descriptions is capable of decoding what is undoubtedly a very important message. Using such a jargon without prior verification of the decodability of these words is the essence of poor communication.

Messages can of course be transmitted in non-verbal ways. A policeman on traffic duty transmits non-verbal signals to drivers. An angry person conveys his feelings in various non-verbal gestures. But now one must recognise that a gesture which the Englishman will decode as a sign of fury may well be

---

* Wilbur Schramm (ed.), *The Process and Effects of Mass Communications*, University of Illinois Press.

interpreted by the Chinese as a sign that the No. 2 bus is arriving! In other words the encoding of messages entails much more than just translating them from one language to another. All the cultural, political and economic factors that make an environment must be looked at with great care when the message is prepared. A fascinating example of the subtleties that one has to build into a multi-cultural message is the famous Esso tiger. The aim was to develop the tiger as an international symbol of Esso's petroleum. Nonetheless the tiger had to undergo 'plastic surgery' in a number of countries, insofar as the original tiger appeared too ferocious and unpleasant in a few cultural environments. By softening the tiger's features, providing him with longer eye-lashes and depicting him in a toy-like form the obstacle was overcome. Subtle changes made the communication process more effective by simply matching better the sender's message to an acceptable norm at the buyer's end. The encoding/decoding process was thus improved.

How is the message transmitted? The word *channels* is shown in Figure 43. In the sphere of marketing the channels available are:

Advertising: Any paid form of non-personal presentation of products, services or ideas placed in one or more of the commercially available media by an identified sponsor.

Sales promotion: These are the so-called 'below-the-line' activities such as demonstrations, sampling, displays, shows and exhibitions which do not utilise media.

Publicity: The stimulation of a mention in the media of significant news items about the firm, its products and its activities without actually paying for such a favourable presentation.

Personal selling: Oral presentation with one or more prospective buyers, deciders or influencers.

These channels can be used as part of a communication mix or the marketer may choose to concentrate his effort on one or two of them depending on circumstances. The ability to select the most appropiate message channel for a given set of objectives is one of the most skilful tasks of marketing. Such a selection depends on a myriad of considerations that differ from country to country, from industry to industry and from product to product. In international marketing one has to cope with the environmental ingredients of the marketing mix. The external elements of the mix, (namely the environment itself, competition, institutions and legal systems), differ enormously from market to market. Their influence is not only significant on the message but also on the choice of the transmission channels. As a simple example to illustrate the point: in a country in which the environmental studies indicate a large level of illiteracy it is unwise to select a daily newspaper as the channel of communication for transmitting information about a new product. Similarly in a market where television advertising does not exist it is impossible to rely on this medium.

This is where the marketing profile analysis is such a useful tool. If assembled with care it should provide the marketer with the basis for identifying pertinent data not only about the message and its contents but also about the channels available and their appropriateness to the firm's communication objectives.

Figure 44 illustrates the kind of questions that this type of analysis should yield.

The most rudimentary marketing profile analysis of Angola would have saved British Aircraft Corporation the following embarrassment:

On the 26th January 1973 the Times reported:

'The British Ambassador in Lisbon has apologized to the Portuguese Foreign Minister for an incident in which the British Concorde hoisted the flag of anti-Portuguese rebels at Luanda Airport in Angola.

The aircraft had landed at Luanda for refuelling on Wednesday during a trial to Johannesburg. As it was about to take off it hoisted the Union Jack and the red, black and yellow flag of the People's Movement for the Liberation of Angola. Instantly jeeps were sent to block take-off and the test pilot had to pay a fine before Concorde was allowed to leave.

The aircraft's makers, the British Aircraft Corporation are reported here as explaining that the flag had been bought in London in the belief that it was the Portuguese national flag. The intention had been to honour Angola.'

Communication Objectives

The source, the seller, starts with a set of objectives. The message aims to help him to meet these objectives. Without clear objectives the whole purpose of the communication effort is futile. But what is the purpose of the communication process?

We talked about commonness between source and destination but how does this commonness of information or ideas help the marketing task. Nobody seems to have managed so far to define the purpose of communication in general, and advertising in particular, in such a way as to be universally acceptable. In his *Madison Avenue* Martin Mayer put it very succinctly: 'Only the very brave or the very ignorant can say exactly what advertising does in the marketplace'.*

In spite of these difficulties it is important that a communication strategy is based on a conceptual framework which is capable of general applicability. Without derogating in any way from the various behavioural models that have been propounded over the years the writer favours the model developed many years ago by Lavidge and Steiner.* The model is reproduced with some adaptation in Figure 45. The main aim of the adaptation is to show how the

---

* Martin Mayer, *Madison Avenue, USA* Harper & Row, New York.

† Robert J. Lavidge and Gary A. Steiner, 'A Model for Predictive Measurements of Advertising Effectiveness' *Journal of Marketing*, XXV, October 1961.

A possible checklist for the Communication portion of the Marketing Profile Analysis

	Communication			
	The Promotional Mix			
	Advertising	*Sales Promotion*	*Publicity*	*Personal selling*
ENVIRONMENT	Language details; literacy levels: readership details: response to symbolism; general attitude to advertising; details of buyer, decider, influencer patterns; various segments; demography	Same language, culture, demographic details as in the case of advertising. Consumer's attitude to 'below-the-line' type activities	Details of consumer response to publicity. Readership details broken down to socioeconomic, demographic segments. Kind of stories sought	General attitude in the market-place to salesmen and salesmanship. Expectations of the channels of distribution as to salesmanship
COMPETITION	Identify competitive advertising practices; their expenditure and ratio to sales over a period. Research strengths and weaknesses of competitors' advertising policies	Competitive practices and expenditure; identify quantitative relationship between expenditure on advertising and sales promotion. Observe for creative ideas	Details of publicity 'mentions' gained by competitors. How were they achieved?	Obtain full details of the kind, size and effectiveness of competitors' sales forces. Identify areas of weakness in competitive practices; also areas of creativity
INSTITUTIONS	Total advertising expenditure in country; media available and growth in expenditure patterns; technical facilities (e.g. colour). Media details—circulation, readership and segments, media costs, frequency. Any special media; research bodies; code of advertising; various organisations	Institutional facilities available to help in performing promotional activities. Barbour Index type organisation (calling on specific professions such as architects)	Public relations facilities available in market; appraise cost and effectiveness. Bodies controlling code of practice and message	Bodies controlling the quality and professionalism of salesmen. Organisations available to help in performing the selling task. 'Sales force to Hire' systems
LEGAL SYSTEM	Trade description legislation. Special rules pertaining to various products (e.g. cigarettes, drugs, fertilisers). Laws limiting expenditure. Use of languages	As with advertising	As with advertising	Laws against selling practices. Laws against inertia selling. Legislation on 'cooling off' periods (e.g. insurance or hire purchase deals)

Fig. 44 The communication (promotion and selling) portion of the marketing profile analysis

main emphasis of the communication process shifts during the product life cycle from awareness/knowledge building at the introduction stage to conviction/purchase in the final stages of the product's life. Moreover, the removal of the cognitive dissonance is shown as a permanent objective of the communication process throughout the life cycle. The model illustrates how communication aims to generate in the target buyer (the destination) the following sequence of responses: *awareness, knowledge, liking, preference, conviction.* It is only when all these have been achieved, either instantaneously or in a tortuous way that the consumer is ready to *purchase* the product. Where the product is of the type likely to generate a certain amount of *cognitive dissonance* the marketer should also incorporate the objective of alleviating these after-purchase doubts. Attaining this objective should help to maintain loyalty in the buyer which is what is needed for future relationship.

It is evident that different emphasis must be placed on different objectives of the communication process during the various stages of the product life cycle. When the product is first launched it is necessary to create maximum *awareness* and *knowledge* of the product and its characteristics. This would normally coincide with the introduction stage of the life cycle and would

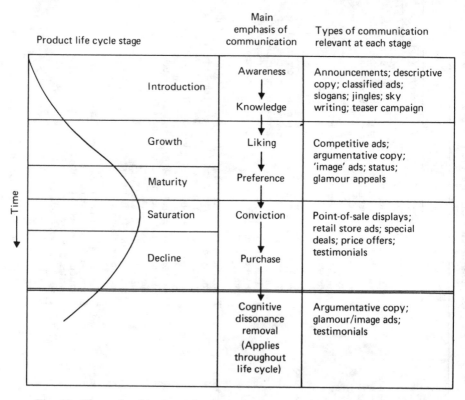

Fig. 45   The main objectives of communication at various stages of the product life cycle

continue until the growth stage is reached. At that point awareness is fairly high and it is the *attitude* of the target buyer which becomes important—one works towards the development of a favourable attitude among those who are aware of the product. This will continue until the end of the maturity stage. At that point the product is well known and is either liked or not liked but having reached the saturation or decline stages it is important to get quick results viz. *sales*. The product is fighting for its life and there is no time to waste. It is important to stress that the demarcation is not as clear-cut as all this: even at the decline stage one should be thinking of raising the level of awareness, and indeed throughout the life cycle one must aim for the ultimate objective of the marketing effort, namely *sales*. The main implication of the aforesaid is that at different stages of the life cycle different emphasis must be placed on the communication objectives which are relevant for the attainment of optimum results of the moment. It is perfectly obvious that without awareness one cannot expect to achieve sales; similarly where the attitude to a product or its maker is negative no sales could be attained.

The behavioural model described above is particularly relevant in international marketing, insofar as the same product may have different life cycle characteristics in various markets. When discussing product policy and planning in Chapter 6,. . . . we saw in Figure 27 how a product that has reached the decline stage in one market, may be approaching the maturity stage in another market, growing in a third market and may be totally unknown in a fourth market. In other words the same product could be at four different stages in its life cycle at the same time. This perforce means that different communication objectives would need to be selected for each country. This is illustrated in Figure 46. It will be noted that in market A the emphasis is on awareness building; in market B on the development of attitudes viz. liking and preference and in market C the objective is action-orientated towards purchase. In market D the product is yet to be launched.

We emphasised earlier in this book the fact that the gap between the time a product reaches its decline stage in the most advanced market and the introduction stage in the slowest market is narrowing. If this trend continues the point will be reached where the pattern of the life cycle in a domestic market will become identical with the pattern in foreign markets. This will of course have a tremendous impact on the communication strategy of firms operating internationally. It would mean that in time it would become possible for the communication objectives of such firms to become more and more homogeneous, thus allowing for a larger measure of standardisation. In other words if the trend continues it should become possible for the same campaign, subject to the manipulation necessitated by linguistic and cultural variations, to be undertaken in all markets. This is indeed the kind of standardisation that Coca-Cola has achieved in world markets. This strategy stems in the main from the fact that the product life cycle profile of Coca-Cola is pretty homogeneous throughout the world.

The move towards more homogeneous product ageing characteristics has

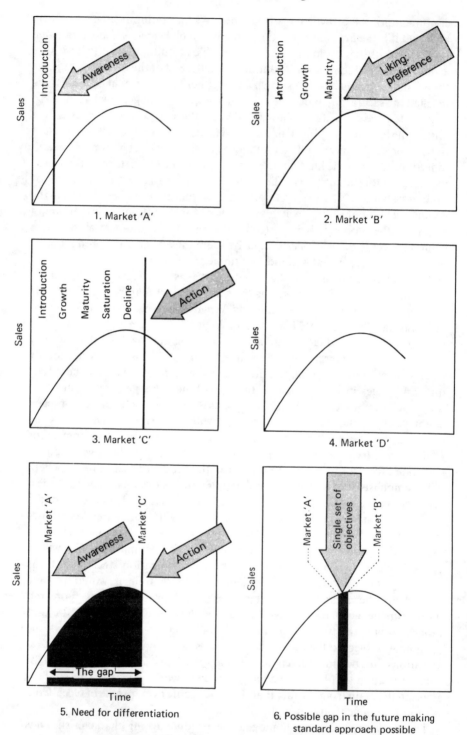

Fig. 46   The changing communication needs as the product life cycle progresses
from introduction to decline

important connotations for the way the firm organises its communication on a global scale and also on the kind of advertising agency assistance that it ought to harness. Obviously where the product profile justifies communication standardisation, it may be advisable to use the services of an international advertising agency with offices in all main markets. This latter point is of great importance: the emergence of international agencies has certainly acted as a great stimulus to better international communication. Many firms operating on an international level have managed to cope with the complexities of international communication owing to the judicious selection of experienced and knowledgeable agencies. Hoping to attain the same results by using a host of local agencies with no international expertise is a formula for waste in world-wide marketing.

International Considerations

An effective communication programme in a firm operating internationally can be affected by a large number of problems. The following are examples of the kind of problems that may arise:

How far should Head Office concern itself with the communication activities of foreign subsidiaries?

Should there be a centrally-formulated policy regarding corporate image, colouring, logotype, etc?

Who should determine communication budgets?

In the event that budgets are determined centrally how should priorities be decided upon?

Should the firm employ one international agency or allow each subsidiary abroad to make its own arrangements?

Who should determine the communication mix?

Where a number of languages are involved who is responsible for executing and controlling the translation work?

Who should be responsible for measuring communication effectiveness?

Where policy and objectives are centrally-planned how does one cope with the variations in media availability?

These are just a few questions that confront most firms operating on a multinational scale and answers must be found to all of them unless the firm is prepared to muddle its way through the maze of international communication problems in a haphazard way.

Factors Affecting Communication Strategies in International Marketing

The major considerations that affect communication decisions in international marketing fall under the following headings:

1 The overall objectives of the firm
2 The nature of the business and its products
3 The firm's organisation
4 Legal constraints
5 Media availability

1 THE FIRM'S OBJECTIVES

This is almost a truism—until we know what a firm's objectives are it is virtually impossible to determine the kind of communication approach it should adopt. To take an extreme example: the owner of a firm who wishes to build the business rapidly in order to dispose of it as a going concern and thus capitalise on his effort will have totally different communication objectives from the firm that seeks to develop a long-term international image for the company and its products. The former will have very limited communication objectives and mostly of a very short-term nature. The latter will have to define the firm's objectives within the framework of a well-balanced long-term plan. Similarly a firm that does not wish to build its international commitment beyond the supply of the ten largest potential markets will, perforce, have different communication objectives than the company that has plans to operate in every part of the globe. Thus IBM will have entirely different objectives from a manufacturer of executive aircraft.

2 THE NATURE OF THE BUSINESS AND ITS PRODUCTS

The consideration is closely linked with the previous one. Once we know what the firm's overall objectives are we must have a close look at the type of products or service that the firm offers. These may determine the kind of communication strategy the firm should adopt. Certain types of goods lend themselves to a highly standardised style of promotion; others by their very nature call for a high degree of differentiation. The important thing is that the firm develops a policy with its eyes open and is not pushed into it by sheer inertia. Highly technical products such as X-ray equipment, computers, processing plants, etc. normally lend themselves to a higher level of standardisation of communication policy than fashion-based products, decorative materials or confectionery.

3 THE FIRM'S ORGANISATION

The way the firm is organised for international operations in general and for international marketing in particular has a very significant impact on its communication strategy. It is quite evident that a highly centralised firm would handle its communication activities in a totally different way from a decentralised firm. Whatever the rationale behind the organisational pattern selected for the company as a whole, it has a definite influence on every aspect of the firm's operations including, of course, marketing communication.

Thus it is normally true to say that a firm that has opted for macropyramid structure is likely to approach its communication effort with the following characteristics:

(a) A strong centralised communication department that lays down rigid rules regarding the company's policy on promotion and selling activities.
(b) Budgets are determined at the centre or carefully scrutinised and approved by a central department.
(c) Pressure to have a standardised and centrally-controlled communication policy.
(d) Whilst on paper the local communication personnel are responsible to the local marketing boss, in practice a strong link exists direct to the centre. This often generates friction and misunderstandings.
(e) Numerous complaints from local management arise regarding lack of sensitivity in the centre towards local needs of the customer.
(f) Total expenditure on communication is kept within economically measurable proportions. In other words, waste is reduced to a minimum throughout the world.

On the other hand the 'umbrella' style organisation would manifest the following characteristics in relation to its communication effort:

(a) Communication decisions vest almost entirely in local management.
(b) Budgets are normally determined, scrutinised and approved at local level.
(c) Very little standardisation exists in style and message quality.
(d) Managerial communication between the centre and the local personnel is quite poor.
(e) A central communication department may exist within the 'umbrella' approach but its role is purely advisory.
(f) Aggregate expenditure can rise to phenomenal proportions.
(g) Little exchange of ideas takes place among the various subsidiaries.

In the case of the interglomerate the situation will, of course, differ from firm to firm. It will depend on the size of the organisation and the diffusion of activities and products. However, by and large one would expect to encounter considerable freedom and decentralisation in relation to products, but fairly rigid centralisation of policies in relation to corporate image and central objectives.

4 LEGAL CONSTRAINTS

The legal system of a country often has an important impact on what can and what cannot be done in the field of communication. It is too wide a subject to cover in detail in a book on marketing. Nonetheless it is important that the marketer gains a broad understanding of the legislation that may affect his decisions and strategies. In case of doubt he must seek legal advice. The number of pitfalls in this area can be enormous and any infringement of the law can lead to considerable embarrassment.

Examples of legislation that one encounters with some frequency:

(a) Trade description legislation, which is quite common in many countries, seeks normally to bar:

Statements containing the slightest deception regarding price, contents, origin, composition, qualities of effectiveness or of service offered.

Quotations from testimonials or certificates which are not accurate or factual.

It will be found that in countries where no legislation exists one often comes across a fairly strong code of advertising operating as a self-disciplinary system of control.

(b) Specific prohibition to advertise certain products. A few products seem to meet more hostility by the legislators than others:

cigarettes and tobacco

drugs and other proprietary medicines

products pertaining to family planning

In a few markets the prohibition is total; in others the law demands that certain statements or conditions are attached to each promotional instrument. Thus in some countries the law demands that products containing poisons must state so in every advertisement as well as on the product itself.

(c) Prohibition on using certain words or expressions that may be misinterpreted by the consumer.

Thus in a few countries it is prohibited to use such words as pasteurised or sterilised unless permission is granted from a governmental body. In the Netherlands, for instance, statements such as free from sugar or low salt content with a medical purport may not be used without prior consent by Royal Decree.

(d) Limitations on expenditure

Whilst this is not prevalent at the moment in free economies the prudent marketer must watch this point, insofar as in many countries one encounters rumblings against the heavy and extravagant cost of advertising. Talk about limiting such expenditure has been mounting and the international marketer might as well check the legal position in each market when substantial expenditure is planned.

In this connection it is also important to investigate the tax position pertaining to promotional expenditure. Turnover taxes, value added taxes and straight advertising taxes may have a significant influence on the media selected for a given set of circumstances.

(e) To the extent that packaging laws may affect promotional policies one must pay careful heed to such regulations.

In some countries containers for specific goods must be of a certain shape.

In the Netherlands at one point, for instance, margarine for home consumption had to be packed in the shape of a rectangular parallelepiped. This seems a pretty useless bit of information to the average marketer. On the other hand a person who was charged with the marketing of margarine in the Netherlands and was unfamiliar with this regulation could easily run into costly and embarrassing promotional misadventure.

(f) Content and style of advertisements

In Germany, for instance, superlatives and comparative claims are forbidden by law. In Sweden, misdemeanours by advertisers may be charged under the criminal law with severe penalties.

5 MEDIA AVAILABILITY

An international marketer must never assume that the type of media he had been accustomed to at home are likely to be found in foreign markets. Admittedly one can expect to meet more or less the same type of media in most industrialised countries but even there the differences in institutional quality and communication value can be quite significant. Much more complicated are those situations where certain media are simply not available.

In some countries there is no television advertising. In others radio as a medium is totally unknown. Trade journals may be limited to certain activities only. Cinema advertising may be popular in one country but totally non-existent in a neighbouring market. Other fairly obvious omissions may exist in each market. Another difficulty that may occur: demand for television advertising time can be so substantial that time has to be rationed to certain products. That can present some difficulties if the advertiser or his agent wish to buy space at short notice for a special campaign.

It is not difficult to obtain full information about the media of a country. Most reputable advertising agents possess such data and in fact many of them issue booklets that set out all the relevant details. Alternatively, one can normally obtain comprehensive information about local media from the country's association of advertising agents. Most countries have such a body and whilst some of them are less effective than the IPA in the UK they are nonetheless a useful source of information about media.

Translating for Communication

A communication message originating in one country very often has to be put to work in other markets. The question of translating the message to suit the environmental conditions of each market can confront the copywriter with overwhelming difficulties. We are not concerned here with those cases where a 'free-for-all' climate exists among the foreign companies in the multi-national group, in the sense that each unit is responsible for its own communication effort. Our main concern is with those situations where the promotion or advertising department in one country has to prepare a copy that is intended to be used in other markets. The number of pitfalls here can be very large.

Where an advertising copy may be used in a foreign language it must be written and designed accordingly from the very outset. The following are a number of useful guidelines to be borne in mind:*

1   Idioms jargon, English 'buzz-words' must be avoided.
2   Layout and artwork should be designed with enough 'free area' to expand the text where necessary.
    Foreign languages often use more words than English to communicate the same message. Latin languages take up 20 per cent more space and German and Slav languages 25 per cent. Pictographic languages like Chinese and Arabic may need up to 50 per cent more space than the English equivalent.
3   Legal requirements or recognized codes of conduct that control the content of advertising material must be checked very carefully.
    As was suggested earlier infringements of local laws can involve the advertiser in serious problems.
4   The translation must be carried out by competent and professional translators.
    In this connection it is important that the translators used are familiar with the every-day language of the country in question. It is well known that UK English differs in many respects from American English. Spanish spoken in the Argentine is marginally different from the language used in Spain. With oriental languages like Arabic one often encounters as many dialects as countries that speak such languages.
    In the UK the Institute of Practitioners in Advertising keeps a register of translation bureaux.
5   Translators must be thoroughly briefed.
    It is not enough to hand over a document to a translator and ask him to carry out the assignment. He must be fully conversant with the details of the product, its nature and purpose. Technical phrases and points of special significance must be explained to him. It must be remembered that the translator's true function is the production of a *total translation* of the original thoughts and ideas rather than that of the exact words appearing in the original text. Otherwise one may get the absurd mishap that 'out of sight, out of mind' in English may translate into 'invisible lunatic' in Turkish!
    The translation must be checked by competent linguists or by the local distributor, agent or personnel of the local subsidiary.
    In this connection translating-back the copy into the original language can be a very effective safeguard. Any anomalies that might have crept into the translation should be detected by this simple device.

*Translating for Advertising, Institute of Practitioners in Advertising, 1972.

Having the final checking done by the local distributors or agents is a useful participative method for ensuring that those who will have to use such material will have an opportunity of voicing their criticism before it is too late.

6 Typesetting and printing must be undertaken by specialist foreign language printers. It is most unwise to use typesetting specialists and printers who have had no experience in carrying out this type of work in a foreign language. The smallest error can make the whole copy look embarrassingly unprofessional. One encounters from time to time sales aids or other communication devices translated from foreign languages and typeset overseas which can only make the reader squirm with discomfiture at the travesty of message they purport to convey. The professional marketer never falls into this trap.

Chapter 10

Marketing Planning on an International Scale

Planning on an international scale is a vast subject and justifies a separate book. Nonetheless one cannot explore international marketing planning without a brief discussion of the total company planning process. The development of marketing plans in isolation from the total company plans is as futile as the production of plans for an infantry force without a national military plan.

Planning has been defined as *the process of reconciling a firm's resources with present and future opportunities*. Thus in its simplest form planning means that a firm seeks to look at itself with the view of identifying what it is capable of doing and choosing a direction which would enable it to exploit such capabilities within a given environment. Because of the futurity of opportunities and because of the necessity to deal with an immense set of interrelated dimensions which are external to the firm the planning process often appears to overwhelm managers and indeed often gets abandoned after a poor start. This is particularly true where after an initial enthusiasm the firm's managers discover that owing to sudden changes in market conditions the actual results attained bear no relationship to the plans.

Nonetheless many firms have come to acknowledge that planning is a vital ingredient in the way the company determines the path it should take for its future destiny and success. Alfred R. Oxenfeldt in his *Executive Action in Marketing** summarised most succinctly the benefits that a firm can derive from the adoption of the planning process:

1 The co-ordination of the activities of many individuals whose actions are interrelated over time.
2 Identification of expected developments.
3 Preparedness to meet changes when they occur.
4 Minimisation of non-rational responses to the unexpected.
5 Better communication among executives.
6 Minimisation of conflicts among individuals which would result in a subordination of the goals of the company for those of the individual.

In other words, there are a number of intangible benefits emanating from

* Alfred R. Oxenfeldt, *Executive Action in Marketing*, Wadsworth Publishing Co., Belmont, California, 1966.

the planning process which probably exceed the immediate expectations of those responsible for introducing such a discipline into the firm. These *fringe benefits* must never be overlooked. What is important to remember is that planning is not just a discipline of spelling out future intentions in a written form. In its most refined form it is a highly responsive process for guiding a firm through the hazards of a rapidly changing environment. It is a sophisticated instrument, like a radar, which enables the firm's pilots to detect deviations from a pre-set path and the need to correct course.

The 'Root' and 'Branch' Concept in Planning

Before discussing the planning process in detail it is useful to highlight a dilemma that faces most planners sooner or later and which has a major significance in international planning activities. Where does one start? Does one start the planning process at the lowest operating levels and then work one's way from *bottom-up* or does one start on a *top-down* emphasis? The supporters of the first orientation suggest that quite often people at operational levels are far closer to the business realities of the firm and therefore can determine objectives which are attainable. Moreover, they claim that having objectives set by those who have to achieve them is a better motivational practice than imposing them from above.

The propounders of the top-down approach claim that logically there is only one starting point, namely the strategic level of the firm. After all, they claim, the aim of the firm is to satisfy a number of *stakeholders* with conflicting demands and expectations and the only people who are in the position of striking a balance among these demands are the strategic level. They express the needs and expectations of the various groups of stakeholders in *corporate objectives* and these are the trigger point from which the firm's planning starts. In other words, according to this school of thought, the firm exists in order to meet certain expectations of various groups such as employees, shareholders, bankers, governments, etc. and the summation of these expectations is enunciated in corporate objectives—until these have been defined no meaningful planning can be performed at the lower levels of management.

The implications of these two fundamentally different philosophies are significant when one approaches planning in a firm operating in many countries. According to the first approach planning must commence at the various operational units throughout the world and then be brought to the centre for distillation and aggregation. According to the second school of thought the strategic centre is the 'trigger point' from which the firm's objectives are transmitted like the Tablets from Mount Sinai. The corporate objectives are defined at the centre and each operational unit and/or functional area throughout the world is allocated a proportion of the overall task. Whilst participation in the whole process is recognised as a good thing, the main idea is that the objectives as declared at the centre are sacrosanct.

Anybody who wishes to spend a lot of time intellectualising upon the two philosophies and their respective merits and drawbacks will finally come to the conclusion that the ideal arrangement is a combination of the two approaches. A planning cycle based on the transmission of rigid objectives from the *top* may easily fail to take notice of the environmental pressures that may affect the attainment of results at the *bottom*. In the opposite situation planning that starts its cycle at operational levels often ignores the fundamental expectations of the total corporation as expressed in the corporate objectives.

The truth is that the top and bottom are totally interrelated and planning must somewhat form a cycle which allows a free flow of information, ideas and proposed strategies between the corporate plan (the top) and the various sub-plans (the bottom).

The whole process may be compared to a tree. The tree has a root and branches. For survival the tree needs both. It obtains nutrition from the earth via the roots and from the atmosphere via the branches. Somehow all this 'input' provides the tree with the opportunity to be healthy and grow. The parallel can now be drawn: the tree is the corporate plan; the root of the tree is the set of corporate objectives; the branches are the sub-plans with their respective objectives. Each sub-plan (each branch) can have further sub-branches—product plans, advertising plans, etc.

The environment which fosters and/or hampers the growth of the tree (the soil, the air, the sun) is represented in the business planning world by the external environment of the firm including the threats and opportunities which may affect the firm's future.

Sound planning means of course that all the branches add up to a healthy tree capable of living in harmony with a strong root. (See Figure 47.)

The analogy of the tree is used to illustrate the inter-dependence of the root and branch in corporate planning. Indeed to most corporate planners the concept is well known and in fact even the terminology root and branch is often used in this connection.

The fundamental message is that it is almost futile to undertake a marketing planning activity in isolation. Marketing is a branch, albeit a very important one, and whatever planning one decides to carry out must be dovetailed with the planning undertaken at the root as well as at all other branches. Marketing planning which ignores production planning or manpower planning, etc. is a pretty sterile exercise.

The tree analogy can now be extended to cover the very much more complex problem of planning on an international scale. One can have a large tree with many branches, each representing a country or a cluster of countries. This would be a fair description of a firm structured on the macropyramid lines.

Alternatively, we may have a number of trees of the same species in a wood. Here the analogy is closer to the 'umbrella' type firm. Each tree symbolises a quasi-independent subsidiary with its own strategic root. The wood needs some sort of a 'keeper' to control the growth and health of the wood as a whole as well as its individual trees. The keeper may develop a number of facilities for

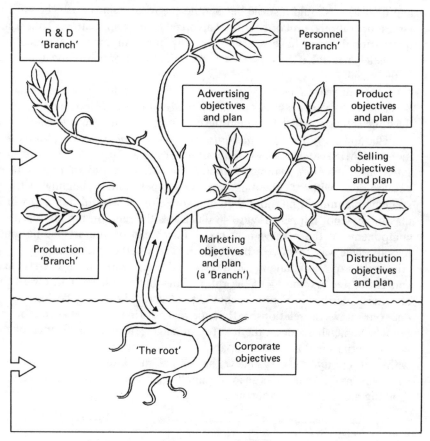

Fig. 47   The corporate plan—the root and branch approach

helping each tree to overcome specific difficulties. Some trees may not need any such help; nonetheless it is there for the asking.

The third possibility is the interglomerate which is more reminiscent of a forest (sometimes verging on a jungle) in which trees of different species grow in their multitudes. A few of these trees grow in total isolation; others grow in bunches as mini-woods; yet others grow in a semi-wild state.

To be able to plan international operations in a systematic and meaningful way one must attempt to conceptualise first as to the type of firm with which one is dealing. Until such a framework is developed and agreed upon it is difficult to determine how the planning process and its supportive procedures should operate. Furthermore it is difficult to motivate those responsible for preparing the various sub-plans if the total edifice is beyond conceptual comprehension of such managers. Planning can only work well when people understand what the whole process is all about and what it seeks to achieve. A framework also helps to determine the location and role of the planning 'centre of gravity'. Should the firm appoint a corporate planner at the centre and if so what should his role be? Should the focal point be attached to the largest operational unit or be totally divorced from profit centres? Thus some international firms have set up planning units in locations which are completely neutral in the sense that no manufacturing or marketing units exist in the vicinity.

One more reason as to why a clear framework for planning must be developed: the various stages of planning are inseparable links in a chain of dynamic activities which represent the way a firm is managed. *Planning* (both strategic and operational), *organisation development, management information systems* (MIS) and *business appraisal* form part of a logical cycle of interrelated activities. Planning without sound MIS is as futile as organisation development without planning. Similarly operational planning without strategic planning is no more than an expression of wishful thinking which may or may not happen. Figure 48 illustrates the relationship among these components of the management cycle. Firms can of course muddle quite happily their way to success but it is doubtful whether they can face major crises or rapidly changing market conditions without a crystal-clear conceptual understanding of the rules of the game. Where and how all the activities described in Figure 49 should be structured can only be determined once one knows the relationship that one wishes to maintain between root and branch. Somewhere along the line top management must take stock of the firm's international activities, capabilities and constraints and seek to define with some clarity how they believe that they should interrelate. In a dynamic environment this represents an important 'trigger point' for future conceptual thinking and not a finite posture.

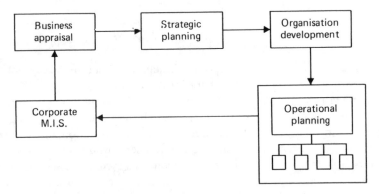

Fig. 48   The interrelationship between the planning cycle, organisation development and MIS

Planning as an 'Iterative' Process

Whether one opts for a top-down or a bottom-up approach one needs a 'trigger point' upon which the process of planning can be built. This helps to

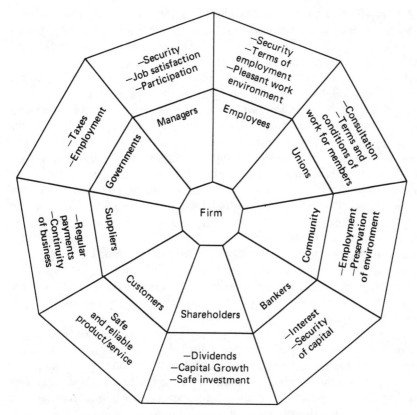

Fig. 49 Typical stakeholders and their expectations

eliminate the circuitous dilemma which so many firms encounter when introducing planning for the first time. The 'trigger point' is a basic enunciation of what the firm feels that it wishes to achieve and what it thinks it is capable of achieving. It is normally expressed in terms of fundamental criteria such as profits, return on investment, market share, growth, personnel policies, etc. Many of the goals thus expressed may be pure fantasy but they must represent senior management's perception of what the various *stakeholders* expect out of the business.

The stakeholders are the starting point for any attempt at determining corporate objectives. Whether these objectives are capable of being achieved needs to be validated by analysing and aggregating an enormous amount of 'input' from root and branches and their respective environments. Nonetheless a 'trigger point' is as essential as saying 'We want a holiday' when one is starting to plan a holiday or 'We intend to win the war' when one is planning the nation's defence during wartime.

The stakeholders in a firm are numerous and their expectations can be difficult to reconcile. Moreover these expectations are dynamic and they change with time.

Figure 49 shows the main stakeholder groups whose interests must be considered and safeguarded. The ability of reconciling these conflicting interests in a dynamic way and in a rapidly changing world is one of the major tasks of the strategic level of the firm.

We shall see later how this task of reconciling conflicting expectations can assume a formidable proportion in international operations.

Having defined the 'trigger point' one can now transmit it to all functional and/or operational branches. This is how the iterative cycle begins. The branches prepare their sub-plans bearing in mind their respective strengths and weaknesses and environmental conditions including threats and opportunities. These sub-plans are sent back to some focal point at the centre, say a corporate planner, for interpretation and aggregation. The final document may not fully meet the initial 'trigger point' as communicated from the top. Through constant multi-directional dialogue between the representative of the strategic level (in most instances in the form of a corporate planner) and those responsible for functional or divisional plans, the sub-plans are moulded into a shape which is not only consistent with the expectations of the stakeholders as initially expressed in the 'trigger point' but also with the realities of the environments within which the units have to operate.

A corporate plan which is based on a truly iterative and participative dialogue can be a most potent tool for planning the future of a firm with many international branches. Each branch is closer to the market-place than people working at a remote head office or where the many sub-plans are interpreted and aggregated. Ignoring the knowledge and experience of local management is not only a serious demotivator but it also an unfortunate way in which to try to develop a meaningful plan.

Conditions for Successful International Planning

Planning on an international scale is a complex process. The larger the number of countries in which a firm operates the more intricate planning becomes. The process and its concomitant procedures can be imposed upon people in such a way that it is no more than a mechanical activity whereby a large amount of figures are assembled and transmitted to a central focal point. The result is a conglomeration of pious hopes. This is not the aim of planning nor is such an approach of any practical value.

The successful introduction of planning into a firm operating internationally depends on the fulfilment of a number of basic conditions:

1 A Total Philosophy

The philosophy of planning must be widespread throughout the firm both at home and abroad. It is impossible to assemble a satisfactory plan in an environment in which the commitment to planning is only partial. This is largely an educational matter and calls for a persistent and systematic development effort internationally.

Developing the planning philosophy or creed in a large international firm can be a mammoth task especially where the company operates not only in many countries but also in a multi-product and multi-market involvement. At the same time it must be emphasised that without such a widespread philosophy the planning process could not possibly attain its proper role in the shaping of the firm's future destiny. Many well-intentioned attempts at introducing a planning process in large international firms collapsed, after an abortive introduction, and for no other reason than the lack of understanding and commitment on the part of the managers of the various operating units throughout the world. Planning cannot be successfully undertaken in a state of solitary isolation in the company's nerve centre without the wholehearted participation of the firm's many managers. A close parallel exists between the need to indoctrinate managers in the philosophy of planning and the propagation of the marketing concept. Neither can be successful unless it becomes part of the firm's culture.

A firm that wishes to introduce planning into its life in a serious fashion must couple it with a highly imaginative and systematic 'brainwashing' programme at all levels of management. This is probably a more difficult task than the planning process itself!

2 'Input'/'Output' Procedures

The development of procedures for gathering data ('input'), distilling and interpreting such data with the view of yielding meaningful and comparable 'output' is another vital condition for a sound planning process in an international environment.

Planning can fail either because the 'input' is inadequate or irrelevant or does not lend itself to intelligent processing. The 'input' that planners require must match the needs of the decision-making process envisaged by the planning task. Thus in international marketing planning the marketing profile analysis is a vital 'input'. It must be prepared in a homogeneous fashion and in accordance with a consistent format. Failure to do so will only mean that the planners, wherever they may be located, will have difficulties in processing the information gathered and deriving comparable conclusions in relation to international markets. This comparability is essential for effective planning and it can only be achieved where data is collected and communicated in accordance with a systematic and consistent 'input'/'output' procedural framework.

In this connection it is important to recall that one of the major planning decisions in international marketing is the choice between *standardisation* and *differentiation* of the marketing programme. To be able to take such decisions careful 'input' has to be assembled from every market and if the content of this 'input' does not conform to a pre-set pattern it is virtually impossible to develop the appropriate 'output' which makes an adjudication on the problem possible and comparable.

3 Systems

Two major aspects must be considered here:

(a) THE SUCCESS OF PLANNING DEPENDS ON THE PLANNER'S ABILITY TO GENERATE A DYNAMIC PROCESS

This means that the plans must be capable of rapid changes and adjustments in the face of dynamic pressures. A plan which is not capable of coping with sudden environmental changes is a poor plan. Environments are dynamic and it is very rare for a plan to remain over a period an optimum representation of the firm's endeavour to match resources to opportunities. A change in a country's economic growth pattern, which is a frequent occurrence, will inevitably deflect the plan from the course set. A sudden change in a country's legal system or fiscal rules may have a similar result. In other words planning, by its very nature, is a representation of what the firm thinks it can achieve in the future within a given set of environmental conditions. If any of these conditions do not in fact materialise, the plan needs steering towards a better matching relationship with the new conditions. A mechanism must be created for adjusting the plan to a new set of circumstances. A planning system that fails to do that will soon disappoint its creators and get the whole process into disrepute.

In practical terms a series of contingency procedures must be developed not only for monitoring performance but also to react to events that may affect results in international operations within a planning period. The planning process thus gains a *systems* approach rather than an inflexible projection of pious hopes. A smart, leather-bound document with gold embossed letters on the front page saying 'The Five Year Plan of ABC Company Ltd.' is not necessarily a proof of a good planning instrument. A loose-leaf folder setting out in detail environmental assumptions on the one hand, and unit/functional plans on the other hand, with a dynamic mechanism for up-dating the matching-up of resources with changing external circumstances is a much more potent document.

(b) THE NEED FOR A TOTAL SYSTEM APPROACH TO PLANNING

This point is fully consistent with the condition described earlier that planning must be based on a total philosophy of planning throughout the firm. Planning can take many different forms and can cover every aspect of the firm. There is no one correct way in which planning should be carried out. If one tries to compare the planning process in a large number of firms one soon discovers that it takes many different forms. However, the important point to remember is that meaningful planning in a modern organisation must be an all-embracing total system which encapsulates a host of interdependent sub-plans into one logical assemblage viz. the corporate plan. Whilst one can always admire the marketing man who endeavours to plan his particular function in isolation from the rest of the organisation, it is difficult not to perceive the futility of such a quixotic effort.

The Planning Process in International Business

From everything that was said earlier it becomes evident that there is little point in discussing marketing planning without fitting it neatly into the corporate planning framework. Enough was said to emphasise the interrelationship between root and branch and obviously the international marketer can perceive the implications where the planning is carried out internationally.

The most important point to remember is that there is no magic format for planning and no sacrosanct procedures. Many marketers dread the whole notion of planning because they find the various procedures recommended in many textbooks as overwhelming. The best process of planning is the one evolved to meet the needs of a specific firm in a given set of circumstances. Trying to follow blindly the procedures laid down in a book or in a manual can detract from the whole purpose and value of the process. It is much more valuable for the procedures to emerge naturally from the conceptual framework and its underlying thinking. The framework which fulfils the conditions listed in the previous section and which caters for the interrelationships between root and branches is what is wanted and not just a batch of ostensibly sophisticated forms!

Without attempting to impose a framework on any potential planners two diagrams are incorporated here: Figure 50 describes a possible planning framework at the corporate level (the root) and Figure 51 describes the form that the planning process would assume at one of the functional branches namely, marketing.

Briefly the process covers the following steps:

1   *The stakeholders' expectations* (What the various stakeholders want to get out of the firm.)
2   *Internal audit* (What are we capable of achieving in the light of our past performance and our particular strengths and weaknesses?)
3   *The external environment* (What are the future opportunities that we are likely to meet; and what are the potential threats against which we must protect ourselves?)
4   *Corporate objectives* (What we want to achieve in the light of our capabilities and perceived opportunities.)

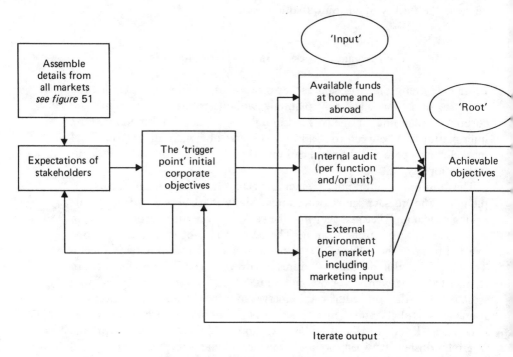

Iterate output

Fig. 50   A descriptive framework for corporate planning (functional approach)

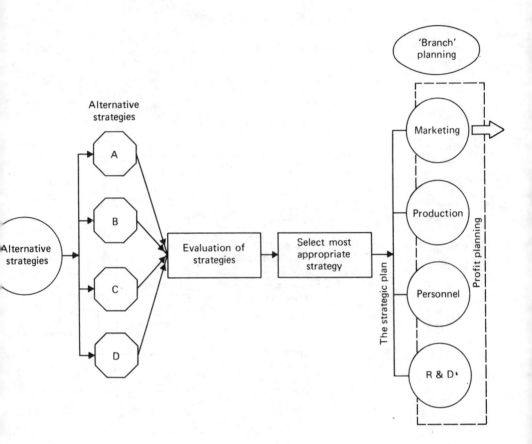

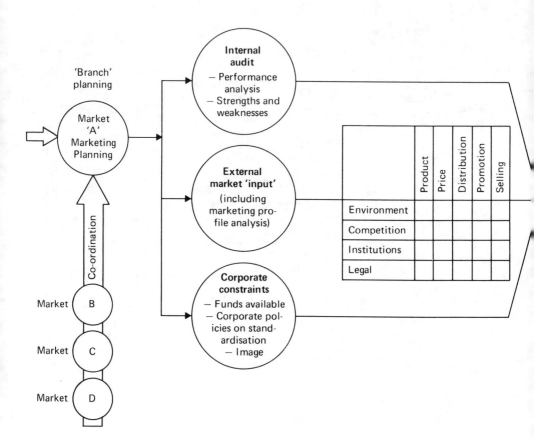

Fig. 51   A descriptive framework for marketing planning in each market

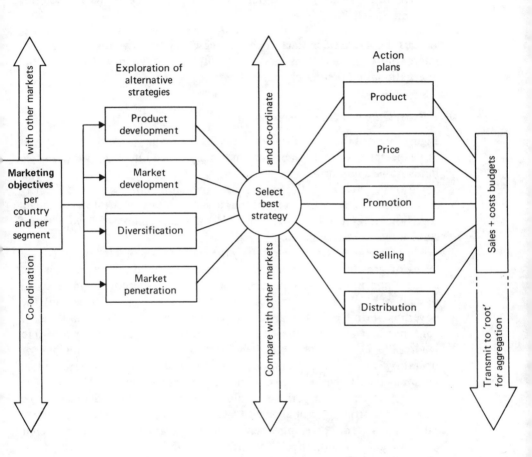

5   *Exploration of alternative strategies* (How can the objectives be best achieved?)
6   *Selection of the most appropriate strategies* (Which is/are the best and most profitable way(s) to achieve our objectives?)
7   *The strategic plan* (What should each function of the business do to meet our goals?)

Let us now consider each one of these ingredients and explore the international implications and especially the way they relate to the international marketing planning effort:

1 Expectations of Stakeholders

Figure 49 listed the kind of stakeholders that a firm has to satisfy and the type of expectations that one can normally encounter in western-style industrialised countries.

However, in international business the situation becomes extremely intricate insofar as the firm not only has to satisfy the expectations of the main stakeholders at the home-base but also the expectations of every set of stakeholders in every market.

Thus General Motors has to satisfy the expectations of its shareholders (in terms of growth in earnings and dividends), its bondholders (in terms of security and punctuality of coupon payments), its employees (in terms of security of employment, terms and conditions of work, job satisfaction), the government (in terms of safety and pricing policies), Mr Nader (in terms of consumerism), etc. At the same time the company's planners cannot afford to ignore the expectations of stakeholders in other countries, regions or operating units. The expectations of the stakeholders in the UK and in Germany have to be considered with as much care as those in the USA. The UK Government as a peripheral, albeit important stakeholder, has to be satisfied (in terms of employment, safety regulations, pollution, exchange satisfied (in terms of employment, safety regulations, pollution, foreign earnings and so on); the UK consuming public has to be satisfied (in have to be satisfied (in terms of employment and conditions of work for their UK members). Evidently it is not easy to find a formula which can satisfy everybody all the time. However, the aim must be to attain 'the greatest happiness of the greatest number' whilst taking full cognisance of every conceivable and identifiable set of expectations. This process has important marketing connotations and it may indeed be appropriate to harness the help of the marketing personnel in this connection. Their contribution in identifying the myriad of conflicting expectations on a global scale can be a most valuable 'input' to starting the corporate planning and also the marketing planning processes in a balanced fashion.

Whilst on the subject of stakeholders and their expectations it is relevant to emphasise that this is one more area in which top management must undertake some heart-searching: is the company prepared or desirous to meet all the expectations of all the stakeholders throughout the world? The answer to this question will have an important bearing (in addition, of course, to other important considerations) on whether the firm will opt for a centralised or a decentralised approach to its international activities. As we saw earlier this in turn will influence, to a great extent, decisions on standardisation or differentiation of the marketing effort. Centralisation with a propensity towards a macropyramid approach inevitably will sacrifice a large number of expectations of many stakeholders especially those located in remote markets. On the other hand the 'umbrella' structure, which by its very nature favours differentiation, is better equipped to meet the expectations of the firm's decentralised stakeholders.

The route that the international firm chooses for satisfying its stakeholders is deeply intertwined with strategic decisions taken in relation to marketing and organisational patterns. This is a 'chicken and egg' dilemma; which comes first is often a matter of post-event rationalisation. Nonetheless, it is an area in which corporate planners of large international firms must seek guidance and clarification from top management.

A useful starting point for those responsible for the international planning process is a simple matrix like the one illustrated in Figure 52. It seeks to list the expectations of the various stakeholder groups in the countries in which the firm is operating or is hoping to operate in the future. The aim of this simple methodology is to show the information in a standard format which is capable of comparability and aggregation.

2 Internal Audit

This phase of the planning process has been called by a large number of different titles and is fraught with jargon. It is not surprising that the newcomer to planning is overwhelmed by the literature on the subject. *Corporate audit, situational analysis, diagnosis/prognosis* are among the terms used to describe the same process.

The aim of the *internal audit* is two-fold:

To *analyse past performance* of the firm with the view of gauging achievements or the lack thereof and highlighting trends.
To identify the range of *skills, competences and strengths* in juxtaposition with the firm's inherent *weaknesses*.

Planning seeks to improve on or at least maintain past performance through building on the firm's strengths and minimising the impact of its weaknesses. The internal audit is an honest attempt at analysing the firm's capabilities and limitations in a factual and realistic way. Glossing over weaknesses and magnifying strengths are the kind of attitudes that can only detract from the real value of the process. Planning calls for integrity and maximum self-

Stakeholder groups	Countries				
	U.K.	Germany	France	Spain	etc.
Shareholders					
Bankers					
Managers					
Employees					
Unions					
Governments					
Community					
Suppliers					
Consumers					

Leave blank if inappropriate. Attach schedules where space inadequate

Fig. 52   Stakeholders and their expectations on an international scale

awareness and these can often be maximised by quantitative analyses. Quantitative information is normally less likely to mislead.

It is not intended to discuss in depth the internal audit task in relation to the *corporate level* within the framework of an international marketing book. Our main concern is to list the area of analysis which pertains to the marketing function. However, having emphasised the interdependence between root and branch, it is not practical to list internal audit 'inputs' relating to the marketing function without mentioning briefly the data needed at the corporate level. After all if the root of the tree is rotten the branches will soon collapse. If the root is healthy even sick branches stand a chance of eventual health.

At the corporate level the following range of topics and data are normally relevant within an effective internal audit exercise:

(a) Major financial ratios over a period to identify trends:
             Return on capital employed
             Profits
             Profits in relation to sales
             Sales as a multiple of capital employed

Sales as a multiple of fixed assets
Sales as a multiple of inventory
Sales per employee
Profits per employee
Liquidity
Cash flow
Dividend
Share performance (where the firm has a quotation)
and price/earnings ratio

(b) Interfirm comparison of management ratios
This is a very valuable tool of planning. The underlying principle of Interfirm comparison is that the systematic comparison of certain accounting, financial and other performance yardsticks of one firm with other companies in the same industry helps to discover otherwise unnoticed weaknesses or dangerous trends.
The use of such comparisons is gaining popularity in most industrialised countries. However, as yet in most countries the planner must undertake the appropriate research and analysis himself. In a few countries, notably the UK and the USA, organisations specialising in the provision of up-to-date comparative studies have been set up. In the UK the Centre for Interfirm Comparison is carrying out a very useful job. In the USA the American Appraisal Interfirm Comparison offers a similar service.

(c) Functional audit including:
Marketing
Production technology
Personnel
Research and development.

(d) Operational units audit including:
Full subsidiaries (companies that manufacture and market their products) in the various parts of the world.
Manufacturing units
Marketing units in the various countries.

Those responsible for the internal audit portion of the planning process cannot ignore the interface between root and branch which we have attempted to emphasise so strongly in the previous sections. In order to be able to proceed to the ultimate task of formulating achievable corporate objectives the corporate planner (or whoever else may be responsible for developing plans at the corporate level) must harness the flow of 'input' from all branches whether they are functional or operational units as is often the case in international business.

Figure 53 illustrates the way 'input' stemming from the various functional internal audits flows towards the summit where the future direction of the firm is shaped. Any attempt at plotting the future course of the enterprise without

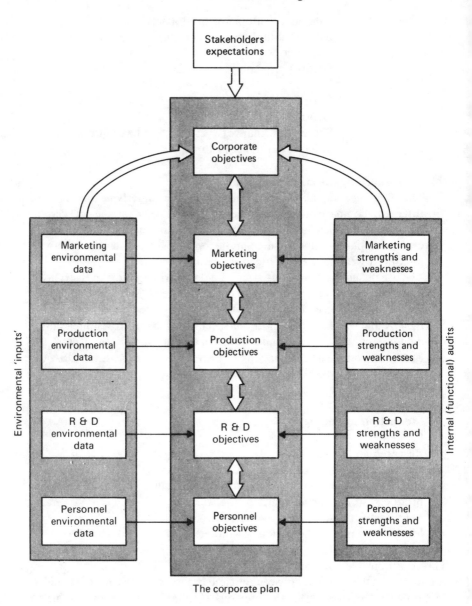

The corporate plan

Fig. 53   The flow of 'input' from functions to the corporate level in the planning
process

such data is of doubtful validity. Where the firm is structured as a collection of
operational units, the flow of data from such units will substitute the
functional boxes shown in the figure.

At the marketing branch internal audit, in an international context, would
normally include:

(a) Past performance—general

List of products and their performance for several years, or for a sufficient period to establish trends.

Market segments and quantified relationships among them (using Pareto analysis).

Breakdown by countries, models, periods and customer types.

Trends as to shift in geographical centre of gravity may thus be identified.

Previous performance versus marketing objectives.

In particular such an analysis should include:

Net profit per product and per country
Net profit as per cent of sales
Market share per country and globally.

Ratios (per regions, per country and by product over a period and interfirm):

$$\text{Ratio} \quad 1 = \frac{\text{Marketing contribution}}{\text{marketing assets}}$$

Marketing contribution = sales − (marketing costs + variable manufacturing costs).

Marketing assets = finished goods stock + debtors + distribution facilities.

$$\text{Ratio} \quad 2 = \frac{\text{Marketing costs}}{\text{Sales}}$$

$$\text{Ratio} \quad 3 = \frac{\text{Sales}}{\text{Marketing assets}}$$

$$\text{Ratio} \quad 4 = \frac{\text{Warehouse costs}}{\text{Sales}}$$

$$\text{Ratio} \quad 5 = \frac{\text{Distribution costs}}{\text{Sales}} = \frac{\text{Home distribution costs}}{\text{Home sales}} + \frac{\text{International distribution costs}}{\text{International sales}}$$

$$\text{Ratio} \quad 6 = \frac{\text{Advertising costs}}{\text{Sales}}$$

$$\text{Ratio} \quad 7 = \frac{\text{Selling costs}}{\text{Sales}} = \frac{\text{Home selling costs}}{\text{Home sales}} + \frac{\text{International selling costs}}{\text{International sales}}$$

$$\text{Ratio} \quad 8 = \frac{\text{Sales office costs}}{\text{Sales}}$$

$$\text{Ratio } 9 = \frac{\text{Sales office costs}}{\text{Number of orders or invoices}}$$

$$\text{Ratio } 10 = \frac{\text{Finished goods stock}}{\text{Sales}}$$

$$\text{Ratio } 11 = \frac{\text{Debtors}}{\text{Sales}}$$

$$\text{Ratio } 12 = \frac{\text{Debtors}}{\text{Average daily sales}}$$

Many other useful marketing ratios can be identified to measure a firm's marketing effectiveness as well as highlight specific areas of strength and/or weakness. It is up to the planner to rationalise the significance of such ratios. The important point to remember is:

(i) Ratios must be used over a long enough period to be meaningful in establishing trends.
(ii) If used on an interfirm or interdivision basis in an international context the data used must be of comparable nature.

On the more qualitative side of the marketing internal audit the investigations should look at:

(b) The level of marketing orientation in each market.
(c) Quality of information (at all levels) and its relevance to marketing decisions in the various countries.
  Quality of market/marketing research.
  The cost/benefit of research in the various markets.
  Control procedures for measuring effectiveness.
(d) Quality of forecasting methods
  Who uses information.
  Frequency.
  Levels of accuracy attained in the past.
(e) Organisation effectiveness
  The competence of the organisation to meet marketing objectives per country and per unit.
  Clarity of jobs and inter-personal roles.
  General communication qualities (both inside units and among units).
  Quality of personnel—how are they trained and motivated:
    List of key personnel and their qualifications.
    Amount and quality of training and management development.

Having completed the internal audit of the marketing function in general terms the planner should now assemble data about each ingredient of the marketing mix. This process should normally include such information as:

(a) Products

Assessment of product quality and standing in each market.

Life cycle performance per product (sales, profit, investment recovery versus anticipated life per product/market).

Quality of innovation.

Rate of successful product launches.

Wherever relevant, success in standardisation of products internationally.

(b) Pricing

Quality of pricing decisions taken in the past in the firm's international markets.

The firm's behaviour in the face of competitive pricing practices.

Information available, if any, on price elasticity in the various markets served.

(c) Promotion

Expenditure over, say, five years compared with sales per product.

Methods for determining budgets.

Quality of media planning.

Costs of promoting each product and in each market.

Quality of sales aids and expenditure thereon.

Interfirm comparison in relation to the above calculations.

(d) Selling

Selling costs as per cent of sales (a ratio listed earlier).

Accuracy of past forecasts.

Quality of sales planning in the past.

Quality of sales force and its management in measurable norms.

Quality of recruitment, training, development and motivation.

Average cost per call for each salesman.

Quality of information, its frequency and appropriateness in each market.

Expenses of selling activities as a percentage of sales:

(i) per market

(ii) per product

(iii) per order (an average figure)

(iv) per salesman (adjusted for exchange variations and cost of living conditions prevalent in each market).

(e) Distribution

The organisation of distribution and quality of personnel responsible for this task throughout the world.

Channels of distribution and their performance. In this connection the performance of the various middlemen must be gauged against:

(i) their own past performance
(ii) each other.
Distribution cost analysis.
The firm's logistics facilities and the effectiveness with which they are utilised. This investigation should normally cover:
  (i) Warehousing
  (ii) Packing
  (iii) Despatching
  (iv) Transport
  (v) Delivery
  (vi) Service.

The analysis should deal with these facilities in each country and seek to appraise the following details in relation to each facility:

  (i) Level of utilisation
  (ii) Level of service offered and expected by clients
  (iii) Competitive practices (interfirm analysis).

3 The External Environment

The aim here is to identify the kind of environmental forces which are likely to have an impact on the future direction of the firm. Some of these forces may represent opportunities for the firm's future effort; others may represent threats against which the firm needs to protect itself.

The planners must analyse available data about the environment of the countries in which the firm is expecting to operate and must also forecast future conditions, assumptions and contingencies. Figure 54 lists the most important environmental areas that one has to consider in relation to a selected number of countries. This table illustrates the enormity of the job. Each rubric represents an important environmental 'input' pertaining to a specific country. The form illustrated in Figure 54 is a useful starting point for the appropriate investigations. It is important that where the planning process covers a large number of countries clear instructions are communicated from those responsible for collating all the data regarding the exact nature, quantity and format of such information. One must attempt to obtain 'input' of comparable nature otherwise collation can become a nightmare.

Environmental studies can cover such a large number of forces that it is essential for every company, large and small, to decide which 'input' has a high probability of significant impact, favourable or unfavourable, on the future results of the firm. Evidently an international company manufacturing military aircraft will investigate and forecast the military environment of its markets. A detergent firm will not. A pharmaceutical firm will gather 'input' about the medical/health environment of its markets.

In determining the relative importance of the various areas for study one

	Level of Importance			Country					
	1	*2*	*3*	*Germany*	*France*	*Italy*	*Spain*	*Portugal*	*etc.*
Economic									
Political									
Social									
Demographic									
Religious									
Educational									
Legal									
Tax									
Foreign Trade Legislation									
Technological									
Medical									
Military									

Level of importance:
   1 = High   2 = Medium   3 = Low

Fig. 54   List of important environmental forces that need to be explored and forecast in each foreign market

can attach a simple screening device at the side of the form illustrated in Figure 54. It is a simple tool which should help those responsible for collecting environmental data to identify the main areas for exploration. The main aim must be to detect relevant threats and to try to quantify real opportunities. It is the quality of the environmental 'input' which is important and not sheer quantity.

At the international marketing planning level a most valuable data gathering methodology is the marketing profile analysis which was discussed fully in earlier chapters. It is a systematic tool for identifying the impact of the external environment on the various marketing ingredients. The completion of such an exercise can certainly ensure that the international marketing plans are based on relevant assumptions and constraints emanating from the external environment.

4 Corporate Objectives

Enough was said earlier in this chapter about the importance of having clearly defined corporate objectives for the planning period. Without this step planning procedures covering functional/operational units sub-plans would have little practical purpose. It was aptly suggested: 'If you do not know where you want to go, any road will take you there'.

Where the firm has a homogeneous range of activities it should endeavour to respond to the classical question: 'What business are we in?' This is not just an intellectual exercise. It is an attempt at defining the outer perimeters of the firm's quest for strategic frontiers. It is a logical limitation to commercially unsound adventures stemming from unbridled creativity. At the same time such a definition of the firm's 'business' must not be so narrow as to stifle progress and innovation.

The search for a clear definition as to the business that a firm is in can be of course very difficult in situations where the company's activities are highly diverse or where the firm is an interglomerate. In this latter case the concept becomes meaningless, insofar as such firms are in the business of making money out of managing many heterogeneous businesses.

Corporate objectives should include quantitative as well as qualitative norms:

Examples of *quantitative objectives* are:

Profits.
Growth (in money and/or quantity terms).
Returns on capital or investment or some other measurable ratio.
Productivity (in terms of revenue per employee).
Market share (per country, per product and/or per segment).
Number and type of countries which the firm wishes to serve within its international goals.
Dividends.

Examples of *qualitative objectives* are:

Survival (a very fair objective in many present-day situations).
Being *good employers*.
Acting as *good citizens* of the various nations in which the firm is currently operating or seeking to operate during the planning period.
Maintain a *good image* throughout the world.
Safeguard the environment of every country.

The latter objectives may sound over-pious but the trend is certainly to pay more attention to those areas which pertain to social responsibility. Firms operating in international markets have certainly come to recognise that success, without adherence to what society considers is a fair deal for the community at large, can be very short-lived.

Corporate objectives must be clear, simple and universally understood. In a multi-language environment it is important that top management takes the trouble of ensuring that all those who have to contribute to the international planning process fully understand what the firm as a whole is aiming to achieve. Failure to communicate effectively the goals of the firm to local managers can only lower the quality of the ultimate plans that emerge.

5 Exploration of Alternative Strategies

'How do we get there?' The options may be numerous and good planning demands that all logical alternatives are explored. The strategy or strategies selected at the corporate level virtually dictate the direction that marketing strategies (and obviously other functional strategies) will have to take. Bearing in mind that marketing 'input' flows into the strategic thinking at the top this is not surprising.

Thus, if one of the alternative strategies considered at the corporate level is *contraction* in the firm's international presence, inevitably the marketing planners will have to respond to such a direction in their own evaluation of marketing strategies.

Strategies must be specific and practical. Vague strategies can only help to blur the main issues. Planning is a very logical process and any activity which interferes with this logic will eventually weaken the total process. In other words the person responsible for planning the marketing function must ensure that the strategies he is exploring are fully consistent with what the planners at the corporate level are investigating. The final planning package that emerges must be so well balanced that the two pairs of strategies—the corporate and the marketing strategies—are in full sympathy with each other.

Examples of possible strategies at the corporate level are:

> Acquisition
> Merger
> Divestment
> Rationalisation
> Contraction
> Deeper penetration of international markets
> New products for existing international markets
> Diversification
> Liquidation (in extreme cases)
> Vertical integration

Examples of Marketing strategies which can be explored are:

> Market penetration
> Market development
> Market segmentation
> Market concentration
> New product development
> Deletion of existing products
> Up-trading or down-trading of existing products

It is not difficult to perceive how corporate strategies can be paired with marketing strategies. A logical nexus exists between each corporate strategy and one or more marketing strategies. Thus, if at the corporate level the planners feel that the firm can only achieve its goals through *contraction,* it is more than likely that the marketing plan will incorporate a strong leaning towards *deleting* products which have ceased to show adequate returns. At the same time, if the word contraction has a geographical meaning in the sense that the planners feel that the firm must reduce its international commitments, the marketing strategy which needs to be studied carefully is *market concentration.* If efficiently implemented it may help to achieve the contraction strategy which in turn will help to achieve the corporate objectives.

The various terms are probably self-explanatory and need little elaboration. However, the terms product development, market development and diversification often cause confusion among managers and a brief definition pertaining to these terms may help communication.

Market development means the introduction of an existing product (subject at times to minor differentiation) to a new market or segment. Selling a product to international markets is in effect a market development strategy within this definition.

Thus, for example, Philips who have been marketing an electric shaver for men, Philishave, decide to introduce a slightly modified shaver for women, Ladyshave. This constitutes a market development strategy, insofar as in essence it is the same product which is being marketed to a different segment of the market.

Product development occurs when a firm introduces new products to a market in which it is well established.

Thus, when IBM introduce photocopying equipment for the business world, which is their main market, they undertake a product development strategy.

Diversification occurs when a firm seeks to enter a new market with a completely new product.

When Unilever try to enter the photocopying field it is tantamount to diversification. For them it is a new product, new technology, and the market is also totally new to them.

Figure 55 illustrates the relationship between these strategies in a simple schematic form.

It is important to recall at this point that a firm seeks to build its future on its strengths. In exploring strategies the planners must constantly bear in mind the strengths which have been identified. If the firm's main strength lies in marketing competence, rather than product development, it must try to exploit this strength before indulging in technological adventures. If, on the other hand, the firm possesses considerable technical skills but only knows one market well, it should try to add as many products as possible to that market. Finally, diversification implies that the firm is seeking to enter a new market with a new product. Such a strategy is probably the most difficult to implement successfully insofar as the firm neither possesses the marketing expertise nor the product knowledge. That is why so many firms fail with their diversification strategies. *Diversification* can of course be coupled with *acquisition*. The idea being that a safe way to enter new markets with new products is by buying another firm which is well established in such a business. Here the planners must make sure that, before trying to acquire a company with the view of diversifying, they enunciate very clearly the type of firm they are looking for and the criteria which it should meet. The process of screening which we discussed fully in the chapter dealing with product development and planning can be applied here with equal validity.

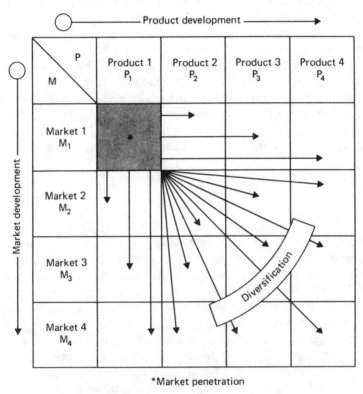

*Market penetration

Fig. 55   The relationship between various marketing strategies

6 Selection of the Most Appropriate Strategies

The next step is to try to evaluate each strategy or collection of strategies in a systematic way in order to identify the best and the most profitable choice.

Once again whichever strategy one decides to choose must be consistent with the information collated in the earlier stages of the planning process and with the corporate objectives that resulted therefrom.

In international marketing planning where so many options may be open to the firm it is useful to develop evaluation procedures which help the planners to quantify the cost/benefit implications of each strategy. Such procedures can be quite simple but once again it is important that marketers round the world understand the procedures and their underlying rationale. The main aim must be to select the best and the most profitable strategy (depending on the firm's overall objectives) and this can be best evaluated in monetary terms. In this connection having evaluation forms which are used by all planners round the world is highly desirable. Otherwise the comparability of the evaluation results can become very difficult. It is not uncommon for firms to select the wrong strategies for no other reason than the fact that at the planning stage financial implications were not clearly understood or correctly tabulated.

Figure 56 illustrates a simple form for attempting to carry out the evaluation task in a consistently systematic way. Each firm should develop its own procedures in this connection. The procedures need not be complex and work involved need not take too much time to undertake. On the other hand these procedures must seek to make managers appreciate the full implications of the strategy which they are recommending. Reducing the details of such courses of action to quantitative calculations is one of the best ways to attain full managerial appreciation of the financial implications within the planning period.

7 The Strategic Plan

The planning cycle is now ready for final aggregation and submission to top management for approval or additional iteration. It represents the firm's future intentions in a written document. It lists what the firm wishes to achieve both as a total organisation and as a family of units operating all over the world. It further enumerates in detail how each function proposes to go about achieving the firm's overall goals.

Action programmes in the shape of annual budgets and operational plans can now be prepared. These are practical implementation schedules showing the details and timetable of market introduction plans, advertising and sales promotion activities, sales training, etc. Action plans must contain clear details of deadlines and responsibility for each step.

It is not uncommon for marketing plans to include specific statements of tasks to be undertaken by field sales force in each market, promotional personnel, marketing research department, brand management and others within the marketing organisation.

Marketing plans can be presented in a host of different formats. Considerable thought must be given to the design of an efficient format to ensure that:

1 Communication of the details is easily understood on an international scale.
2 Review and control are facilitated.

EVALUATION OF ALTERNATIVE MARKETING STRATEGIES
(Details to be assembled from each region/country)

Planning period _____

Planning area	Strategy 'A'					Strategy 'B'					Strategy 'C'				
Performance estimates/other criteria	Year 1	Year 2	Year 3	Year 4	Year 5	Year 1	Year 2	Year 3	Year 4	Year 5	Year 1	Year 2	Year 3	Year 4	Year 5
* Feasibility															
Capital required – in £															
Skills – are they available?															
'Know how' – can it be obtained and at what cost?															
† Marketing environment															
Demand (in units)															
Demand (in value)															
Estimated share in %															
*† Pro forma calculations															
Sales – units															
Sales – value (total)															
Costs – (total)															
Profit															
Return on investment %															
Estimated investment recovery (in years)			[years]					[years]					[years]		
Estimated level of probability of achieving results (in %)			(%)					(%)					(%)		
Probability % x 5 years profits			( )					( )					( )		
General comments (Qualitative)															
Assess scope of synergy															
Long term prospects															
New technical vistas															
New marketing vistas															

Explanatory notes:
*Provide all supportive data. Translate capital required into £ sterling †Attach market research details ††All calculations to be based on DCF at prevalent rate of discounting

Fig. 56 Procedure for evaluating alternative marketing strategies

3 The quality of the plans is improved through familiarisation with a standard approach.
4 Each plan covers fully all elements pertaining to future performance.

It is certainly difficult to see how resources can be intelligently allocated to a host of marketing units round the world without each unit adhering to a certain degree of conformity in the format and approach to its individual plans.

In small firms or in companies in which only a few individuals are concerned with planning the strategic plan can take a pretty informal pattern. On the other hand, in a firm operating in many countries and possibly with many products, formal standards must be laid down. It is the only guarantee that the output will be comparable, understandable and capable of logical aggregation. This means that somebody must set down written guidelines, accompanied by forms and specimens of what is required coupled with clear explanations as to how one should go about complying with such instructions.* In some firms such guidelines are imposed in a mandatory way. In others the process is much more persuasive and advisory. This, as we shall see later, depends on the type of firm one is dealing with and its organisational structure.

Organisational Aspects of International Marketing Planning

Assuming that the planning process is fully understood throughout the firm and at all levels, and that a total commitment to the planning philosophy has been developed, a major problem still exists: who should be responsible for the procedural aspects of the process and for distilling an approved set of plans?

Planning needs some sort of focal point. In theory corporate planning is the task of the chief executive. He often delegates the procedural aspects of this task to a corporate planner or planning officer or a member of his team who enjoys a similar title. The fact still remains that a corporate planner is no more than an extension of the chief executive who must never abdicate from this all-important task. Marketing planning is the task of the marketing director who has to dovetail his plans for the marketing function with the firm's overall plans.

So far this is simple enough. The position becomes much more complicated where the firm operates in a multi-environment world. Who should act as the focal point in such a situation? This is a very important problem and it calls for

---

* An excellent selection of examples of marketing planning guidelines, schedules and excerpts from marketing plans is included in a research report from the conference board: David S. Hopkins, 'The Short-Term Marketing Plan', The Conference Board Inc., New York, 1972. The report is based on a survey of current planning practices in 162 US and Canadian firms that engage in formal marketing planning and routinely commit their plans to writing.

considerable creativity on the part of senior management. There is no easy answer inasmuch as a large number of factors affect decisions of this nature. One of the major considerations is the way the firm is structured. Whilst in theory the plans come first and the organisation is set up to meet the needs of the plans, in reality most firms have existing structures with inherent policies and attitudes and these cannot be brushed aside at will. In other words, where the planning focal point should be located within an international firm depends to a great extent on the kind of organisation we have.

A firm that has opted for a radically centralised approach will probably find a strong planning team at the centre a fairly simple solution. Managers at the various local outposts will have to comply with requests for data emanating from the central planning personnel and will have to fill in all the forms that will be transmitted to them from time to time. Technically such an approach can work quite well, but it is seldom easy in such circumstances to attain maximum commitment to the planning task among distantly located personnel. At best they will co-operate with the whole process; at worst they will fill in the forms in a spirit of suppressed distaste. Inevitably the quality of the 'inputs' in such circumstances cannot be of the highest!

In a decentralised structure the position is very much more complex. By definition a decentralised firm allows freedom to the various operating units. Freedom means that each unit wishes to plan its own future. At the same time some central control of the planning process must exist unless the firm is prepared to allow each branch to grow wild. Referring back to the tree analogy, even a wood needs a keeper to ensure that the various trees in the wood do not interfere with each other's growth. Moreover somebody must collate the various sub-plans. Where should this be done and by whom?

Different solutions have been developed for this problem by various companies. The success of these solutions seems to hinge around the personality of the people selected for the task of co-ordinating this vast input from all over the world. They cannot order or direct, they can only advise, persuade and communicate ideas. To be able to cope with such an ill-defined task one must possess personal attributes which virtually make such an individual capable of walking on water! Choosing the right person as a focal point is much more important than his location. In fact a few creative firms have decided to rotate the responsibility for collating and interpreting data in the process of preparing international marketing plans from one main market to another. The pay-off can be substantial: first it helps to develop promising managers in the art of planning in various parts of the world; secondly it helps to generate a better understanding of the planning philosophy in remote offshoots. Knowing that for the next two years the person responsible for planning the marketing effort is one of 'our boys' has a tremendous morale boosting value in a complex decentralised international firm.

It is very difficult to offer an easy formula which will enable every firm to decide how it should organise its corporate and marketing planning activities on an international basis. Every firm must evolve its own solution and on the merits of each situation. However, a few basic principles must be borne in mind when attempting to find a solution to this problem:

1   Where planning is a new concept in a firm the initial task is *educational*. The choice of the appropriate 'focal point' and his location must stem from the need to train the organisation in the art of planning.
    In practical terms, this need to develop the planning philosophy is likely to mean that the process will be located close to the headquarters of the organisation. After all, the development of the philosophy has to start at the top.

2   The interface between root and branch must be carefully safeguarded in an effective planning process. This can be best achieved by using individuals who are in no way committed to operational prejudices stemming from a long involvement in an executive line management role.

3   It is often suggested that the secret of successful management of international companies lies in the simple principle: 'centralise responsibility for strategic planning and decentralise responsibility for local planning and operations'.* This theory must be treated with some caution, insofar as in extreme cases of decentralisation a substantial amount of strategic planning has to be undertaken at local level. However, it is fair to say that wherever possible the separation of strategic planning and operational planning must be clearly defined and the organisational implications formally communicated and explained to everybody concerned.

4   Whilst there is absolutely no harm in having separate marketing planning officers in each marketing unit, it is important that their activities are co-ordinated. Each such planning officer is responsible to his respective marketing director. Nonetheless a co-ordinative function must be developed in order to:
    (a) help to lay down planning guidelines and procedures.
    (b) act as an interface between the marketing functions of the various units and those responsible for corporate planning at the centre. This can save a lot of unnecessary points of contact.
    (c) identify and communicate ideas for possible synergy among units and/or functions.
    (d) assist in interpreting 'input' from the various units.
    (e) maintain a reservoir of information about the markets that the firm hopes to serve.
    (f) stimulate creativity through cross-fertilisation of ideas from the various marketing units round the world.
    The concept of *co-ordination* can be a very useful instrument in the management of the planning process in a complex international marketing environment. However the exact role of so-called co-

* George A. Steiner, *Top Management Planning*, Macmillan.

ordinators must be defined and communicated. Invariably the idea of having co-ordinators becomes troublesome where the job incorporates hierarchal connotations. In such situations the abuse of the word can be the source of misunderstandings and irritation.

Chapter 11

The Application of the 'Business Portfolio' Concept to International Marketing Decisions

In seeking to launch a product on the international scene the marketer often has to grapple with the problem of deciding as to which countries ought to rank in his plans as the priority markets for development. Clearly among the 200 or so countries in the world a few countries are bound to represent excellent target markets whereas others should be avoided at all cost. Most well-informed businessmen can list countries which in their opinion are attractive markets and those which should be avoided like the plague. However this kind of instantaneous judgement has its danger inasmuch as some countries offer useful opportunities for a specific product in spite of their adverse image among international marketers. In fact if every marketer would reject a country as an unpromising market for development the one who is foolhardy enough to step in may find fairly rich pickings. This is the essence of market segmentation: the one who can attain a dominant penetration of a small market or segment is often better off than the firm that attains a minute market share of the total market. The firm that manages to dominate an ostensibly poor and small geographical market is not necessarily silly. If the figures prove that the marketing effort is justified, so be it.

Another point that must be remembered in seeking to choose the priority countries for development. A country may be an excellent opportunity-market for one firm yet be the complete opposite for another firm. For instance, there are some countries where a British firm would be able to attain an excellent position in the marketplace partly because of the flag which it represents. In the same country a French company may find the going very hard simply because the local population is out of empathy with French culture and method of operation. In other countries the complete opposite may apply. There may be many reasons for such phobias such as political, historical, educational and religious. Nonetheless this is a fact of life and no marketing effort can brush aside such constraints. The reader may remember the problems that British businessmen encountered in Saudi Arabia during and after the fracas that resulted from the showing of the film 'The Death of a Princess'. On the other hand it appears that most British companies find trading conditions in Portugal very supportive. This emanates from many centuries of strong political and commercial amity. The international marketer's job is to identify those countries which offer more empathetic and supportive environments for development and avoid those which tend to present impediments and blockages to a happy relationship with the marketing firm.

It is evident therefore that when a company decides to pursue a selective international marketing strategy it ought to identify the countries which offer the following:

1   Attractive commercial/marketing opportunities
and
2   Marketing environments and institutions which are compatible and empathetic with the firm itself.

A country which fulfils the first condition without the second is an unsatisfactory target market. So is the one that fulfils the second criterion without offering a tangible marketing opportunity. Many marketers tend to forget the very important second criterion described. They take the very simple view that the larger and richer markets are the ones that should be pursued with vigour. They often apply the Pareto Law by dividing the world into discrete segments. The 20% of the countries of the world which represent 80% of the wealth or the consumption levels are considered as the most suitable opportunities to exploit. Alternatively they take a graph paper and plot a correlation diagram. On one axis they place such a parameter as 'per capita income' and on the other axis they might record 'consumption level of product x or commodity y'. Obviously where the product consumption depends on the level of living standard a fairly linear scatter diagram should emerge. The richer countries would show higher levels of consumption on a per capita basis. At this point the marketer may often fall into the trap of concluding that the top 10 or 20 countries on his scatter diagram represent his best opportunity markets. Of course this is not always a sound marketing policy. Firstly high consuming countries are often the sort of markets that a newcomer with limited resources should avoid owing to the excessive competition that probably prevails there. Secondly as stated earlier the fact that a country seems to be an attractive market does not necessarily mean that it is attractive to a specific marketing organisation. It may be totally incompatible with the marketing firm's specific strengths and resources. After all this is precisely what the planning process is seeking to establish. An opportunity can only be classified as one when the firm has the resources, skills and competence to take advantage of it.

The ability to match the two dimensions—the external one and the internal one—is what the marketing planner must aim to achieve. The external dimension is the quantitative data about the marketplace and the potential opportunity that it offers. The internal dimension is the thorough and up-to-date assessment of the firm's ability to cope with the opportunity that the marketplace is presenting.

The 'Business Portfolio' concept that emerged during the last few years seems to offer a useful methodology for matching the two dimensions thus described. In the next few pages the logic of this method will be explored and its application to international marketing decisions considered.

The 'Boston Effect'

The tool which we call nowadays the 'Product Portfolio' or more broadly the 'Business Portfolio' started its life under the title of the 'Boston Effect'. It emerged a few years ago as a result of work carried out by the well-known firm of consultants the Boston Consulting Group. Like most effective tools of management it is a very logical and simple concept to apply. In analysing the relative performance of clients' products/activities mix the Boston Consulting Group sought to categorise such products into four groups as described in Figure 57.

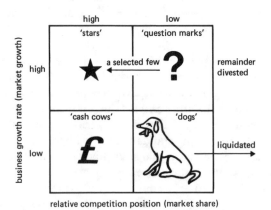

Fig. 57   The Business Portfolio or Growth-Share Matrix

Each quadrant of the diagram represents the relationship between the *market share* that the product and/or activity has achieved and the *market growth rate* that the market itself enjoys. For convenience the market share level has been divided into 'high' and 'low' and so has the market growth rate. The theory is that most products and/or activities are capable of being slotted into one of the four boxes depending on their performance in the marketplace vis-a-vis the behaviour of the marketplace itself. Obviously the basic concept is simplistic in the extreme. However it does not need too much imagination to perceive that when designating the terms 'high' and 'low' one can ascribe well-defined and highly quantifiable criteria to each of the dimensions. Thus 'low' market share may be defined as 'less than 10%' and 'high' a figure in excess thereof. Once again 'low growth ratio' can be defined as 'up to 10% growth per annum' and 'high' as a figure in excess of 10%.

Thus the four quadrants that emerge are '*high/high*', indicating products enjoying a high market share in a high market growth business; '*high'/'low*' namely a situation where a high market share exists in a low growth market; *'low'/'high'* where the market share is low but the market is growing fairly fast; and *'low'/'low'* when both the market share and the market growth are low. This is all a bit of a mouthful. For ease of communication quaint titles were given to the four groups: *'Stars'* for the *'high'/'high's'*; *'Cash Cows'* for the *'high'/'low's'*; *'Dogs'* for the *'low'/low's'* and *'Question Marks'* for the *'low'/high's'*. Other descriptive titles were given to the last quadrant such as 'Problem Children' and 'Wildcats'. For the purpose of this paper we shall stick to the title 'Question Marks'.

The four categories can now be described in greater detail:

'Stars' are relatively new products and often in the growth phase of the product life cycle. They are enjoying high shares of the markets in which they operate. Obviously they represent precious opportunities for their companies and need to be looked after with attention and skill. They are today's breadwinners. At the same time one must recognise that they may require heavy investment in order to ensure that the high share so far attained in a growing market is maintained.

'Cash Cows' are the products that have achieved high market shares but in markets that have ceased to grow. They are often the successful 'Stars' of yesteryear. Most probably they have reached the maturity phase and by and large they require limited investment and financial support. On the other hand the 'Cash Cows' are very useful generators of cash, hence the title.

'Question Marks' refers to products under the disadvantage of low market share yet operating in growth markets. They may be former 'Stars' whose position has eroded or products that simply have failed to maintain their share of the market in order to preserve their 'Star' status. They offer a useful potential for exploitation but require the addition of funds as well as marketing talent before they can enter or re-enter the desired quadrant, namely become a 'Star'.

'Dogs' labour under a dual disadvantage: not only do they have a low market share but they also suffer from the fact that they operate in low growth markets. Prospects are on the whole poor and a strong case for divestment exists. On the other hand if properly managed and with a suitable level of austerity they may be able to generate a positive cash flow whilst they are kept in the firm.

The tool is simple and extremely helpful especially in complex multi-product and multi-market environments. It enables the planner to slot the myriad of products/activities/subsidiaries into four distinct pigeon holes, each of which has different managerial/marketing/financial prospects. Such a categorisation can be dovetailed into every aspect of the planning process. Thus manpower planning can benefit from this kind of analysis in so far as one can match individual talents to the specific needs of every unit. The person who is best suited to run a 'Cow' is not necessarily the most competent individual to run a 'Question Mark'. The former must be a manager who can run a tight ship in the most cost-effective manner. The latter must be a highly creative and experienced marketer with strong diagnostic and analytical skills!

Similarly the planner can use this approach for calculating and evaluating cash flow levels of products falling into each of the quadrants. The aim must be to divert cash from areas that enjoy a short-term flow to those that can yield longer-term prospects of success. Figure 2 illustrates an imaginative approach to the cash flow management of products in the portfolio. It is based on the assumption that 'Cash Cows' are the vital sources of short-term cash flow whereas 'Stars' are cash hungry. 'Question Marks' generate little or no cash but their cash needs are high especially if a higher market share is aspired for. The planner can attempt to calculate and quantify the cash that can be diverted from one quadrant to another. Cash picked up from the 'Cash Cows' can go into research and development in order to improve the product mix and also to endeavour to ameliorate the market share of the 'Question Marks'. The whole idea is based on the need to identify the sources of cash on the one hand and the best recipients of that cash on the other. After all this is the essence of good planning and the 'business portfolio' approach helps to reflect upon the appropriate options open to the strategist.

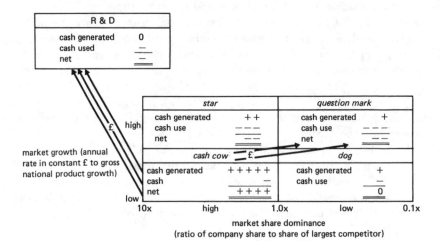

Fig. 58   Cash flow management

Number of +(s) indicates level of cash flow
Number of –(s) indicates level of cash needs/use

There is a major cash flow from 'Cash Cows' into R & D to improve the product mix and a secondary cash flow diverted into 'Question Marks' to maintain or revive some of these products.

Source: George S Day Diagnosing the Product Portfolio; Journal of Marketing April 1977. *Adapted by the author.*

The Application of the 'Portfolio' concept to Managerial Decisions

The 'Product Portfolio' concept has triggered the imagination of businessmen, consultants and academics alike. In its simplicity it paved the way for a host of modifications, extension and developments. The basic concept sought to match two dimensions on a matrix. In fact there was nothing new about analysing complex problems through the use of matrices. However the elegance of the 'Boston Effect' was in the way two parameters were chosen: one internal to the firm, namely its own performance, and one external, namely the marketplace itself. This is the main value of the whole concept to the planning process. As stated earlier planning means the matching of one's own resources to the opportunities offered by the marketplace. In other words one must attempt to dovetail internal resources and capabilities to perceived and if possible quantified openings in the market.

At this point it is important to emphasise that whilst the original 'Boston Effect' approach sought to divide the portfolio into four quadrants there is nothing sacrosanct about that division. There is no reason why the matrix cannot be divided into nine or sixteen or even more 'pigeon holes'. Moreover whilst the original concept attempted to match market share with market growth rate there is no reason for not attempting to match other disparate dimensions.

Before exploring how the concept can be applied to international marketing problems it is useful to consider the versatility of this tool and examine some of the modifications that have taken place over the years.

'Business Portfolio' in Corporate Planning

An ingenious evolution of the 'Boston Effect' can be detected in the so-called 'Directional Policy Matrix' used in the Shell organisation. The purpose of this matrix is to identify the most interesting strategic business units in which the firm should invest additional resources and those areas which ought to be considered for a policy of divestment.

Two parameters are selected for study:

1   The commercial/marketing attractiveness of the various industrial sectors in which the firm is operating. These are of course commercial facts capable of measurement and quantification.
2   The firm's own competitive capability.

The former is divided into three sectors: *attractive, average* and *unattractive*. The latter is divided into *strong, average* and *weak*. The combination of the two axes gives the planners nine areas for analysis and strategic consideration. Succinct titles were given to each of the 'pigeon holes' as shown in Figure 59. 'Leader' is self-explanatory; 'Avis' stands for a sector in which the firm appears to be 'second, but is trying harder' ... Once the management accepts the terminology and understands the full implications the tool gradually becomes extremely meaningful within the planning process. The manager of a 'cash generator' should appreciate the financial, marketing and managerial implications as much as the manager of a 'cash cow' in a Boston-orientated firm does . . .

prospects for sector profitability

		unattractive	average	attractive
company's competitive capabilities	weak	disinvest	phased withdrawal/ custodial	double or quit
	average	phased withdrawal	custodial/ growth	avis
	strong	cash generator	growth/ leader	leader

Fig. 59   Directional policy matrix

Developing a Sales Aid for a Transport Company

A large road haulage company has come to realise that in the context of its operations there are some cargoes which are more cost-beneficial than others. For many years the company has been offering an 'undifferentiated' product in the sense that it consented to carry all cargoes irrespective of their nature. A new marketing manager took the view that it should be possible to run a much more profitable and effective operation by concentrating the firm's marketing and selling activities upon a range of cargoes capable of utilising the firm's capacity, as far as it was possible, to the optimum. Thus the underlying objective was to determine what would constitute an optimum 'cargo mix'.

Moreover the marketing manager felt that the outcome of such an analysis could form the basis of an excellent sales aid. If salesmen could be provided with a 'hit parade' list of cargoes in a descending scale of 'desirability' it would enable them to decide how much sales effort was justified *vis-à-vis* each prospect. Cargoes at the top of the 'hit parade' would be worth fighting for; those at the bottom should be avoided like the plague.

At the same time the marketing manager realised that a cargo which was generally attractive to the transport industry was not necessarily the most suitable for his own firm's capacity owing to vehicle configuration, route structuring and depot location.

A simple screening device was compiled with the view of matching:

1 Cargoes and their commercial attractiveness, and
2 the firm's own infrastructural characteristics and needs.

Figure 60 illustrates the results of the study and the numerical quantification ascribed to each cargo analysed. Salesmen knew that cargoes marked with '9' (3 ×3) were the 'Star' cargoes and '1' (1 × 1) were the 'Dogs'.

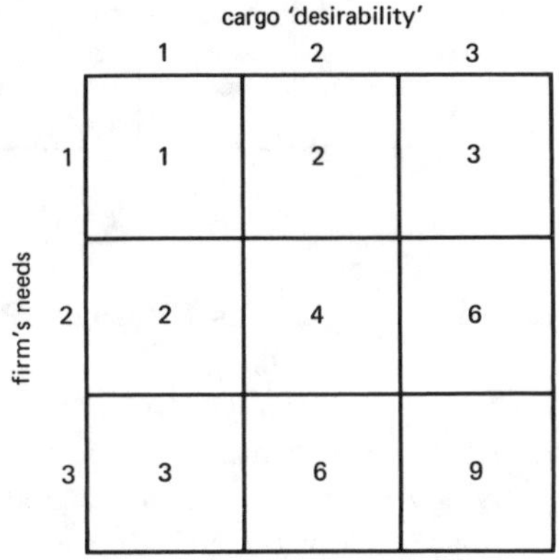

cargo 'desirability'

	1	2	3
1	1	2	3
2	2	4	6
3	3	6	9

firm's needs (vertical axis label, rows labelled 1, 2, 3)

Fig. 60   Cargo analysis

Branch Selection in a Bank

This case study represents another imaginative application of the 'Portfolio' concept to an important managerial decision. A bank with many thousands of retail outlets wished to develop a screening method for determining whether any of its existing branches were unattractive and also defining fresh criteria for the selection of new branch locations in the high street.

The success of a branch normally depends on the combination of two factors: 1. the size and characteristics of the catchment market and 2. the bank's own ability to provide a service compatible with the needs of the target market thus defined. The former includes such elements as size of market, its socio-economic and demographic nature; level of business/commercial activity in the area etc. The latter encompasses the expertise and personal resources available to the branch; the bank's image; and of course the bank's own objectives and aspirations. The former dimension is external to the firm. The latter is internal to the firm and its organisation. The ideal location is the one that offers a sizeable market and which corresponds as far as possible to the bank's capabilities and objectives. Both are capable of quantification and screening.

Figure 61 shows the kind of matrix that emerged after considerable external study as well as internal self-flagellation.

THE MARKETPLACE

	high	medium	low
high	'high—flyers'	possibles	?
medium	possibles	?	'dead loss'
low	?	'dead loss'	'dead loss'

bank's aspirations and capabilities

Fig. 61

International Marketing and the 'Business Portfolio'

It does not require too much imagination to perceive how the 'Business Portfolio' concept and its various derivatives can be applied to international marketing decisions. As stated at the beginning of this chapter the international marketer must attempt to select those markets that offer the best commercial and marketing opportunities whilst they enjoy, at the same time, maximum compatibility with the firm's own capabilities, resources, style and method of operation. The former is external to the firm; the latter is internal.

An example would help to illustrate how the marketer can approach such a task. A firm wishes to market a new and highly sophisticated electric shaver on an international scale. It realises that it would be too ambitious a task to attempt to sell the product in all countries. It therefore seeks to identify the most promising countries in which to develop its international presence.

As a first phase an arbitrary decision is taken to restrict the firm's marketing objectives to countries that enjoy a 'per capita income' in excess of $2000. It is recognised that the product, being a luxury item, is more likely to attain a penetration in countries that enjoy a certain standard of living. Thus one can narrow the field of concentration into a more manageable catchment portion of the world.

Now comes the big problem: having identified a few score countries that fall into the desired 'typology' one must accept that some of them are not necessarily the most suitable opportunities for the marketing company in question. 'Country A' may rank very high on the 'per capita income' league and also have a high population. Yet the same country may rank as a poor opportunity for our specific marketer owing to an inherent weakness in the firm's structure and/or capabilities *vis-à-vis* that country. The firm's image there may be an insurmountable barrier to market penetration. Similarly lack of experience in managing an intricate distribution structure may be another constraint. On the other hand 'Country B' which appears a less attractive market may prove a lot more compatible with the organisation's skills and strengths. The ideal target market is of course the one which offers the highest objective and quantitative opportunity coupled with the highest compatibility with the marketing company's specific strengths and capabilities.

A modified version of the 'Business Portfolio' concept can be a most valuable aid to a structured screening effort. All one has to do is design a matrix with two dimensions:

1 *The Countries Explored*
   We can divide countries by their level of commercial attractiveness into three groups: 'high', 'medium' and 'low'. Each of these terms can be supported by measurable criteria encompassing such items as population size, economic development, stability, level of industrialisation, consumer habits, local competition etc. All these are facts which can be quantified.

2 *The Firm's Compatability with each Country*
   This is an internal assessment of the firm's own inventory of strengths and weaknesses *vis-à-vis* each country in the short-list assembled during the earlier phase. Once again 'high', 'medium' and 'low' can describe the firm's perceived compatibility in relation to each country.

A 'box' with nine 'pigeon holes' as described in Figure 6 can form the basis upon which the most promising countries for development can be identified.

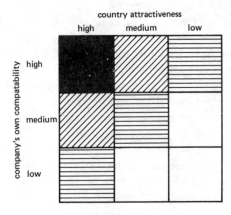

Fig. 62   Choice of country

Chapter 12

Organising for International Marketing

When a firm starts operating for the first time one tends to ignore organisational problems. The general attitude normally is that spending too much time on developing an organisational fabric is a luxury to be left for a future date when the firm is profitable and successful. This is particularly true of the company which derives its energy and stimulus from an entrepreneurial personality. Unfortunately this common attitude is the source of many organisational weaknesses which can plague a firm's career for many years to come.

Most firms would readily acknowledge that if they could start life afresh they would organise their structure differently. With hindsight it is relatively easy to perceive what went wrong and how the approach to organisational matters could have been better planned.

The trouble with organisation development and planning activities is that managers often forget that an organisation is purely an instrument with the help of which the firm can hope to achieve its objectives. It is not an end in itself. An organisation that looks elegant on a chart is not necessarily the most appropriate one for a firm's needs if it fails to attain the defined goals. By the same token a structure that looks chaotic in relation to accepted norms may prove highly effective in terms of practical results. It is not always the sleek and smart army that represents the most effective military machine! It has been known, even in present-day conditions, for an army to resemble a disorganised rabble but yet be exceedingly effective in the field. The same happens frequently on the business scene. A company must first establish what its goals are and only then can it embark on the task of deciding what kind of organisation would help the firm to attain those goals.

In other words managers should resist the temptation of designing a structure which looks appealing in terms of elegance and tidiness. Furthermore one must refrain from changing an organisation which is working well in terms of results. The idea that a 'change is good as a rest' is totally fallacious in the context of organisation development activities. The setting up of an organisation is a vital stage in the total corporate planning process and must never be undertaken in isolation. *Organisation development* has to follow the *strategic planning* stage of the total planning process and strategic planning, in turn, must follow the *business appraisal* or diagnosis phase of the process. Casting one's mind back to the diagram shown in

Chapter 10 dealing with planning (Figure 48) might help to clarify the point once more. It is a vital point to remember and losing sight of its implications can only lead to unnecessary organisational upheavals. 'Do not attempt to organise until you know what the organisation is meant to do' is the moral that should be deeply engraved on a manager's mind.

What a Marketing Organisation Must Cater for

Before exploring the international aspects of an effective marketing organisation it is important that the various sub-functions that form the total marketing process are identified and listed. A 'home' must be found for each one of these sub-functions within the framework of the structure. It is often the absence of a suitable 'home' which is the main cause of organisational problems.

In line with an earlier description of the firm's conceptual framework (Figure 1) we can divide the various marketing activities of the firm into the four categories: 'INPUT' gathering; OBJECTIVES setting; OPERATIONS and CONTROL. This division is consistent with the way any activity, whether large or small, domestic or international, is managed.

Now we can endeavour to list the various activities into which the marketing function can be divided and place them under each of the four headings. This is shown in Figure 57. The list is not comprehensive but it covers most of the more important sub-functions. Any omission identified can be added to the appropriate column.

What the list is actually trying to convey is: for the marketing function to be effectively constituted and organised it is essential that a number of tasks are performed. The firm must possess the capability of performing these tasks. Some of these activities can of course be delegated to an external resource. Market research need not be carried out by the firm's own people; nonetheless it is the responsibility of the firm's management to ensure that the task is efficiently performed. Although the market research activity may be carried out by outsiders, the firm's own organisation must be in the position of planning, authorising and directing such an 'input' gathering effort. The essential concept here is that whoever is responsible for the marketing function must be aware of the fact that the marketing process entails a cluster of activities which are capable of being segregated into fairly clear-cut compartments. It is not intended to imply that each activity shown in Figure 63 calls for a separate person or a department. In many firms the same person can be responsible for a number of activities. Indeed in very small firms one person may have to undertake the total process. The fact that one person may have to perform the full marketing effort does not mean that the job ceases to be multi-faceted. A person may find himself gathering information about his markets ('input'); the same person then determines his objectives; he then goes out to sell his product and finally he appraises

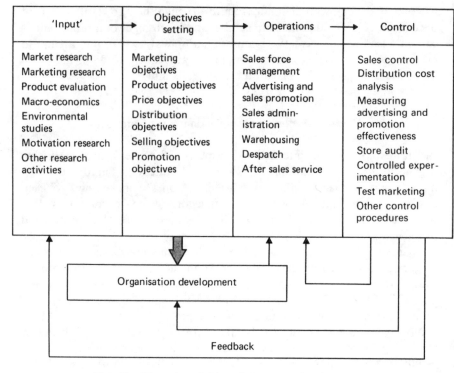

Fig. 63　The sub-activities of the marketing function

the results and ponders about improvements. However, it may be still true that he performed a sound selling job but failed miserably in the process of collecting market data or interpreting information. To that extent the marketing function has been only partially effective.

In summary, therefore, a firm must find a way for accommodating in its structure the various sub-functions described earlier. This can be a fairly easy task in a small company operating in a single domestic market. It is more complex in a firm operating in a large number of markets. It can become literally a nightmare in a company that has to serve many markets, with a large number of product groups and on a multinational scale.

The number of organisational options can be astronomical and selecting the most appropriate one is a job calling for an enormous amount of skill, patience and clear-thinking.

Organisational Options

It is appropriate at this stage to enumerate briefly the basic options that are open to the organisers of the marketing function. They will be shown in their simplest form and under each heading the complexities that may occur in international situations will be highlighted.

It will be noted that the various structures discussed below encapsulate the activities listed earlier (Figure 63), although it is not always apparent from the titles shown. Thus, for instance, the title marketing intelligence manager is often used in the charts as a substitute for marketing research manager. Similarly marketing planning manager is a useful title for the person responsible for the process of planning the marketing function and determining its objectives and those of the various ingredients of the mix. The reader should try to look beyond the titles and appreciate the functional roles that each title seeks to convey.

The alternative organisational patterns illustrated hereunder tend to be 'purist' in character, insofar as no account is taken here of the many possibilities of developing hybrid structures encompassing two or three of the options in one 'cocktail' type organisation. Furthermore, space does not allow to list all the permutations that can occur where a firm chooses a combination of structures to cater for different product groupings or market expediencies.

Marketing organisations can be based on:

> Functions
> Product groupings
> Markets or customer groupings
> Geography
> Channels of distribution
> Matrix approach

Each of these options has its inventory of qualities and disadvantages. All that one can hope to do here is illustrate them as organisation charts and highlight the salient characteristics of each. Moreover the special implications surrounding organisations covering multi-national activities will be emphasised.

The six options listed above are illustrated in Figure 58 (Charts 1–6). It will be noted that an endeavour has been made to place each sub-function under its proper heading viz. 'input', 'objectives', 'operations' and 'control'. However, for the purpose of this classification 'input' and 'control' were bulked under the one heading; after all those who research markets and how to reach them are well equipped to measure results.

1 Functional Organisation

(Figure 64 Chart 1)

In its simplest form this structure includes the following sub-functions:

Marketing intelligence or marketing research

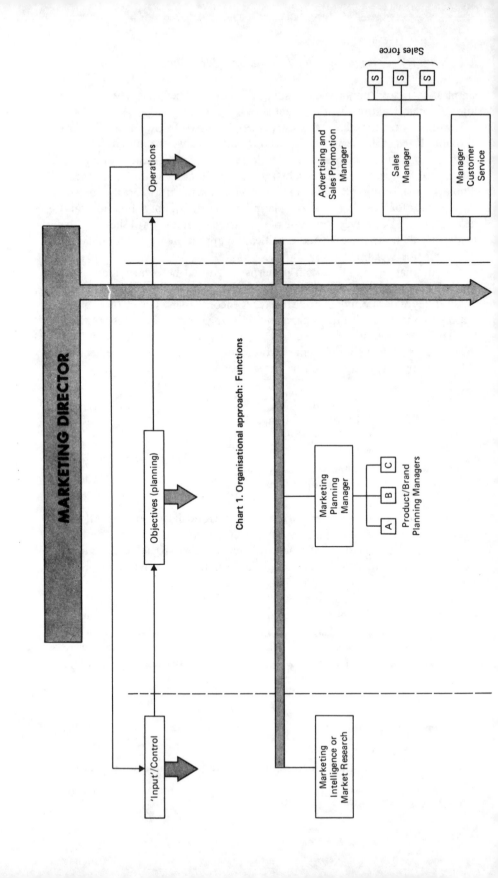

Chart 1. Organisational approach: Functions

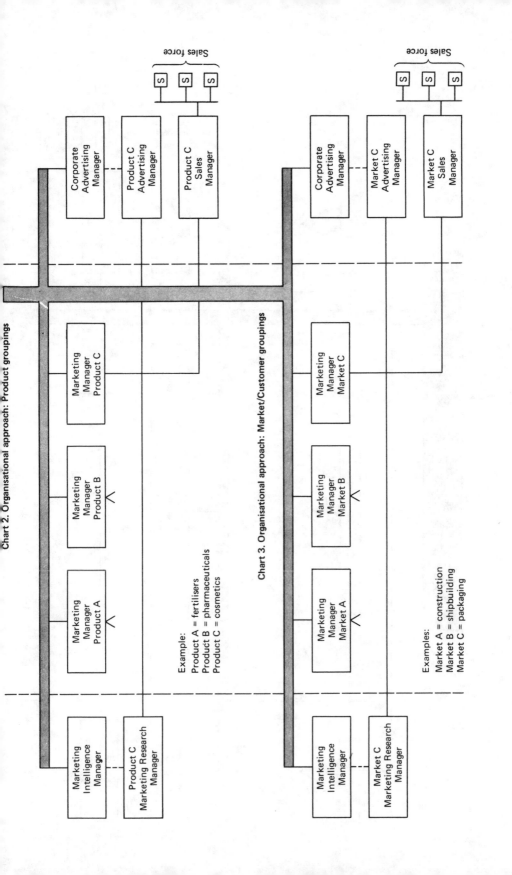

Chart 2. Organisational approach: Product groupings

Marketing Intelligence Manager

Product C Marketing Research Manager

Marketing Manager Product A

Marketing Manager Product B

Marketing Manager Product C

Corporate Advertising Manager

Product C Advertising Manager

Product C Sales Manager

Sales force

S S S

Example:

Product A = fertilisers
Product B = pharmaceuticals
Product C = cosmetics

Chart 3. Organisational approach: Market/Customer groupings

Marketing Intelligence Manager

Market C Marketing Research Manager

Marketing Manager Market A

Marketing Manager Market B

Marketing Manager Market C

Corporate Advertising Manager

Market C Advertising Manager

Market C Sales Manager

Sales force

S S S

Examples:

Market A = construction
Market B = shipbuilding
Market C = packaging

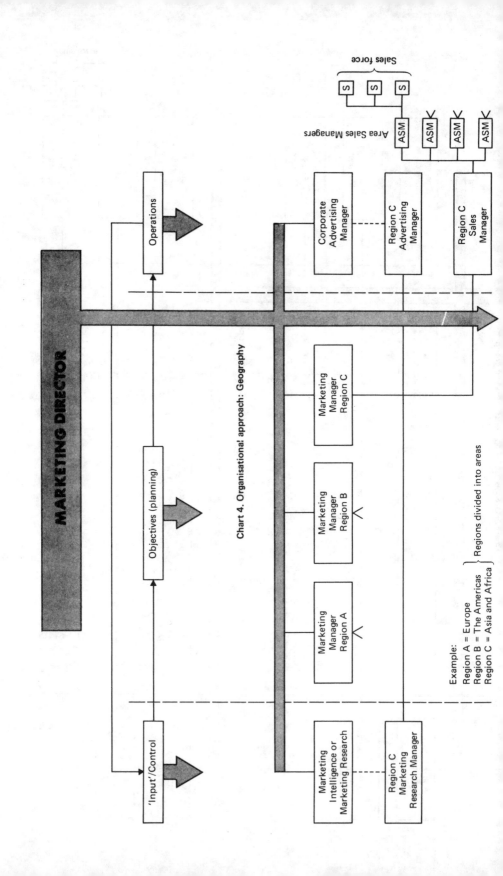

MARKETING DIRECTOR

'Input'/Control

Objectives (planning)

Operations

Marketing Intelligence or Marketing Research

Region C Marketing Research Manager

Marketing Manager Region A

Marketing Manager Region B

Marketing Manager Region C

Corporate Advertising Manager

Region C Advertising Manager

Region C Sales Manager

Area Sales Managers

ASM ASM ASM ASM

Sales force

S S S

Chart 4. Organisational approach: Geography

Example:

Region A = Europe
Region B = The Americas
Region C = Asia and Africa
} Regions divided into areas

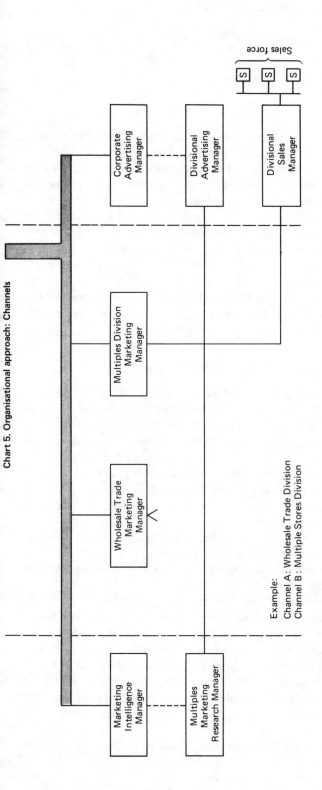

Chart 5. Organisational approach: 'Channels'

Marketing Intelligence Manager

Multiples Marketing Research Manager

Wholesale Trade Marketing Manager

Multiples Division Marketing Manager

Corporate Advertising Manager

Divisional Advertising Manager

Divisional Sales Manager

Sales force

Example:
Channel A: Wholesale Trade Division
Channel B: Multiple Stores Division

Chart 6. Organisational approach: 'Matrix'
Details shown in figure 60

Fig. 64   Organisational options for the marketing effort: functions, product grouping, market/customer groupings, geography, channels, matrix

Marketing planning; this task can be subdivided into products/brands
planning activities
Advertising and sales promotion
Selling
Customer Service (if appropriate)

This kind of structure is simple and allocation of responsibilities fairly
straightforward in most situations. It becomes troublesome where the firm has
a large number of products or where the geographical spread is wide. In the
former one runs the risk that the interests of specific products may be
neglected owing to the personal likes and dislikes of the various personalities
involved. In the latter case the risk is that important geographical catchment
areas are not adequately covered. Another difficulty that may occur is where
the firm serves a number of user groups via different channels of distribution.
For instance, a glassware manufacturer supplies the catering trade on a direct
basis and the public via 'cash and carry' outlets. It is difficult to see how the
same sales force can cope with both activities. The nature of the selling task,
the frequency of calls and the difference in negotiating skills required make it
difficult for the same force to cope with both streams of activity.

INTERNATIONAL IMPLICATIONS OF THE FUNCTIONAL APPROACH

First it must be recognised that where the firm is organised for an 'umbrella'
style decentralisation it is, in the main, inappropriate to think in terms of an
international marketing function. Marketing becomes in such situations a
local affair and the management of the foreign company will decide how its
marketing function should be organised. The centre, as part of the 'umbrella'
philosophy may have certain staff services such as corporate advertising,
international marketing research, marketing training. These services tend to
be more advisory than operational and the minute they try to exert some
influence on local decisions they create conflicts. Basically one must
appreciate that once the firm has opted for decentralisation and the
independence that goes with it, any interference with the way the local
company decides to organise its marketing effort is a serious infringement of
such an independence.

It is a different situation with a macropyramid type company where major
decisions are taken at home. The main strategic direction is determined by the
marketing management at head office. Here the functional approach can
make sense. Every sub-function at headquarters will have counterparts
abroad who will be subordinated to them. Thus the marketing research man
will have people responsible to him in a number of major markets; the
advertising manager will have a number of subordinates abroad, etc. The
main difficulty here is the communication problems that distance and
geography entail.

Furthermore, the fact that each member of the local marketing team is responsible to some manager at head office may create co-ordination problems in the subsidiary company. It is perfectly conceivable that the marketing research man and the advertising man in a Spanish subsidiary of a UK company are in more frequent contact with their counterparts in London than with each other. This is of course an absurd consequence of a functional approach when it is allowed to develop to extremes.

2 Product Groupings

(Figure 64 Chart 2)

This structure is particularly useful where the firm has a large number of products or product groups. The main objective of this approach is to satisfy the special requirements of the products and their supportive technologies. If the same firm manufactures cosmetics, pharmaceuticals and fertilisers it is difficult to see how a functional organisation can cope with all the complexities of the different product groups.

A rudimentary product-orientated organisation normally consists of:

At corporate level
　Marketing intelligence or marketing research
　Advertising
At product groups marketing management
　Marketing research facilities
　Selling activities
　Advertising and sales promotion
Each product group will repeat the last three functional capabilities in relation to its own operational needs.

INTERNATIONAL IMPLICATIONS OF THE PRODUCT-ORIENTATED APPROACH

Once again the suitability of this structure depends to a great extent on the way the total organisation is set up for international operations. It can be a potent structure in companies organised as macropyramids. Afrer all the whole idea behind the product type approach is to treat product management as the heart of the marketing task and it makes good sense for this sub-function to be centralised in those firms that have opted for maximum centralisation. This in turn means that products in such firms tend to be fairly standard throughout the world inspite of the inevitable complaints from local distributors and/or agents.

A weakness of this structure is the fact that quite often product groups tend to develop a total independence from each other in world markets. This entails duplication of selling/distribution infrastructures in the various countries. Whilst this can be fully justified in the larger markets it is a costly method in the smaller countries.

In the example we looked at earlier it is conceivable that the cosmetics, pharmaceuticals and fertilisers divisions would each have a separate presence and distribution arrangements in the same countries. The waste that can stem from this development for the total corporation must be carefully watched.

It is a different story with a company which has opted for the decentralised approach as characterised by the normal 'umbrella' type structure. Endeavouring to duplicate the product-orientated approach in every country is a formula for maximum differentiation and proliferation of products. Yet this is the underlying philosophy of the 'umbrella' structure and anybody who opts for this approach must recognise its strengths as well as its weaknesses.

Another danger with the marketing organisation which is based on a decentralised product-orientated structure is poor communication among the various marketing units around the world. It is almost inevitable that considerable creativity will be lost though this kind of structure. Great ideas created in one market will be lost unless a special system is established for transmitting such ideas from country to country.

Finally the 'umbrella' staff services at the centre are rarely of real value to a marketing organisation which is product based. Their role is seldom recognised as very useful to the various units. At best they are advisory, co-ordinative; at worst they tend to be impotent and treated as a bit of a joke among operational units. When this kind of image develops around these central services that is the time for some serious reappraisal of their role within the structure.

3 Market or Customer Groupings

(Figure 64 Chart 3)

The word *market* here must not be confused with the narrower meaning which implies a country or part thereof. The meaning ascribed to the word market here is the one used in planning viz. clearly-defined user-groups, industries or segments. Thus construction, packaging or shipbuilding are *markets*. Hotels, schools or hospitals are *customer* groups. Products are normally designed to meet the needs of specific markets or customer groupings. Whether changes in products are substantive or minor depend on the marketing merits of each case. The market or customer orientated structure seeks to ensure that these needs are accurately identified and acted upon.

The structure normally contains the following sub-functions:

At corporate level
   Marketing intelligence or marketing research
   Advertising
At markets/customers groupings level
   Marketing research facilities
   Selling
   Advertising and sales promotion

The last three sub-functions will repeat themselves in respect of each market or customer grouping into which the marketing function is divided.

Undoubtedly this approach to marketing organisation is desirable where clearly-defined groupings exist and especially where the nature of the business is such that a small number of markets and/or customer groups are being served by the firm. The structure becomes clumsy where the number of markets is large. Moreover the system is slightly inflexible, insofar as it cannot accommodate at short notice new product opportunities which do not fit into the organisational groupings in existence. Thus if the firm has organised its marketing effort into construction, shipbuilding and packaging it is difficult to see where a new opportunity to serve the *catering* industry could be accommodated. It will need a new grouping and that in turn will require the establishment of a new organisational set-up. All this may involve the firm in considerable waste of time and expense.

INTERNATIONAL IMPLICATIONS OF THE MARKETS/CUSTOMERS APPROACH

Once again we have to ask ourselves whether we are dealing with a macropyramid or with an 'umbrella' type organisation.

With the former the markets-orientated structure has the advantage that specific knowledge pertaining to the markets served is located at one place viz. the centre. The marketing expertise on the construction industry and so on will be under one roof. This of course has also its point of weakness: the knowledge available at headquarters will be, in the main, based on information stemming from the country in which the centre is based. Knowledge of other countries and their specific characteristics will be rather superficial.

Most marketing decisions will be taken at the centre. The only marketing sub-functions which will be adequately represented and manned in the foreign outposts will be selling and distribution. There is a high probability that the marketing boss of each markets division will want to make his own international arrangements. In other words little synergy will exist among the various divisions. It is not uncommon for firms organised on this pattern to have a number of totally independent local offices in the same country. To overcome this problem and the duplication of cost large multinational firms often set up single local office buildings in which all the marketing personnel are stationed. Such infrastructural arrangements are convenient, but in organisational terms it is true to say that those responsible for serving a specific market or customer grouping are still in the 'line' to a boss at headquarters and not to a boss in charge of an office block in country X.

In an 'umbrella' type firm the markets/customers-orientated structure means once again that a certain atmosphere of organisational *laissez-faire* develops. In fact it is not unusual to find a markets structure in one country and a *functional* structure in another. The greatest weakness, as in the previous options, is the fact that knowledge and expertise of local conditions, although very thorough in each country, seldom get communicated to other parts of the international organisation. Moreover, the corporation as a whole seldom enjoys the benefit of cross-fertilisation of creativity.

4. Geography

(Figure 64 Chart 4)

This organisational option seeks to meet the need of the geography and provide a broad coverage of a country, a region or indeed the world. It is an ideal structure for firms operating in one product or in a homogeneous range of products that need fast and efficient countrywide (or worldwide) distribution. The marketing of milk, produce and bread are examples of products that can be best marketed through a geographical structure.

A typical structure would include:

At corporate level
  Marketing intelligence or marketing research
  Advertising
At regional level
  Regional marketing research
  Regional advertising
  Selling

These last three sub-functions will repeat themselves in every region and sometimes even in sub-divisions of the regions.

INTERNATIONAL IMPLICATIONS OF THE GEOGRAPHY-ORIENTATED APPROACH

On the face of it the geographical approach is a natural one for international marketing. After all the underlying aim of such a structure is to cater for the needs of large and widely dispersed catchment areas. What can be a larger market than the total world? Indeed this approach is quite popular with large international firms: the world is divided into regions such as Europe, the Americas, the rest of the World. Regions can be subdivided in turn into areas or simply into countries. The important feature of such a structure is that regions are fairly self-contained and possess their own functional infrastructure in terms of marketing research, marketing planning, advertising and of course selling. Often it is the selling sub-function which is subdivided into smaller geographical areas of responsibility.

This structure is easily managed both within a centralised and a decentralised philosophy. The main difference between the two approaches is that in the former strategic decisions will be taken at the centre and in the latter they will be delegated to the various regions. The macropyramid firm will decentralise the selling and distribution tasks within clearly-defined objectives. The 'umbrella' organisation will delegate the total marketing task including the planning and setting of objectives to the various subsidiaries.

The weakness of the geographical organisation in international operations is that insufficient attention is normally given to the needs of specific markets and the development of products to match these needs. For example, a firm manufactures a range of packaging machinery and sells it throughout the world via a network of regional subsidiaries. In other words the organisation is geography-orientated. The main markets served by the firm are cigarettes, razor blades, bread and confectionery. These four represent different markets for the firm's range of packaging products. Obviously the specific needs of each one of these markets in each country may be somewhat different. The firm would seek to maximise sales to the best of its ability. If the company is organised as a macropyramid the aim will be to standardise the product as far as possible; in the case of the 'umbrella' firm a certain amount of differentiation will be inevitable. However, in both instances the likelihood is that inadequate attention will be paid to the collation, comparison and interpretation of data about each market on a worldwide scale.

What are the influences that affect bread consumption in each country and how is that likely to affect this segment of our business in the world? This is a typical question that the total organisation needs to ask itself from time to time. Bits of the answer may be available in each country. However the geography-based organisation is unlikely to have the appropriate organ for dealing with such diagnostic problems. Moreover the geographical organisation often faces the difficulty of coping with the problem of determining priorities in situations where the demands of the various markets within the various regions exceed supplies. Who decides as to whether the emphasis should be placed on the razor blades market rather than confectionery? The technology is similar, the product is more or less the same, the profit may be the same; nonetheless there must be marketing justification as to why one market should receive priority over others. In a macropyramid organisation such decisions are normally taken at the marketing director's level. On the other hand in an 'umbrella' structure organised on a geographical basis, the mechanism seldom exists for dealing with such important decisions. In the absence of such a mechanism the tendency is for decisions regarding the allocation of output to be taken by production personnel and this is unlikely to be based on the best principles of marketing.

We shall see later how the *matrix* approach can help to resolve problems of this nature.

5 Channels of Distribution Structure

No discussion of the various basic options for organising the marketing function can be complete without referring to a structure which is based on channels of distribution.

A structure based on channels would normally include:

At corporate level:
  Marketing intelligence or marketing research
  Advertising
At channels marketing level
  Marketing research
  Selling
  Advertising and/or sales promotion

An example of channels-orientated approach is a situation where the firm has decided to have two parallel marketing organisations: one to cater for the wholesale trade and one for the multiple stores groups. It may take a different form by calling the first division branded goods division and the second one private label division. In practice this is a subtle way for organising the firm by channels. It is a case again of trying to look behind titles which quite often help to fog the whole issue.

The channels-orientated approach is seldom applicable to international situations. With the great variety of channel options that exist in international markets it is unlikely that a channels structure would make organisational sense. Nonetheless, one does come across, from time to time, multinational firms that divide their marketing organisation into a retail products division and an industrial products division. This is probably the nearest that a channels-orientated structure can apply to international marketing.

The various comments made in relation to the *markets/customers* approach apply with equal validity to this kind of structure, subject to the overall observation that this is an organisational option that should be used in exceptional situations only. A firm that has, for instance, developed a novel type of channels of distribution such as Tupperware or Avon Cosmetics is entitled to explore an international structure based on such channels strategy.

It is very difficult though to see how a channels structure can operate effectively within a macropyramid organisation. The variations that exist in world markets are such that only in special circumstances would it make sense to have a structure of this nature planned and controlled from the remote vantage point of the centre.

It is easier to envisage the large-scale use of the channels structure within the 'umbrella' approach, although it is not likely to be imposed or recommended by the centre. One or more units in the international structure may simply opt for this approach because it meets the special marketing needs of the country they serve. As with all 'umbrella' organisations it will be a matter of local choice.

6 Matrix Approach

This approach seeks to combine two or three orientations in one structure. The underlying concept is that by judicious dovetailing of two structural systems one can achieve the 'best of both worlds'. Thus by combining a product management approach with a market-orientated specialisation one can meet both the needs of markets and of products. The notion that structures must be based on 'pure' systems has been slow to die. The propounders of the *matrix* approach feel that if marketing effectiveness demands that a multi-faceted structure is established, a method must be found for accommodating such a flexible orientation.

The matrix approach aims to synthesise the demands of a number of parameters and by doing so add strength to the organisation.

The easiest way to illustrate this organisational concept is by looking at a simple case:

Southern Aluminium Limited manufactures a range of products that fall into three main categories: *sheet, extrusions* and *film.*

The Company supplies these products to a large number of markets. However, the main users come under three industry headings: *construction, aircraft* and *packaging.*

Furthermore the Company markets its products in many countries.

Advise how the marketing function should be organised.

Many organisational options unfold themselves. Each option has its advantages and disadvantages. Organising by products would mean that the needs of the specific markets served may be neglected. It is not possible for all three product groups to have in-depth expertise of the three markets all the time. Organising by markets makes marketing sense but the needs of the products will not be adequately covered. The construction marketing man may have a blind prejudice against film as a suitable product for the construction industry and that of course means that there is little chance for this product to achieve any penetration of that industry. A geographical structure will be highly results-orientated but little or no development progress will be achieved into new applications. A functional structure seems totally inappropriate because it will develop little or no marketing concentration on either products or on markets. And all this has to be done within an international scene.

The matrix structure seeks to solve this dilemma. 'Why not have a double-pronged organisation that meets the needs of the products as well as the needs of the markets?' say the propounders of this concept. In fact the approach can be best illustrated in the following matrix from which this method obtains its name (Figure 65).

The main implication of this structural concept is that there are nine functional inter-sections. At these points one gets the benefit of maximum knowledge and expertise of a product group and a market group. The hope is that no opportunity can be lost as a result of inadvertance, insofar as the infrastructure is there to look after both products and markets.

The actual organisation chart would look fairly conventional. The matrix would be shown as two parallel streams of functional activities (Figure 66).

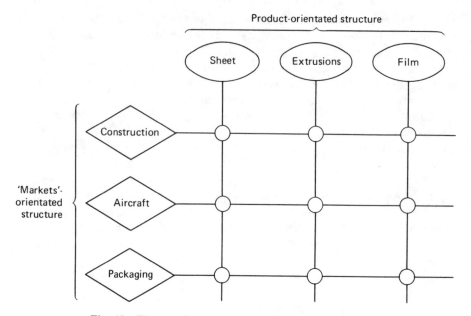

Fig. 65   The matrix approach to a marketing organisation

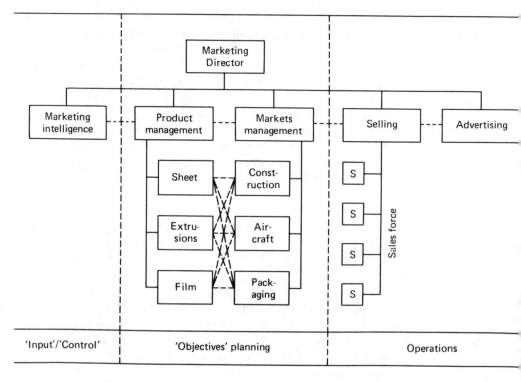

Fig. 66   A matrix style structure based on product/market approach

Thus within a set of marketing objectives the firm possesses two teams of planners/thinkers: one orientated towards the firm's products; the other towards markets. Between them the firm should know all there is to be known both about the needs of specific markets and the products the firm manufactures. In a highly technological environment such as an aluminium fabricator the firm may decide that one of the two streams described should also be responsible for the selling task. In other words, it may be felt that those responsible either for markets management or for products management are capable of carrying out the selling. In such an event one stream becomes a 'line' responsibility and the other stream becomes a 'staff' position.

Experience has shown that where the matrix approach is used it is important that clear job descriptions coupled with individual standards of performance are defined. The nature of this organisational option is such that conflicts can easily arise. What happens if a period of shortages occurs? Who gets priorities of supply—those who look after products or those who seek to satisfy the needs of markets? This problem can be avoided if the answer is defined in advance in clear job specifications.

Furthermore if top management decides to attach the selling function to one marketing stream rather than the other it is important that the ultimate responsibility for the attainment of results is attached to that group. The other group which has gained a staff function has an important role in advising, persuading and even cajoling but cannot be held responsible for results. In such an event one must also recognise that different types of managers are needed for the two streams of activity. The 'line' stream must consist of active and dynamic 'doers'; the 'staff' stream calls for thinkers who 'can walk on water'.

The matrix approach has opened new vistas in organisational development thinking. However, it must not be used indiscriminately. It may be ideal for firms capable of coping with sophisticated inter-departmental communication problems. It must be avoided by others.

THE MATRIX APPROACH IN INTERNATIONAL MARKETING

The matrix style structure has opened many creative solutions to organisational problems in international marketing. The mere fact that one can superimpose a number of organisational 'layers' upon a basic structure means that one need not feel constrained by purist solutions. We discussed in the example shown earlier (Southern Aluminium Limited) two streams of marketing activity running in parallel viz. products management and markets management. It does not require much imagination to conjure a situation where the organisation could cope with three or possibly even more dimensions.

If we take the Southern Aluminium Limited case we can add the international dimension as a third geographical axis on the chart. It will represent a third layer responsible for the marketing needs of geographical units such as regions or countries as distinct from the marketing needs of products and/or markets. This may seem a formula for chaos. However, it need not be: firms that have learned the art of defining jobs, attaching standards of responsibility and performance to each job and identifying 'interface' problems ahead of them occurring, should find a multi-dimensional structural approach manageable. In fact it offers a creative solution to problems which often seem intractable. Pictorially the three dimension matrix approach could look like a cube with many cells as described in Figure 67.

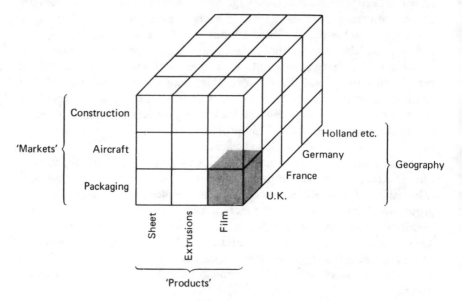

Fig. 67   Three dimensional matrix approach to international situations

In the diagram described we have three products, three markets and four countries. This represents $3 \times 3 \times 4 = 36$ cells. Each cell represents a product/market/country marketing cell. If the team responsible for results in each 'cell' knows how to optimise their individual knowledge and experience into a single effort they should achieve optimum performance. The theory is sound; the results will only be as sound as the human material of which each cell is constituted. As stated earlier the one essential precaution is to identify which dimension of the 'morphology' is ultimately responsible for the attainment of the firm's marketing objectives. This is particularly important in an era when there may be shortages of raw materials and/or productive capacity. In such circumstances it is not possible to meet the full demands of all three dimensions. It is therefore imperative that one dimension has the last word.

We have endeavoured to explore the various organisational options in general terms. Each option has its merits and each has its weaknesses in a given set of circumstances. Before one can organise or reorganise for international marketing the manager responsible for this task must look at as many options as possible, chart them on paper and try to list the advantages and disadvantages of each. **Being** methodical and painstaking in exploring alternatives normally pays dividends in the form of fewer problems and obviously better performance.

Figure 68 attempts to summarise the options discussed and lists the implications where the structure is of the macropyramid or the 'umbrella' type. This is the kind of tabulation which the person responsible for an international marketing structuring activity might find useful.

Main Considerations

The quality of an organisation can only be measured in its ability to meet the firm's total or functional goals. Pretty charts are not a guarantee that the organisation will achieve the desired results. Similarly, structures which do not fully adhere to the fundamental principles of how organisations should be developed often perform very effectively in practice. Nonetheless it is important to enumerate a number of considerations which the international marketer must bear in mind before finally committing himself to a structure which will enable him to attain his marketing goals internationally:

1 Authority and Responsibility

Lines of authority must be clear and unambiguous. There must also be no doubts as to who is responsible for what and to whom. A firm that operates in a multitude of markets can easily run into serious confusion as to where authority lies. This, in turn, is bound to weaken the value of the organisation pattern selected and its ability to operate effectively.

The definition of authority and responsibility is particularly important in a matrix type structure which by its very nature is based on a multi-dimensional division of both. Failure to grapple with the definition of these two aspects may nullify the value of the matrix type approach and should be avoided.

2 Communication

An effective organisation in international marketing must be capable of efficient, speedy and accurate communication. An organisation operating in international markets which is not capable of transmitting and receiving information and ideas is less likely to succeed than the one that can do so.

This means that the marketer must consider very carefully the communication implications of every organisational option that is open to him. In this connection the question of clustering sub-units in accordance with language convenience is an important aspect which must not be forgotten. After all one communicates through languages and an organisation that is set up in such a way that people have difficulties in communicating, simply

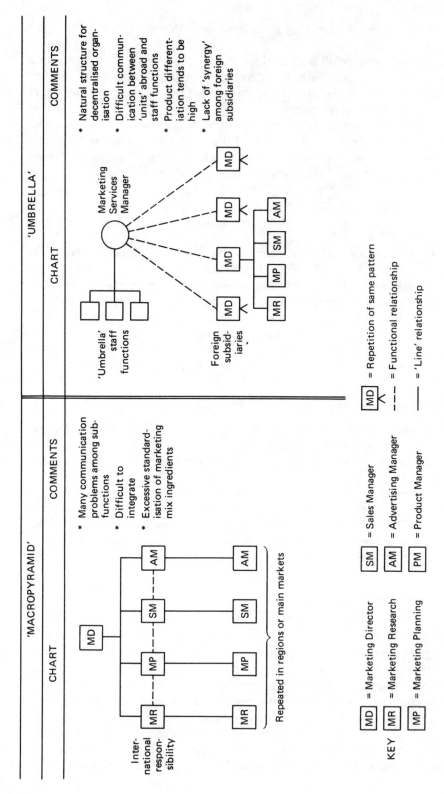

Fig. 68(a) Organisational style—Functional

'MACROPYRAMID'

CHART

International responsibility

Repeated in regions or main markets

COMMENTS

* Many communication problems among sub-functions
* Difficult to integrate
* Excessive standardisation of marketing mix ingredients

'UMBRELLA'

CHART

Marketing Services Manager

'Umbrella' staff functions

Foreign subsidiaries

COMMENTS

* Natural structure for decentralised organisation
* Difficult communication between 'units' abroad and staff functions
* Product differentiation tends to be high
* Lack of 'synergy' among foreign subsidiaries

KEY

MD = Marketing Director
MR = Marketing Research
MP = Marketing Planning
SM = Sales Manager
AM = Advertising Manager
PM = Product Manager

MD = Repetition of same pattern
- - - = Functional relationship
——— = 'Line' relationship

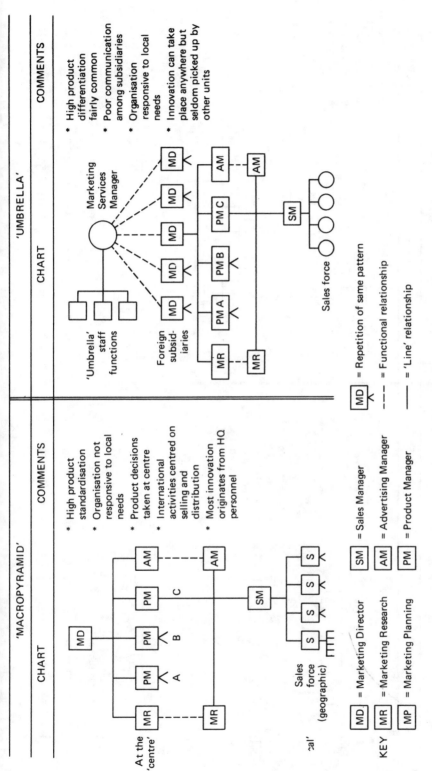

Fig. 68(b) Organisational style—Products

'MACROPYRAMID'

CHART

At the 'centre'

MD

PM A   PM B   PM C   AM

MR

MR ---- AM

Sales force (geographic)

SM

S   S   S   S

COMMENTS

* High product standardisation
* Organisation not responsive to local needs
* Product decisions taken at centre
* International activities centred on selling and distribution
* Most innovation originates from HQ personnel

'UMBRELLA'

CHART

Marketing Services Manager

'Umbrella' staff functions

Foreign subsidiaries

MD   MD   MD   MD   MD

MR   PM A   PM B   PM C   AM

MR ----   AM

SM

Sales force

COMMENTS

* High product differentiation fairly common
* Poor communication among subsidiaries
* Organisation responsive to local needs
* Innovation can take place anywhere but seldom picked up by other units

KEY

MD = Marketing Director
MR = Marketing Research
MP = Marketing Planning

SM = Sales Manager
AM = Advertising Manager
PM = Product Manager

MD = Repetition of same pattern
- - - = Functional relationship
——— = 'Line' relationship

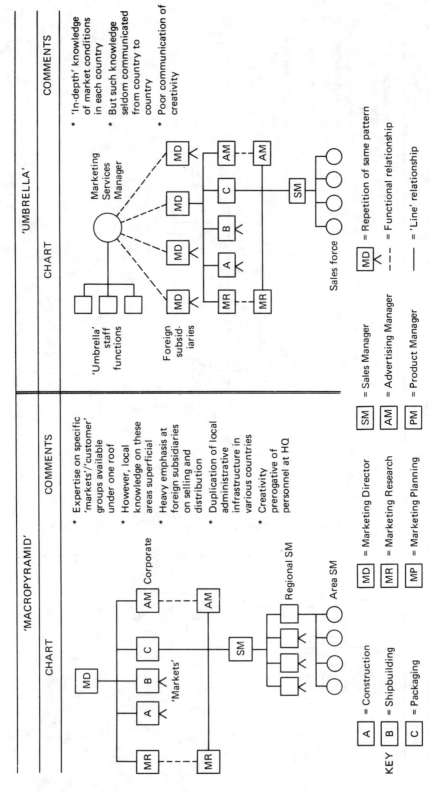

Fig. 68(c) Organisational style—'Market'/'Customer' Groupings

'MACROPYRAMID'

CHART

COMMENTS

* Expertise on specific 'markets'/'customer' groups available under one roof
* However, local knowledge on these areas superficial
* Heavy emphasis at foreign subsidiaries on selling and distribution
* Duplication of local administrative infrastructure in various countries
* Creativity prerogative of personnel at HQ

MD

AM Corporate

AM

C

B

A

MR

MR

'Markets'

SM

Regional SM

Area SM

'UMBRELLA'

CHART

COMMENTS

* 'In-depth' knowledge of market conditions in each country
* But such knowledge seldom communicated from country to country
* Poor communication of creativity

Marketing Services Manager

'Umbrella' staff functions

Foreign subsidiaries

MD MD MD MD

MR A B C AM

MR AM

SM

Sales force

KEY

A	= Construction	MD	= Marketing Director	SM	= Sales Manager
B	= Shipbuilding	MR	= Marketing Research	AM	= Advertising Manager
C	= Packaging	MP	= Marketing Planning	PM	= Product Manager

MD = Repetition of same pattern

--- = Functional relationship

—— = 'Line' relationship

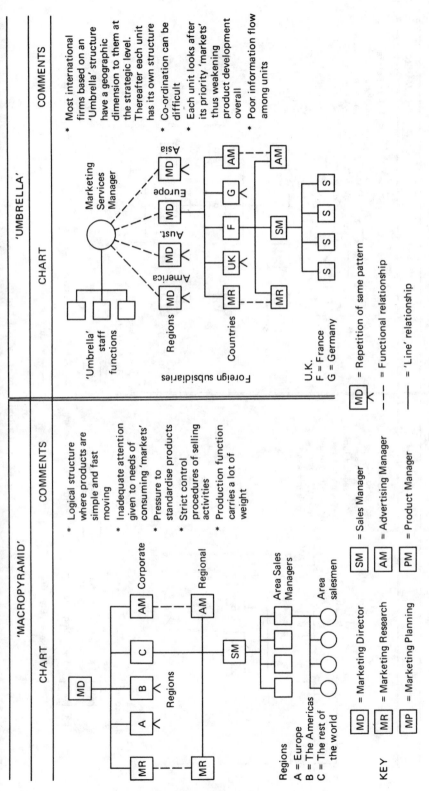

Fig. 68(d)   Organisational style—Geography

'MACROPYRAMID'

CHART

Regions
A = Europe
B = The Americas
C = The rest of the world

KEY
MD = Marketing Director
MR = Marketing Research
MP = Marketing Planning

SM = Sales Manager
AM = Advertising Manager
PM = Product Manager

COMMENTS

* Logical structure where products are simple and fast moving
* Inadequate attention given to needs of consuming 'markets'
* Pressure to standardise products
* Strict control procedures of selling activities
* Production function carries a lot of weight

'UMBRELLA'

CHART

Marketing Services Manager

'Umbrella' staff functions

Foreign subsidiaries

U.K.
F = France
G = Germany

MD = Repetition of same pattern
--- = Functional relationship
—— = 'Line' relationship

COMMENTS

* Most international firms based on an 'Umbrella' structure have a geographic dimension to them at the strategic level. Thereafter each unit has its own structure
* Co-ordination can be difficult
* Each unit looks after its priority 'markets' thus weakening product development overall
* Poor information flow among units

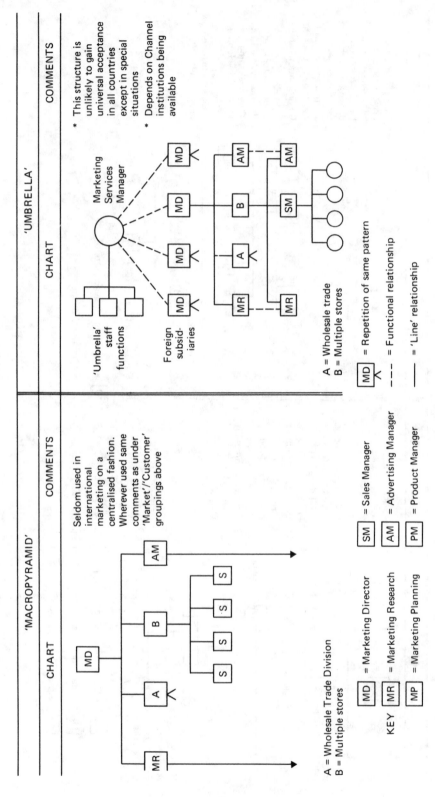

Fig. 68(e) Organisational style—Channels

'MACROPYRAMID'		'UMBRELLA'	
CHART	COMMENTS	CHART	COMMENTS

The 'cells'—concept
 	
The chart
 	
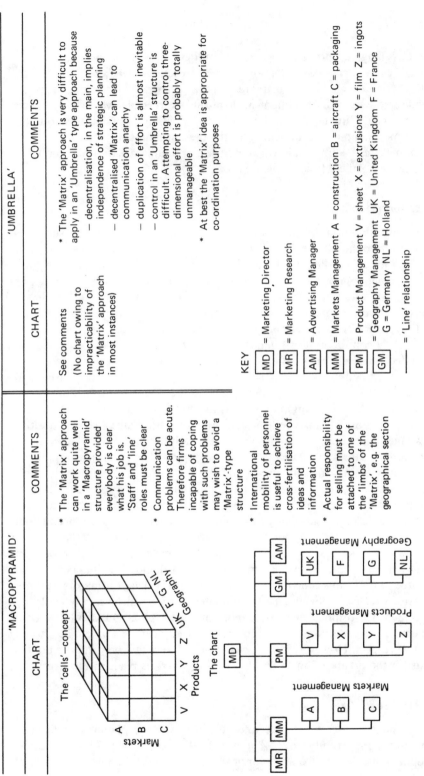
	* The 'Matrix' approach can work quite well in a 'Macropyramid' structure provided everybody is clear what his job is. 'Staff' and 'line' roles must be clear
	
	* Communication problems can be acute. Therefore firms incapable of coping with such problems may wish to avoid a 'Matrix'-type structure
	
	* International mobility of personnel is useful to achieve cross-fertilisation of ideas and information
	
	* Actual responsibility for selling must be attached to one of the 'limbs' of the 'Matrix', e.g. the geographical section
		See comments
		
		(No chart owing to impracticability of the 'Matrix' approach in most instances)
			* The 'Matrix' approach is very difficult to apply in an 'Umbrella' type approach because
			  — decentralisation, in the main, implies independence of strategic planning
			  — decentralised 'Matrix' can lead to communication anarchy
			  — duplication of effort is almost inevitable
			  — control in an 'Umbrella' structure is difficult. Attempting to control three-dimensional effort is probably totally unmanageable
			
			* At best the 'Matrix' idea is appropriate for co-ordination purposes

KEY

MD = Marketing Director

MR = Marketing Research

AM = Advertising Manager

MM = Markets Management   A = construction   B = aircraft   C = packaging

PM = Product Management   V = sheet   X = extrusions   Y = film   Z = ingots

GM = Geography Management   UK = United Kingdom   F = France
G = Germany   NL = Holland

——— = 'Line' relationship

Fig. 68(f)   Organisational style—'Matrix'

because language problems occur, cannot logically be a very wise choice. One often encounters geography-orientated structures where countries are attached to a region for no better reason than proximity on the map. This can lead to very awkward communication problems especially where two markets have very different cultural, linguistic and possibly political backgrounds. Extreme examples are: attaching, at the present moment, Israel in the same region as the neighbouring Arab countries, or South Africa with a number of her more hostile African neighbours.

3 Co-ordination

The co-ordination of the marketing activities of the various sub-units scattered round the globe is one of the important tasks of an effective international marketing. However decentralised a firm may be, top management must recognise that over-fragmentation of strategies cannot be the most economical way of doing business. On the other hand, decentralisation implies a certain freedom to pursue an independent strategic action in each country. The aim of sound co-ordination policies is to mitigate the risk of contradictory strategies emerging round the world. Co-ordination in a decentralised firm does not imply the curtailment of local management's freedom of action. Its role in such situations is in the main persuasive and advisory. It seeks to alert local personnel to the fact that the type of policies adopted and their timing may be harmful to the overall aims of the firm.

In a macropyramid type firm co-ordination often takes a more positive managerial meaning. In some centralised multinational firms the word *co-ordinator* means a lot more than the term implies. The co-ordinator in many situations is tantamount to a product chief executive with wide 'line' responsibilities. The word co-ordinator must be used with some care, insofar as it is fairly nebulous and unless defined clearly can be a source of considerable organisational confusion. It is therefore very important that when a firm decides to appoint managers to positions that carry the term co-ordinators that a clearly formulated job description is prepared. Moreover such a job description must be communicated to all those who happen to be in a direct 'line' or in a functional relationship with such co-ordinators. It is not the title which is important; it is the content of the job which needs to be clearly specified. Co-ordination is an important aspect of a sound international marketing organisation and the co-ordinator idea can be a potent institution in this respect. However, it must be developed in such a way that no doubts exist in the organisation as to what it means and its place in the structure.

4 Marketing 'Centres of Gravity'

A sound structure must take into consideration the planning realities of identified opportunity areas. The organisation must cater for the greatest opportunity countries, markets or products. The structure must be capable of looking as effectively as possible after the firm's priority areas—the so-called 'centres of gravity'. An organisation which is geared to look after the interests of large and small markets in an identical way, and without paying special attention to the needs of the main opportunity segments, is sure to dissipate valuable and scarce resources. Opportunity areas are not necessarily the largest markets in terms of numbers of people or personal disposable income. Opportunity areas must be defined as those activities or sub-activities which are likely to meet the firm's objectives with the minimum cost and effort. If the firm's objectives are expressed in profit terms then one should seek to identify those areas of the universe where profitability can be attained in the most cost-effective way. If the main objective is sales, regardless of profits, then of course one goes for the most highly populated as well as rich countries. The organisation therefore depends on the clarity with which corporate objectives have been defined, but having done that the structure must reflect the direction towards which the firm must concentrate its main attention. Failing to do this can only weaken the organisation's ability to execute the strategies envisaged by the planning process.

In this connection it is worthwhile to analyse one's markets in accordance with the Pareto rule. The aim is to identify the 20 per cent of firm's activities which generate 80 per cent of the total firm's performance. Thus if one can identify those countries which in the medium term or even in the longer term can provide the bulk of the company's sales it would make good sense to build such information into the firm's international structure.

5 Human Factors

Finally one must not forget that organisations have to be manned by human beings. Developing a structure involves a lot more than just placing anonymous titles in convenient pigeon holes. One is dealing with people and invariably they have wishes, expectations and ambitions. These must represent an important element in the way work relationships are structured. Obviously the interests of the firm and those of its human resources must be reconciled. A structure which ignores the feelings of those who will have to make it work is unlikely to attain the tasks expected from it.

In an international setting this aspect gains enormous complexity. Whilst one wishes to build an organisation pattern which will conform to the personal expectations of most employees round the world this is not always possible. One has to balance these expectations with the other considerations which we listed above. Nonetheless a genuine endeavour to find out the attitudes of individual managers to organisation proposals can, in most instances, be a useful exercise. Seeking to impose a structure which is anathema to most managers is hardly a wise strategy.

In an earlier chapter mention was made of the fact that moving an organisation from an 'umbrella' structure to a macropyramid entails serious demotivation of senior managers who up to that point have been running semi-independent units. Instead of running the show they find themselves subordinated to a boss in the centre. This is the kind of ingredient which can weaken the rationale behind a decision to reorganise and centralise. At the same time a sound understanding of the sentiments of these managers coupled with a judicious rearrangement of their positions, in a way which is capable of offering them the right motivation, can overcome this obstacle. This is common sense but unfortunately organisations are often structured in complete defiance of this important principle.

The study recommended in the chapter on planning whereby the expectations of stakeholders (including employees) round the world should be identified and recorded is an admirable platform from which to test new organisational ideas. Such a study, if properly conducted, can tell the firm's top management and the organisational development specialists what kind of structure is likely to offer happy work relationships whilst maintaining overall effectiveness.

Chapter 13

Creativity and Innovation in International Marketing

Firms operating in international markets often overlook the fact that the sheer exposure to multi-national and multi-culture environments is a spur to innovation. The cross-fertilisation of ideas emanating from different countries can be a source of great creativity and can enrich the quality of the firm's international marketing effort. Unfortunately this opportunity is not always perceived by the international businessman and quite often a wealth of ideas is allowed to drift into oblivion. The notion that great ideas originate at the home-base only is one of the greatest dangers that faces firms hoping to build their prosperity on serving international markets.

The objective of this chapter is to alert the reader to the importance of creativity and innovation to a successful international marketing programme and to identify the various obstacles which must be removed if the firm is to derive maximum innovation from its international presence.

Creativity and Innovation

For the purpose of this chapter we ascribe the following meanings to these two interrelated terms:

Creativity is the thinking process which helps us to generate ideas.
Innovation is the practical application of such ideas towards performing a task in a *better* and/or *cheaper* way.

By definition, therefore, a task which has been performed in a manner which is neither better nor cheaper does not constitute an innovation. Novelty *per se* is not necessarily innovative in character. A manager must avoid pursuing an idea just because it appears creative in its original thought. If it costs more to do the same job or if the results are less satisfactory, the idea does not lead to innovation and must be avoided. An electric shaver which performs the task of shaving in an identical way to the previous model cannot be classified as an innovation simply because it is packed in a more extravagantly designed box. On the other hand, a shaver which shaves better or is smaller or is more aesthetically pleasing would meet our criteria.

No book on international marketing can be complete without a general discussion of creativity and innovation in the context of international operations. Creativity and innovation are vital ingredients in any business. Most firms have come to realise that without these ingredients every aspect and every function of the enterprise will gradually stagnate and become sterile. The subject gains even greater importance in those organisations that seek to derive their fortunes from serving a large number of markets. The larger the marketing coverage the more problems a firm is likely to encounter. The ability to solve such problems in a creative way is the essence of sucessful operations.

It is probably relevant to explode at the very outset the notion that innovation only occurs in relation to new or better *products*. So many managers believe rather mistakenly that the acme of creativity is the emergence of new products. They overlook the fact that whilst products are vitally important to successful marketing the major problem areas often relate to other parts of the marketing mix or indeed the managerial and planning processes. Innovation can take place in any area in which managerial decisions have to be taken and often such innovations can lead the firm to considerable breakthroughs.

Let us explore a few innovations which are not product-based and which have helped their creators to achieve considerable success:

Innovations in the Area of Pricing

The way the Xerox Corporation has priced its products has proved most profitable. Instead of selling its photocopying machines the Corporation has developed the following policy: machines are rented out at a nominal monthly charge. Thereafter an additional charge is made for every copy made on the machine. Furthermore the firm supplies paper and accessories which are an additional source of revenue.

The idea, when it first started, was undoubtedly great; we now take it for granted and see it repeated in other industries. Nonetheless when it first emerged it was a most ingenious pricing innovation which paved the way to a great industrial success. The innovation stemmed from a clever pricing policy. It is difficult to visualise where Xerox would have been today if its policy had been based on the outright sale of photocopying machines.

We take the concept of trading stamps for granted. Whoever developed that idea undoubtedly managed to demonstrate creativity in the sphere of pricing. Giving stamps, after all, is less flagrant than straight discounts.

A few hotel groups offer free accommodation to wives who escort their businessmen husbands. Once again this is a price innovation—it hardly costs the hotel any extra to accommodate a wife in her husband's room; to the business traveller, on the other hand, the saving seems significant and most welcome.

Volvo used to offer a free car insurance for one year to buyers of its cars in the UK. It is certainly less quantitative in its impact than a straight price reduction! Fiat innovated in a different way: they offered a free one-way air passage to Turin to car purchasers. They could fly to Turin and drive themselves back whilst having a holiday at the same time. Fiat of course saved the cost of shipping the car to the UK.

Many creative pricing policies based on *derived demand* can be found around us. The idea is that it pays to sell razors cheaply in order to generate demand for the blades.

Innovation in the Area of Distribution

Once again this ingredient of the mix lends itself to considerable innovative strategies.

Avon Cosmetics opted out of the customary channels of distribution. They developed a novel way for marketing their products through a most effective network of housewives.

Similarly Tupperware have achieved an outstanding distribution success through direct selling via the famous tea parties organised by enthusiastic and highly motivated housewives.

Holiday insurance policies sold through vending machines at airports also represent an innovative channel of distribution. Surely vending machines lend themselves to many other novel possibilities!

Cash dispensing machines outside banks certainly represent a creative and convenient channel for customers who need cash when the bank is closed.

The reader should ponder for a brief moment about the creative thinking that must have gone into developing the *mail order* idea! We take the whole concept of selling through the post for granted. Nonetheless the first person who identified the postal services as a potent channel of distribution was certainly a great innovator.

Innovation in the Area of Communication

Coca-Cola's television advertising campaign based on the song 'I want to teach the world to sing . . .' managed to convey the kind of warmth and feeling of well-being which helps to communicate with a mutinational audience.

The Barbour Index approach to promoting and selling to architects' and quantity surveyors' offices is certainly innovative. Briefly the Barbour Index maintains an up-to-date library in over 2000 architects' and quantity surveyors' offices in the UK. Around sixty librarians visit all these subscribers and up-date their libraries and also introduce and leave details of new products on behalf of manufacturing companies. The architects are happy— they do not have to see hundreds of salesmen; manufacturing companies appear happy insofar as they can promote their products more effectively and probably more economically.

The Esso tiger story and its international nuances has earned, with justification, many accolades as a highly creative international communication programme.

These are just a few examples to illustrate the point that innovation does not necessarily mean new products. The list of creative ideas that have led to profitable innovations can be further enlarged to cover clever ideas in marketing research, organisation development, training and education, controlled experimentation, market segmentation, etc. Indeed there are few areas of management where creativity has not enriched performance. It is a very instructive exercise for managers to observe how other firms, other industries and other nations have achieved creative solutions to specific problem areas. Moreover one can quite often derive creative ideas by simply observing nature at work. It is staggering how often firms manage to miss great ideas which literally stare them in the face. In other words, the power of observation is an integral part of the process of identifying good ideas and after all ideas are the essence of innovation.

The power of creative thinking is an important tool of effective modern management. At the same time it must be appreciated that creativity does not always mean pure originality. The ability to translate a proven idea or method from one sphere of activity to another or from one environment to another is an eloquent proof of a creative manager. This may even include the ability to translate ideas from the world around us. Nature has solved many difficult problems; surely we as managers can draw imaginative and practical analogies from what we observe!

In this connection it is important to appreciate that the mere exposure to world markets offers an immense opportunity to pick up creative ideas. Different nations have different ways of tackling problems and obviously the manager who has the opportunity to travel should be able to discover potent solutions to problems that have appeared insoluble. However, this is only true if the manager who travels has a keen power of observation and sensitivity to everything which is different, new or clever. The manager who travels with his eyes closed is less likely to enrich the international marketing scene than the man who travels with a deep sense of curiosity and alertness. In other words one of the qualities of a roving international marketer must be a well developed observing skill—without it a great part of the opportunity to detect creative ideas is bound to be lost.

Conditions for Successful Innovation in International Marketing

The need for innovation is of course not specific to international marketing. Innovation is the life-blood of every business whether it is domestic or international. Nonetheless it must be recognised by the international marketer that a firm that operates in many countries has this unique opportunity to cross-fertilise ideas from a variety of cultures, styles, attitudes and patterns of human behaviour. To miss such an opportunity is certainly a regrettable failure to capitalise on one of the most important pay-offs of an international presence.

As we saw earlier, it is very important that managers selected for international work must possess a keen observing skill. Some people are born with such a gift; others develop it through conscious effort. One often finds that competent salesmen develop such a skill in the course of their work. It manifests itself in their ability to notice what is happening around them in the course of an interview. They are able to read letters upside-down; they notice pictures and maps on the wall; they detect little snippets of information from which they can glean the buyer's hobbies and interests.

This is an important personal trait in those who might be responsible for innovation in a firm. But at the same time it must be realised that all the observing skills in the world are not enought to ensure that creative ideas are harnessed and innovation attained. A number of additional conditions must exist in the firm itself if creativity will be able to thrive:

1 *The climate for creative thought must be right*
2 *An effective system for communicating ideas must exist*
3 *Procedures for managing innovation must be developed*

1 The Climate

Creativity seldom thrives in an environment in which senior management discourages ideas. Such discouragement can be overt or be subtle in the form of a non-verbal communication. The boss can stifle creativity by simply looking bored when an idea is presented to him. Alternatively, he can dampen the enthusiasm of his subordinate by asking for a written report instead of going to the trouble of listening to the idea exposed. Suggesting to a person that he ought to discuss an idea with a third party is another way for demotivating a creative manager.

Creativity can best thrive in a firm where ideas are solicited and encouraged. Every person in the organisation must feel that his ideas are wanted and that a receptive ear is always ready to listen to what he wants to say. It is very important that the climate is supportive throughout the firm. It must transcend all levels of management and exist in every functional area. Pockets of creativity in limited areas of the company, for example in product management, advertising or in some specific country do not add up to a creative climate. Creativity must start at the top, with the chief executive, if the climate stands the chance of becoming total and meaningful. The fact that the boss preaches about creativity with some enthusiasm is not enough. He must show interest in practical terms: he must participate in idea-generating activities; he must help to manage ideas, screen them and help to lead them towards commercialisation. A boss who participates in such activities is the best formula for encouraging a creative climate. It may be rightly suggested that by taking such an active part in the process of innovation the boss departs from his strategic role and encroaches into the sphere of activity of his subordinates. A happy balance, has to be struck. The aim of senior participation in the process of innovation must be supportive in character and must be seen as such. Nobody can take exception to this kind of contribution so long as it does not amount to a positive attempt to determine policies or take decisions. Thus the boss who is prepared to take part in the occasional brainstorming session organised in the firm and who can act naturally in such sessions is probably the greatest stimulant to the building of a suitable climate for creativity.

The right climate for creativity is vital for stimulating innovation in a firm that is operating in many countries. This is particularly important in a firm which is organised in a centralised fashion. Individuals who operate in remote outposts to a centrally-formulated plan are much more concerned with the performance of their tasks than generating ideas which might or might not be considered useful by some manager who sits a few thousand miles away. By the sheer philosophy of centralisation foreign personnel are seldom encouraged to put forward ideas as to how the business can be improved or managed in a more economical way. This is the kind of attitude that an effective marketing boss must fight if the firm is to exploit the tremendous opportunity for innovation which the company's multinational presence can offer.

A useful piece of advice to those responsible for international marketing activities: 'Improve your personal *attitude spectrum*'.

What does the phrase *attitude spectrum* mean? Every person responds to an idea with a mixture of feelings. This mixture consists of positive and negative responses. Moreover every person has a different mixture of such responses. A critical person will find many faults in an idea presented to him; he will give it hardly any benefit of the doubt. A tolerant person will see in the idea a lot of good before he detects weaknesses. People of course prefer to present their ideas to the tolerant type because he shows interest, enthusiasm and encouragement. Such a person normally has the ability to attract people who have ideas to offer and knows how to draw these ideas out of them even when they are 'half-baked'.

If we can plot the relationship between the *good* and the *bad* inner responses to an idea as perceived by the average man we shall find that in normal circumstances the bad response will occupy the larger part of the spectrum. Pictorially it could look like Figure 69.

The diagram illustrates how the 'bad' segment diminishes drastically in a tolerant person.

Every person is capable of improving his attitude spectrum through self-discipline and self-awareness. Improving one's spectrum does not imply a change in personality or character. It simply means that one forces oneself to focus, however frustrating it may appear at first, one's intellect, feelings and intuitions on that portion of an idea that is worthwhile. Only then one has earned the right to express doubts and highlight weaknesses. The manager

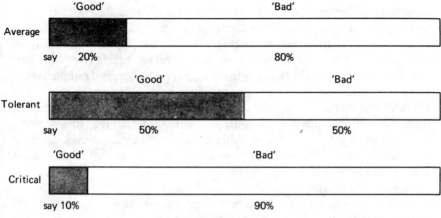

Fig. 69   Attitude spectrum

who can train himself to modify his attitude spectrum from a narrow and negative one to a tolerant and generous one is more likely to obtain a fertile climate for creativity among the various managers who are responsible to him throughout the world. The reward to the firm as a result of such a personal effort can certainly be considerable.

Later on we shall discuss a number of techniques that can be used for generating ideas. The usefulness of these techniques has evoked some controversy. Some firms have found these techniques limited in their value; others have found them highly beneficial in solving problems. The real point to bear in mind is that whether these techniques provide the 'answer to the maiden's prayer' or not is immaterial. If they help to solve problems, well and good. If they do not they are still useful as a stimulus to the development of the climate which we emphasised so strongly. In other words the manager who attempts to use techniques such as brainstorming, synectics or morphological research must realise that there is a far greater benefit in using such methods than just solving immediate problems. The real value of these methods is to act as a prod to creativity and as a manifestation of top management's desire to stimulate the necessary climate for innovation. In this respect a creativity session in which the participants come from various parts of the world can have a miraculous effect on the overall climate.

2 Communicating Ideas

We emphasised earlier how an international firm has an excellent opportunity to derive considerable benefit from the fact that the firm operates in a multi-national and multi-cultural world. We enjoy travelling abroad on holiday partly because we discover new ideas and fresh perceptions about how old routines can be performed. In a firm operating in a large number of markets this process of discovering ideas must be organised in such a way that other parts of the firm can derive full benefit therefrom. Thus if a Unilever subsidiary in Venezuela discovers that Procter & Gamble have undertaken a highly imaginative promotion in the form of a special lottery, it is essential that all parts of the Unilever empire get to know about it. Omitting to communicate such information is of course a serious failure. An alert organisation can probably identify in the aggregate hundreds if not thousands of ideas, schemes and strategies generated in the many countries in which it operates and in the course of a short period. Many of these ideas emanate from the firm's subsidiaries; others originate from the firm's many competitors. A machinery for collating and communicating these ideas must be developed. It is futile to rely on human nature and hope that all these ideas will be communicated through the personal motivation and enthusiasm of the thousands of managers scattered round the globe.

Some international firms have developed a centrally-located department charged with the task of collecting ideas from every company throughout the world and assembling monthly or quarterly bulletins summarising the vast 'input' collected. Such bulletins can be extremely valuable in communicating ideas. However, it is important that the person in charge of this activity knows how to motivate international personnel to send him details of ideas perceived. Offering some sort of reward can help to make people more co-operative, especially in a firm organised as an 'umbrella' structure where the outposts do not feel in any way responsive to the staff services at the centre.

This is an area which in itself calls for managerial creativity. The important point to remember is that without a communication machinery of sorts a vast amount of creative ideas are bound to get lost.

Figure 70 illustrates the haphazard flow of ideas that exists in a firm which has not taken steps to develop communication machinery as against the firm that has decided to formalise the process by establishing a communication channel for ideas. Inevitably the latter is better equipped to 'catch' ideas in a systematic and effective way thus reducing the rate of 'evaporation' of creative thinking.

3 Procedures for Managing Innovation

Having a large number of ideas is essential in a firm that wishes to innovate. When we discussed product policy we mentioned the need for a large number of ideas before the marketer can hope to identify an idea which deserves commercialisation. We emphasised how in some industries one needs as many as thousands of ideas for subsequent screening. This is a pretty formidable raw material.

The various techniques which we shall explore later can help to generate a large number of ideas. Furthermore, collecting ideas from the various operations round the world can also help to assemble a significant creative 'input'. However, an idea is only one bit of raw material; it is not an end in itself. Ideas must be screened and analysed in accordance with clearly-defined criteria. Without such procedures a firm can easily get smothered by an

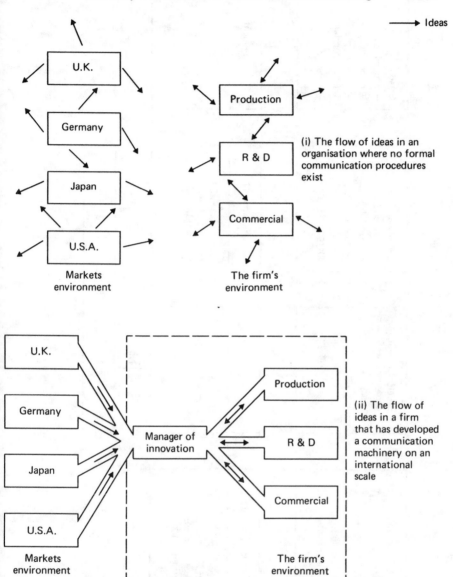

Fig. 70   The flow of ideas
(i) in firms without formal idea communication procedures
(ii) in firms that have developed a machinery for communicating ideas on a global
scale

avalanche of wonderful ideas which are of little practical value.

Figure 71 illustrates a simple and logical procedure which those responsible for managing innovation in an international environment ought to pursue. The flow diagram shown can of course be adapted to the specific needs of each company. However, what is important is that the firm must set up a practical

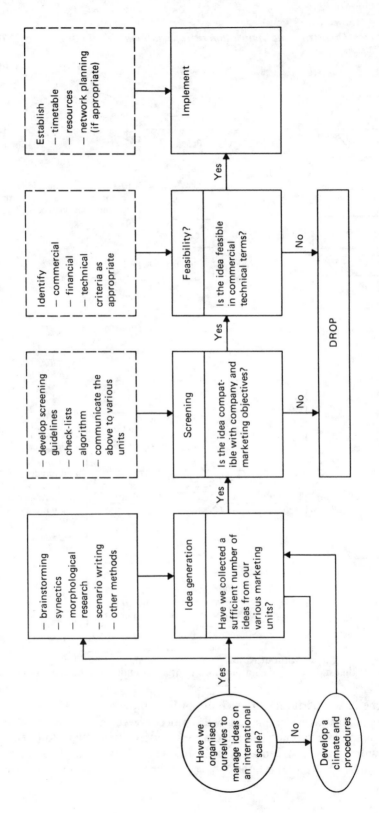

Fig. 71   Procedure for managing innovation

method for dealing with the fruit of the firm's creative climate. Without such procedures many good ideas cannot possibly receive the attention which they deserve.

A novel idea which is gaining some popularity is the appointment of a manager of innovation or a director of innovation. The title is immaterial—the thinking behind this concept is more important. Such a person is a member of the international marketing team and his main duties can be summarised thus:

To take all the necessary steps for developing a suitable climate for creativity and innovation.

To act as the focal point for collecting and disseminating ideas throughout the organisation.

To establish procedures for screening ideas in accordance with criteria agreed with marketing colleagues in the international organisation.

To co-ordinate the implementation of ideas found appropiate during the screening process.

To monitor the success of ideas implemented and make recommendations for the application of such innovations in other markets.

The director of innovation can of course assume a much larger role by dealing with innovation in other functions. In such an event he may have to be responsible for or closely associated with the R & D function. This may create certain problems which are outside the scope of this chapter. For the purpose of our discussions here it is probably better to assume that the role to be ascribed to the director of innovation is a more limited one and relates in the main to innovation in marketing and to other functional 'input' only to the extent that it has a direct influence on the marketing activities of the firm.

Techniques for Generating Ideas

As stressed earlier in this chapter many techniques exist for helping to generate ideas in sufficient quantities to form the basis of subsequent screening. The wise manager does not allow failures in this connection to disillusion him from continuing to use such methods. He should treat the various methods in question not only as idea generating devices but also as stimulants to the development of the appropiate climate for creativity.

Many techniques have been developed over the years and the literature is rife with many variations on a number of basic methods. The person who seeks to use these techniques must not be mesmerised by their ostensible intricacies and must not be afraid of modifying them to suit the style of his company and the specific requirements of a given situation. These techniques exist to help managers and not to obsess them. There are no right and wrong ways of generating ideas and if a manager finds that through a subtle deviation from what a textbook recommends he can attain better results he should feel completely free to do so.

We shall discuss briefly the following methods:

Brainstorming
Synectics
Morphological analysis
The various technological forecasting methods:
   Scenario writing
   Delphi technique
   'Input' 'output' tables

1 Brainstorming

The word *brainstorming* was coined by Alex Osborn and is described fully in his book *Applied Imagination*.

Very briefly the technique is to assemble a small group of eight to ten individuals and give them a specific problem to solve. In other words 'normative' creativity is usually sought. Creativity is said to be normative when ideas are sought to solve identified and detailed needs, problems or objectives.

A few general rules normally apply to brainstorming sessions:

(a) The group must suspend temporarily any judicial thinking. In other words they must learn to suspend judgement.
(b) 'Freewheeling' should be encouraged. The wilder the idea the better; it is easier to tame down than to think up.
(c) Quantity is wanted; the greater the number the higher the probability of good ideas being included.
(d) Combination and improvement should be encouraged. In addition to contributing ideas of their own participants should be encouraged to suggest how the ideas of others may be combined to yield yet another idea.

A long list of ideas should normally emerge from a brainstorming session. A thorough screening and evaluation process should follow for each idea, however absurd it may at first appear. It is very important to remember that an apparently absurd idea can stimulate and lead to useful ones.

2 Synectics

The word *synectics*, from the Greek, means the joining together of differently and apparently irrelevant elements. Synectics as a technique was developed by William Gordon.

Synectics aims at the integration of diverse individuals and disciplines into a problem-stating—problem-solving group. Members of a synectics group should ideally represent as many functions or activities as possible. A person who has held a number of jobs of diverse experience is usually better equipped than the person whose career was concentrated on one job.

Age is unimportant but experience has shown that twenty-five to forty is a suitable range. Under the age of twenty-five a person normally does not possess the breadth of experience; over forty a man lacks the tolerance needed when exploring seemingly unorthodox ideas.

Persons with an independent spirit and some entrepreneurial attitudes have been found more suitable than those whose entrepreneurship has been inhibited. Educational criteria should revolve around the 'metaphoric potential' of each discipline. This means that the discipline in question must be capable of apparently irrelevant analogies which can offer sources of new viewpoints. Thus, if the subject matter is *camouflage*, the zoologist can easily draw parallels from the animal world such as the way the chameleon changes his colours and the way other animals place themselves in backgrounds which hide them from sight. This kind of analogy can be a very fruitful source of ideas and viewpoints. Some disciplines have a better metaphoric potential than others. Biology is probably more suitable than law.

People selected for synectics groups should also possess the following characteristics:

> Emotional maturity
> Capacity to generalise
> High level of stimulation
> Ability to take risks
> Commitment
> Non-status orientation

The first task is to develop a group which is free of the traditional inter-personal tensions and undercurrents that characterise groups at work. This can of course be a fairly long process if the synetics group represents managers from various cultural backgrounds as one would expect such a group to be in an international marketing environment. In a normal group two elements govern the behavioural pattern of its members:

(a) each member perceives a meeting as a contest
(b) each member carries into the meeting a preconceived idea of his own image.

Every endeavour should be made to mitigate the disturbance that these two elements can create on group effectiveness. At the same time the sensitivity of members should be safeguarded if their creativity and participation are not to suffer. This is particularly important in the case of a multinational group. It can take as long as a year to establish an effective synectics group and therefore unlike brainstorming which can be organised on an *ad hoc* basis synectics groups must be of a more permanent nature. These groups are set up to develop solutions to problems submitted from every part of the organisation. However, as managers often imagine problems where in fact none exists the synectics groups must be skilful at diagnosing problems or the underlying causes thereof. The aim throughout is to harness the specific knowledge of each member of the team in identifying ideas and possible solutions from his particular discipline. The botanist seeks to illustrate how the world of plants deals with analogous problems. The zoologist tries to draw parallel ideas from the animal world. The archaeologist extrapolates from his own experience and knowledge.

Synectics is an exciting technique for its participants. It has proved highly effective in evolving solutions to thorny problems. The point to remember is that even where the firm's exposure to the synectics approach has yielded nothing the firm must console itself with the thought that the climate for creativity has been vastly enriched through the use of this method. This is not a' mean pay-off.

3 Morphological Analysis

This technique is also known as *morphological method*. It was devised by Fritz Zwicky, the famous astrophysicist and jet engine pioneer. This method aims to single out the most important dimensions of a specific problem and then examine all the relationships among them. Morphology means structure and the technique seeks to explore all the possible alternatives that a multi-dimensional matrix may yield.

The easiest way to describe this technique is through a simple illustration:

'A firm operating in the immensely competitive packaging field is looking for new product ideas. The aim is to identify something new or cheaper thus escaping from the rigours of competition.'

One dimension of the problem could be the *shape* of the new pack. Another dimension could be the *contents* of the pack. The third dimension could be the *materials* (or combination thereof) from which the pack could be made.

The relationship between these three dimensions can be represented in Figure 72.

Assuming that these three dimensions fully define the problem there would then be $7 \times 7 \times 9 = 441$ cells. Each cell represents an idea. Some of these ideas may be clearly useless—others may be worth exploring. What is important is that this method helps to generate an enormous number of ideas.

The next step is to let the imagination loose on each cell and seek to identify how far it deserves further study and how far it may fulfil the firm's criteria of acceptance within the company's objectives.

Our illustration showed three dimensions. The method is of course capable

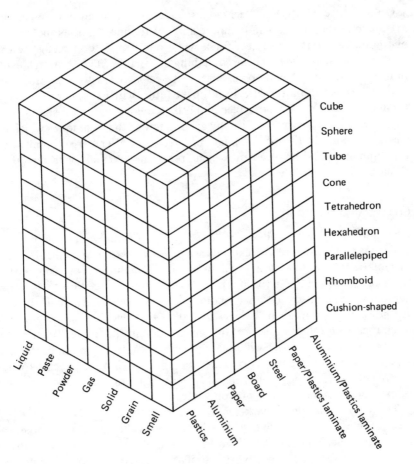

Fig. 72 Morphological analysis of a new pack idea

of having more than three dimensions although at that point they could not be represented in a pictorial form. Where four or more dimensions are defined one has to list all the permutations and these can amount to many thousands. Some companies use a simple computer programme for matching all the cells and listing them. Such lists are indeed a formidable material for creative exploration.

4 The Various Technological Forecasting Methods

These techniques have been devised in the main to assist organisations to forecast future events and/or environmental pressures. The aim of these methods is to help planners to identify how technological, political, social and other types of pressures may affect the direction of the organisations whose future they seek to plan.

On the face of it these techniques have little relevance to creativity, inasmuch as they are aids to planning and not to innovation. Nonetheless if one ponders about the subject for a while one would soon recognise that *planning* and *innovation* do have something in common. They both relate to a futurity which is yet unknown. The first seeks to create a future whilst mitigating risks; the latter seeks to equip the future with new, better or cheaper products or ideas. To be effective both activities need foresight if not entrepreneurial clairvoyance. In any event a few of the techniques which are clustered under the title of *technological forecasting* offer a great opportunity for stimulation and involvement which are so fundamental for the creativity climate.

(a) SCENARIO WRITING

A scenario is a logical and plausible recording of future events with careful attention to timing and correlations wherever the latter are salient. It is a systematic attempt to write about a 'future world' in the form of a summary of the events that are likely to take place in the future in relation to a specific company, an industry or an economic activity. Thus Herman Kahn and Anthony Weiner in their *The Year 2000: A Framework for Speculation* attempted to produce an important scenario about the future. Whether the events described will or will not happen in reality is not important. It represents an intelligent and genuine attempt at writing a forecast for the future with a certain level of probability built into it through using a number of extrapolative methods of proven value.

To the international marketer such a document can be a source of inspiration when seeking to determine a choice for the future direction of the firm's strategic thinking. What can be more useful to managerial creativity than identifying such perspectives? Thus if a scenario prepared by a competent group of people predicts that certain markets will develop more rapidly than others, owing to the anticipated discovery of a certain commodity there, surely, the manager who is lucky enough to acquire such a report is in a better position to innovate in respect of such markets than those who do not possess such information.

(b) DELPHI TECHNIQUE

This technique was originally developed in the USA by the RAND Corporation. It is, in effect, a logical extension of the well-practised method of the 'jury of executive opinion'. It attempts to integrate the opinions of experts without sacrificing or compromising individuals' suggestions and ideas.

A panel of 'wise men' is asked to give judgement on important issues such as 'In what year (if ever) do you expect electric cars to capture 10 per cent of the automobile markets?'

Through iterative questioning, the members of the panel are invited to reconsider and possibly revise their original opinions. Whilst the technique is mainly used for forecasting technological changes, some companies find this technique is a useful vehicle for generating creative climate and innovation inside the firm.

(c) 'INPUT' 'OUTPUT' TABLES

This is a technique developed by W. W. Leontieff, aiming at highlighting the interrelations between industries or sectors of the economy. Leontieff's matrix of the American economy has now been emulated by a score of nations, including the UK. Briefly, the economy of a country is divided into a hundred or so industrial sectors. The matrix shows each sector twice: once in a *row*, as an *output*; once in a *column*, as an *input*. The rows, in other words, show all the sales made by one sector to other sectors including itself while the columns represent the purchases of all sectors in turn from a given sector. Since the classifications of supplier and purchasing industries are identical on both axes of the matrix the 'input'/'output' tables tend to be in a state of total equilibrium.

'Input'/'output' tables have been developed either by governments or by independent research agencies in relation to past economic performances. Tables summarising the past are purely of academic interest. However, a number of such tables now exist in relation to the future of a number of economies. These tables incorporate the synthesis of a wealth of forecasts made by many industries, trade associations and representatives of economic sectors. Whilst the accuracy of such tables cannot be validated until the future has taken place, they form a superb basis upon which to establish forecasts for specific industries and companies. Moreover they are an important tool for helping managers to think laterally about their planning task in general and marketing strategies in particular.

Other techniques exist for helping to generate ideas and enrich the firm's creativity thus leading to successful innovation. The international marketer who recognises the importance of creativity as an ingredient of dynamic, imaginative and profitable marketing should try to manipulate these methods in his endeavour to stimulate an appropiate climate throughout the firm. A climate which tolerates and encourages creativity is probably the greatest safeguard in the firm's battle to remain an acknowledged 'satisfier' of a vast and complex marketplace.

Introductory Note
to the Cases and their Use

The cases incorporated in this book represent fairly typical situations that occur in international marketing. They do not purport to describe examples of effective or ineffective marketing. They are simply meant to provide a vehicle for group or individual exploration of the elements that make decisions on a global scale more complex and very often more demanding. The ideal forum for using these cases is in the context of short courses or seminars on international marketing. A number of these cases cover a wide range of problems and lend themselves to a fairly broad range of discussion. Where the audience has multinational experience the cases can give an excellent opportunity to develop a useful exchange of views and a cross-fertilisation of ideas. Managers from different countries have different ways of tackling problems—these cases are spcifically aimed at the need to ventilate such variances in approach.

A few of these cases are shown under fictitious names although, in the main, the facts represent realistic problems with which the author in his consultancy career has had to grapple.

Following each case a number of suggested topics for discussion are incorporated.

Alimentation Générale SA

A European distributor of fruit and vegetables discovers significant disparities in *per capita* consumption of citrus products in the various countries it serves. This is not an unusual occurrence in international marketing. The case lends itself to an exploration of the way comparative market research should be approached.

Scales Industries Inc.

This case relates to a fairly typical situation where a company operating in a large number of markets has a major educational problem to solve, viz. how to educate the international organisation to accept the *marketing concept*. This is a very difficult problem and there is no easy solution to it. However, it is a topic that should encourage some creative thinking among those responsible for changing a company's orientation on a multinational scale.

Decrolux Limited

This company has developed a new range of high-quality washable wallcovering. Essentially the firm's product is *design* and as such the taste of the international consumer differs enormously. A controversy has developed among the company's senior managers as to whether the range can be standardised for world markets. The case lends itself to a thorough coverage of this important topic. Furthermore a useful discussion of the organisational implications of an effective marketing department seeking to cater for international markets can be derived from this case.

KLM Royal Dutch Airlines—Air Cargo

The True Price of Distribution

KLM have developed a system for helping their international clientele to calculate the *true value of their distribution*. Although air freight is often more expensive than other means of transport if one adds all the direct and indirect elements of effective logistics the true total cost may favour air cargo in many situations. The case describes the KLM system. It is a useful vehicle for discussing the role of physical distribution in international marketing. It offers also an opportunity to explore the whole question as to 'What is our product?'

Medi-Systems International Inc.

An international pharmaceutical company decides, by way of a major diversification, to enter the 'turnkey' hospital business. There are around two hundred countries in the world. The newly appointed managing director of the project has to identify the best opportunity-markets to aim for. He also has to decide on the kind of 'product' to develop.

This case offers an opportunity to discuss the whole question of international market research, marketing profile analysis and product planning.

Pioneer International Limited

A firm operating in a multi-national, multi-market and multi-product environment is facing the problem of how to organise the corporate structure as well as the marketing function. The options are numerous and the aim of this case is to identify the most relevant ideas as to how the organisation should be structured so as to optimise opportunities and marketing effectiveness.

Case 1

Alimentation Générale SA

Alimentation Générale SA is one of the leading European distributors of fruit and vegetables. Most of the produce it distributes is imported from all parts of the world.

Among the many items it handles are citrus products. Market research has recently shown that the firm has a 50 per cent market share of the orange business in country X. However, the information collected is disturbing the management of the firm in so far as it indicates that orange consumption in country X is less than half of the neighbouring countries. In other words whilst the market share is excellent the management cannot understand why concumption figures are so poor. Further research was undertaken to find out the reasons for such a disparity.

The outcome of the second phase of the research was quite inconclusive. Consumer buying habits and eating habits appeared to be similar both in country X and its neighbouring countries. The general attitude to the value of Vitamin C as a means of preventing colds and influenza was identical in both territories. The results were quite puzzling. The problem was simply a smaller consumption *per capita* and a lower primary demand. The marketing management of the firm felt that until the underlying reasons for the lower primary demand were diagnosed it would be difficult to evolve a suitable strategy for correcting the situation.

Topics for Discussion

Disparity in *per capita* consumption among countries is a frequent occurrence. Such disparities often occur as a result of historical supply/demand developments or sources of supply which were specific to one country and not to another, as a result of geo-political circumstances.

This case can be approached in a number of ways:

1 Indentify the kind of information that you would like to have in order to diagnose the reasons for the disparity. The marketing profile analysis is a useful tool in this connection. It can highlight the areas of disparity.

2 A good look at the consumption figures and a study of their comparability is an essential task. It is possible that country X gives figures in tons and the

other countries provide figures in different units. Furthermore the oranges imported by country X may come from a source that grows smaller fruit hence the consumption in terms of weight is smaller but the consumption in terms of number of oranges is not as small *per capita* as was thought.

Case 2

Scales Industries Inc.

Scales Industries Inc. is a large international company operating in about sixty countries in the field of electronics, calculators, business machinery and allied products. The firm employs over 50 000 people throughout the world with about 6000 personnel in managerial and 'white collar' positions.

The firm is organised as an 'umbrella' structure with the result that most marketing decisions are taken at local level. Similarly most management development activities are planned and carried out by the training personnel in each country. A central service is available to assist all subsidiaries in this connection.

By the nature of the business and the large number of scientists and technologists it employs the company has developed a radical production orientation. Products are being developed and manufactured and the commercial side has to go out and sell. Lately difficulties have occurred in so far as a few products that were expected to become major successes have yielded very disappointing results thus generating substantial losses.

The President of the Company has decided to change the firm's orientation from the traditional production orientation which characterised it until now to a market-orientated philosophy. In other words the President has decided to adopt the *marketing concept* throughout the firm. He fully realised the implications and the size of the task. He recognised that to be able to implement such a change in managerial attitude in a highly decentralised firm a far-reaching programme of management development would have to be undertaken.

The centrally located Management Development Adviser expressed serious misgivings about the ability to propagate the marketing creed in a firm where local managers have always been so independent. He feels that about 3000 people will have to undergo training programmes of varying lengths and sophistication to create the basic awareness of what marketing is all about. He believes that until this is done no progress can be made towards changing the general orientation of the organisation on a global scale. The Personnel Director at the centre who is responsible for senior appointments claims that any attempt at training more than 300 people per annum will create havoc in the firm. 'The only two organisations in human history that could do better than this', he claims 'were the early Christians and the Communists'.

The President is not impressed by this argument. He feels that if the change in the firm's orientation is justified in the light of market circumstances an imaginative and possibly a non-traditional approach should be evolved.

Topics for Discussion

This is not an untypical situation. The problem of educating a large organisation to a new philosophy is an enormously dificult task.
Explore:

1 Ideas for training thousands of a firm's managers in modern marketing principles without sending them all on courses.
2 How the marketing concept can be promoted internationally among the sixty companies throughout the world.

The problem presented can be summarised as: 'How can we market marketing on a global scale?' After all if one does not know how to market this concept one is less likely to know how to market products.

Decrolux Limited

Decrolux Limited manufactures a range of decorative products used in the home mainly by 'do-it-yourself' enthusiasts. If offers paints, strippers, adhesives and allied products.

The Company recently decided to launch a range of high-quality washable metallic wallcoverings based on printed aluminium foil/paper laminate.

Whilst the firm's new product had a number of unique features–self adhesive quality, washability, long life—the marketing personnel recognised that the product would only sell well if the actual designs were acceptable to the market-place.

Mr Rowland, a well-known designer, was engaged on a consultancy basis to assemble a collection of designs. He was instructed to develop a range which was 'modern, attractive and saleable'. The Marketing Director felt that Rowland's experience and flair were a safeguard against the wrong designs being selected for the new range. On the other hand, Rowland's experience was based on the UK market and he had very little experience in foreign markets.

The Controversy

A major controversy flared up among the firm's senior personnel regarding the way the wallcovering range should be developed for international markets. Mr Butterworth, the Production Director, felt that an international range should be assembled and that the range should consist of about forty designs—each design reproduced in two or three colourways. He believed that it should be artistically possible to produce a range which would meet the taste of most markets especially those enjoying a high standard of living. 'I do not see the point of trying to satisfy the whims and caprices of potential consumers in every small country' he emphasised.

Mr Butterworth was a great believer in the validity of the Pareto principle and kept stressing that a range should be developed 'capable of satisfying the needs and tastes of the 20 per cent markets likely to absorb 80 per cent of our output'. 'Let us forget the others,' he kept remonstrating. As the new wallcovering product (which did not as yet have a name) was meant to be manufactured initially in the UK factory only, Butterworth's views carried some weight. His main argument was that having one standard range for the whole world would save considerable costs in the following ways:

1 Fewer printing rollers would be needed. The cost of each set of rollers per design was estimated at £1000. He feared that if the international marketing boys had their way the firm would need to invest in as many as 300 designs.
2 A standard range would involve a much smaller inventory problem.
3 Pattern books—an essential promotional tool—could be standardised thus showing an enormous saving.
4 Quality control would be much more economic where a small range is involved.
5 Bigger batches of production would help to ensure consistency of colour and print quality, an important selling point in the wallcovering business.

The opposite view was taken by Mr Foss, the Director of International Marketing. His view was supported by all the Managing Directors of the selling subsidiaries abroad. Foss had conducted research into his main international markets and came to the unhappy conclusion that the tastes of these markets differed so drastically that each one needed a separate range although he admitted that a small hard core of designs had universal appeal. Foss objected most vehemently to the principle that the range must meet the needs of the UK market first. He felt that the international markets which he served offered a greater potential in terms of volume of sales and that each major market such as Germany, France and Benelux deserved a separate range and pattern books. He further went on to suggest that trying to market a UK range on the Continent of Europe was a waste of time.

More specifically Foss was able to produce evidence to show that the French favoured floral designs and preferably embossed. The Germans liked very modern, slightly abstract designs. The Dutch preferred ultra-conservative patterns. The Belgians varied according to whether they were Flemish or French speakers. The man in Australia had totally different needs, although he conceded that half the range shown to him could be incorporated in an Australasian pattern book.

Other Difficulties

In addition to the question of design, research seemed to indicate that in some countries wallcovering was *overlapped* at the joints rather than *butted* as was the case in the UK. This could make a significant technical difference to the type of designs which were capable of meeting the needs of the two joining techniques. When designs are butted they must provide for excellent definition of pattern at the edges; when they are overlapped a blank edge must be provided to facilitate the overlapping process. Certain designs are easier to produce for the one joining process than the other.

Two other important difficulties were identified: one was the question of a universally accepted brand name and the other was the question of languages in which instructions were to appear inside the packs and on the cartons.

Foss was unable to think of a suitable name that might be acceptable, pronounceable, easy to spell and easy to remember in all major languages. However, as he was pressing for different ranges for all main markets he saw no disadvantage in using two or three trademarks. Moreover, he felt that each market should have the printed matter incorporated in the packs written in the language of the recipient country. He saw no difficulty in sticking simple labels on the product in different languages. He fully appreciated the extra cost but emphasised the communication value of such a move in stimulating sales.

The Organisation

The company was organised on a functional basis as described in Figure 73. The Production Director, Butterworth, was responsible for the two UK plants and a Belgian plant. In each plant he had a works manager. The decision as to which plant would produce what was basically that of the Director's planning staff. This was a source of great irritation to the marketing personnel and especially to the foreign distributors.

Marketing was split into two: Marketing Home (Mr Winters) and Marketing International (Mr Foss). Both gentlemen were Directors of the Main Board but by virtue of age, length of service and experience Winters was the more senior of the two. This seniority often manifested itself in Winters having the last word in any disagreement, however unjustified his decision might be. Furthermore the Director of Marketing (Home) was in charge of three product/brand managers and their departments. These departments wielded considerable influence on the direction that their respective products were allowed to take in international markets. This exasperated both Foss (Director of Marketing—International) and the Managing Directors of the selling subsidiaries in France, Benelux, Germany and Australia. Agents and distributors also felt that their specific needs were being relegated to a secondary place and that insufficient attention was given to them by the product managers. Winters took the view: 'Our products must first meet the needs of the very important UK market and only then should they meet the special requirements of other markets. Moreover our policy must be not to incorporate any changes in the products if it involves excessive expenditure.' As we saw earlier he found a great ally in Butterworth who also supported this narrow view.

Facing the Problem

Whilst hitherto the fundamental differences described generated some heated arguments, they never caused major problems because the firm's products

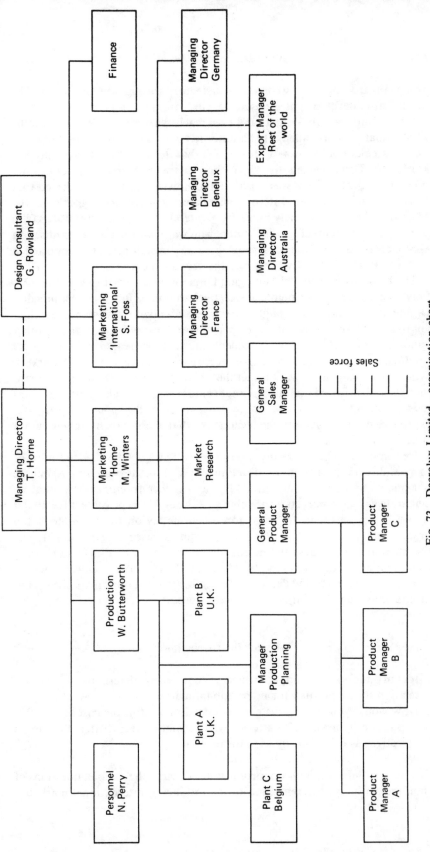

Fig. 73 Decrolux Limited—organisation chart

were standard and sales were very satisfactory throughout the world. The wallcovering development brought the controversy to a head.

Messrs Butterworth, Winters and Foss reached a deadlock. Winters saw the whole situation as a challenge to his authority and sought to exploit it towards solving an old 'hobby horse' of his: he felt that the firm should have only one Marketing Director and the distinction between Home Marketing and International Marketing was artificial and unwise. He further believed that Foss should become an International Sales Manager responsible to the Marketing Director (namely himself—Winters) and should have little say in product policy. In other words Winters who was favouring a standardisation approach translated it into a centralised organisation. Foss supported a differentiation philosophy. This was the crux of the argument.

The boss, Mr Horne, the Managing Director, was forced to intervene. He fully appreciated the two points of view but had some difficulty in taking sides. Of the two schools of thought he tended to favour the standardisation approach; he agreed that it might prove more cost effective. On the other hand, having developed an excellent product he feared that a purely production-orientated approach might jeopardise success in world markets. What worried him most was the fact that this product was a new departure for the firm and he feared that success might elude them through a serious error of judgement. The nature of the controversy and the polarised attitudes expressed by his Directors made him feel that the company might ruin a superb development.

He summarised his misgivings in the following way: 'Our objective must be to maximise our profits on this development. Competitors are sure to imitate our quality and designs fairly quickly and it is therefore imperative that we penetrate as many markets as possible and as quickly as possible. I feel that it would be wrong for us to spend too much money on printing rollers and promotional costs. Surely there must be a compromise range that might meet the maximum happiness of the maximum number. . . . Please stop being emotional about the matter and find out all the relevant facts which would enable us to reach a sound decision. Remember that the objective is maximum profits, minimum investment and speedy success. . . .'

Topics for Discussion

1 Identify the kind of 'input' which is required to determine a policy in relation to the product for international markets.
2 How would you resolve the controversy described in the case?
3 Explore organisational patterns which might meet better the firm's objectives as described by Mr Horne.

The case offers a good opportunity to discuss the whole question of standardisation or differentiation of the product in international markets.

KLM Royal Dutch Airlines—Air Cargo

The True Price of Distribution

In an effort to market its air cargo service more effectively KLM decided to develop a system whereby they could help their international clientele to calculate the *true value of their distribution*. The underlying aim was to compare the total cost of distribution based on air freight as against other means of transport. KLM recognised that although air cargo may appear more expensive than other means of transport such as shipping, if one takes the total cost including packing, documentation, insurance, handling, inventory carrying charges, etc. air freight can yield important savings in many areas. They further realised that such comparisons are quantitative and lend themselves to accurate analysis.

The Test of Time

Under the title the *test of time* KLM developed a computer programme for analysing the total cost of distribution of a product for any given twelve months period. The computer system enabled KLM to compare the cost of distribution of a product in various markets. It could tell the marketer that air cargo would be economical for one segment and perhaps not so economical for another. Furthermore, detailed and confidential print-outs summarising the results of the analysis were made available to the airline's existing and potential customers.

The computer programme sought to compare the following costs:

A Direct Costs

Under this heading all costs pertaining to distribution and procurement were examined. In particular the following items were included:

1 PACKING

It was felt that in the case of air cargo packing costs would be less expensive because less packing was necessary. By the same token unpacking expenses would be lower and probably pre-sale refurbishing would not be necessary.

2 INSURANCE RATES

These would be lower by air because risks were normally less, given the shorter time en route, little or no trans-shipment and less opportunity for pilferage or damage.

3 DOCUMENTATION

The airway bill being the simplest document in transportation it was recognised that the cost of documentation in the case of air cargo would be much lower than in shipping.

4 TRANSPORT TO DEPARTURE POINT

As a rule this item would be less costly in so far as airports were usually closer to factories than seaports.

5 LOADING AND TRANSLOADING

Cost nothing at all at airports; unloading on arrival would be free at airports but charged at seaports.

6 CUSTOMS DUTY

This item would depend on the basis used for calculating duty. It would be lower if the basis was gross weight or FOB value in country of origin. It might be more if the basis was CIF value as indeed is the case in the illustration shown in Figure 68.

7 STORAGE CHARGES

Probably non-existent since goods pass through airports quickly.

8 CUSTOMS CLEARANCE

Savings could be attained in airports because the process was shown to take only a couple of hours.

9 FINAL DELIVERY CHARGES

Thought to be lower with air freight because air shipments normally arrive closer to final destination than surface shipments.

All these items could be studied in respect of each commodity or product and in relation to each country or market, both exported or imported. Given

DIRECT COST COMPARISON PRESENT METHOD VERSUS PROJECTED AIR

CODE A3

NUMBER OF SHIPMENTS		SURFACE AIR FREIGHT	PRESENT METHOD 64 38	WT IN LB CURR IN US PROJECTED AIR 52
WEIGHTS	GROSS		59,943	57,604
	NETT		48,003	48,003
	TARE		11,940	9,601
DIRECT COST	11 INVOICE VALUE		220,590·24	220,590·24
	12 PACKING		365·10	316·11
	13 INSURANCE		766·68	4,032·28
	15 TRANSP TO PORT OF DEPARTURE		4,728·00	979·27
	16 HANDLING ON DEPARTURE		1,222·74	
	18 MAIN TRANSPORTATION		7,626·33	13,876·96
	19 CUSTOMS DUTY		42,792·67	43,610·29
	21 UNLOADING		549·72	
	22 HANDLING ON ARRIVAL		422·28	230·42
	23 PORT STORAGE		366·87	
	24 CUSTOMS CLEARANCE		1,455·57	1,040·00
	25 FINAL DELIVERY		920·52	518·44
	TOTAL LANDED COST		281,806·72	285,194·02

Fig. 74   Direct cost comparison surface versus projected air transport

all the relevant information KLM's computer study sought to report the comparative costs by air and by other methods of transportation. This was the jumping-off point for a deeper study of the indirect costs.

The example shown in Figure 74 demonstrates the comparative direct distribution costs for one commodity, sent during one year, from the United States to Great Britain. The figures actually show that the use of air would be more expensive to the tune of a difference in total landed cost of 1·2 percent. However, it was pointed out by the KLM analysts that this insignificant increase would be more than off-set once the indirect costs were calculated and incorporated in the analysis.

B Indirect Costs

Under this heading the analysis would cover:

1 THE CAPITAL COST OF GOODS IN TRANSIT

The theory here was that considerable capital was normally invested in distribution activities, in inventory in warehouses and inventory in transit.

Whilst goods were en route, the capital invested in them was not available for other purposes. KLM emphasised that air freight's shorter transit time should yield a faster capital turnover and this in turn should save money.

2 INVENTORY CARRYING COSTS

KLM attached great significance to this aspect of the total distribution process of a modern firm. They recognised that successful marketing called for the right amount of goods to be available at the right place without a risk of stocks running out. The need to keep safety stocks especially where a higher demand may occur inevitably involved the firm in capital commitments.

The cost of inventory was influenced by many factors, such as the cost of premises, overheads, personnel and office space. Reserves were needed to hand to cover orders which would be placed while refills were en route and of course the capital employed in such reserves was totally immobilised. Furthermore, it was felt that there were risks of obsolescence, exchange rate fluctuations, model changes. Many of these risks would be reduced if shipments could be acquired faster. Inventory costs could represent as much as 15–35 per cent of the value of goods in stock. Because air transport is faster it could cut back *lead time* and a reduced lead time means lower inventory carrying costs.

In a very well-designed pamphlet KLM described the process of how the size of safety stock should be determined. They stressed the need to look at the length of lead time and market fluctuations. Safety stock was an important portion of total stock. Given a pre-set order pattern, if lead time could be shortened (through the use of air freight), then the period needed to be covered

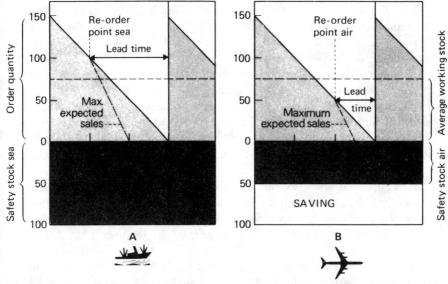

Diagram A pictures inventory stock as it might appear if sea freight were used. Over a period of three months 150 items are ordinarily sold. Two months lead time are needed to get a new order in stock. Thus, under normal circumstances, re-orders must be made when working stock drops to 100. However, sales may soar unexpectedly. Let us assume they may reach 200 items over two months. Since the new order was placed when working stock was down to 100, an additional safety stock of 100 items will be needed to service the maximum possible demand.

Diagram B is an illustration of what happens when the switch is made to air. Lead time is reduced by half. Orders can be placed later, and only half as much need be kept on hand as safety stock.

Fig. 75   Inventory management—surface versus air

by safety stock would be shorter and the size of safety stock could be smaller. Thus KLM's main argument was that using air freight would make it possible to meet market fluctuations better. Moreover, they argued that air freight would promote more efficient inventory management and as a result general stockturn would increase.

Figure 75 is taken from the KLM promotional booklet that describes the methodology that was developed for calculating the *true price of distribution*.

Promoting the Service

A very imaginative and attractive booklet was designed by KLM to explain how their computer model worked and the kind of information that was needed in order to compare total costs by air with other means of transportation.

The list of data collected from customers would include facts drawn from the invoices of exporters, clearing agents (customs brokers) and forwarders. Bills of lading and air waybills, insurance certificates and packing lists wherever necessary would be requested.

The data on the worksheets would go into the computer and the resultant printouts (altogether six of them) would be available to the customer. These printouts would provide a detailed look at an organisation's distribution or procurement systems. They would also form the basis for KLM's final report and recommendation to the client. In other words KLM have in fact taken upon themselves to act as consultants to their customers—a role which would probably be welcome in many situations.

KLM's approach was based on an understanding of the logistics process and the fact that air or shipping transportation are only links in a very much more complicated chain of operations. Their philosophy was succinctly summarised under the heading *KLM as part of the product*:

'Those who know of interesting overseas markets, whose demand would justify overseas warehousing costs—as well as those who use surface freight now and who find that overseas market demand makes the necessary overseas

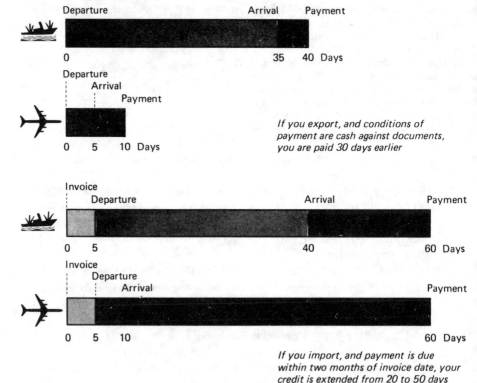

Fig. 76   Cash flow performance in surface and air transport

warehouses too expensive to maintain—often find that air freight simplifies the marketing picture.'

'Those who do business in Europe, who deal with more than one European country, often chalk up substantial savings by working out of one central warehouse. This allows them to take advantage of low bulk shipping rates over intercontinental long-haul routes. Goods can be consolidated at a central warehouse for export outside Europe. Bulk-breaking for import to multiple destinations in Europe, after the long haul, is similarly advantageous. . . .'

'Sound distribution systems add value to products, and it is often true that the fastest distribution systems are the soundest, for they can spell the difference between profitable marketing and loss. This is one reason why, when their aircraft participate in a product's distribution, KLM feel they have become part of that product. . . .'

Among other interesting charts included in the booklet described KLM incorporated Figure 76 which aimed to emphasise the value of air freight as a method of improving cash flow.

Topics for discussion

1 What in your opinion is the nature of the *product* that KLM seek to offer?
2 The booklet issued by KLM represents an interesting way to promote the service which the firm offers. Discuss the promotional value of such a tool on an international scale. Can its effectiveness be measured?
3 Undoubtedly the KLM approach is based on considerable creativity. Explore its applicability to other international marketing activities especially where the firm's product is a service which offers an important link in a total commercial effort. This case offers a good opportunity to discuss the whole question of total logistics in international marketing.

Medi-Systems International Inc. (M.S.I.)

Medi-Systems International Inc. is a subsidiary company of one of the largest international pharmaceutical firms. It was first set up by way of a major diversification from the parent company's over-reliance on a small, albeit exceedingly profitable, range of ethical drugs. The philosophy behind the MSI development was the notion that there is a substantial global need for the development design and building of 'turnkey' hospitals. Brief research has indicated that many countries, especially the emerging OPEC economies, would welcome the opportunity of placing orders for a total hospital system. Such a system would include the total design and building work, equipment, supplies, recruitment, selection and training of personnel, and the actual start-up of the hospital activities.

MSI was organised to run its affairs in an independent fashion from the parent company. Substantial funds were set aside for developing this business. The parent Board's instructions to Dr. Herrmann, the Chief Executive of MSI were:

'Your objectives are:
1 To develop the 'package hospital' concept on an international scale.
2 To attain a break-even point within two years.
3 To attain a 10% return on investment during the next two years.
4 To attain 20% R.O.I. in subsequent years.
    In selecting the most suitable geographical areas for development attempt to ensure that the countries thus selected are:
    (a) Politically stable.
    (b) Large enough to need a number of hospitals over a fairly short period.
    (c) Capable of developing an adequate number of nationals to assume managerial, professional, medical and nursing tasks within a reasonable period.
    Within these constraints you have a total freedom to develop the business in the way which you feel will best benefit the Company's stakeholders.'

Marketing the Concept

Dr. Herrmann was a competent manager with an excellent record in the pharmaceutical industry. He was a qualified doctor and also gained an MBA degree from a well-renowned business school.

On taking control of the MSI project he realised that a thorough study of world needs in hospitals was essential. Whilst he knew a lot about hospitals in Europe, the USA and other developed countries, he knew very little about the kind of hospitals that the less developed countries needed. He was in some difficulty in determining the most promising parts of the world to explore. Moreover a vast number of questions kept cropping up:

— 'What kind of 'product' should we offer: large or small hospitals? General or specialist types? Standard or 'made to measure'? What facilities and equipment should we incorporate?
— 'How do we determine our pricing strategy?'
— 'Is there substantial competition and if so what are the strengths and weaknesses of our competitors?'
— 'What are the special commercial/financial features that the ideal 'package' should include?'
— 'How do we promote our "product"?'
— 'Do we need to appoint middlemen?'

Many other questions arose during the discussions. One thing became clear to Dr Herrmann: before accepting the objectives set for him by the Board, he needed to evaluate the whole project from both marketing and financial viewpoints.

Approach to Marketing Consultants

Dr Herrmann came to the conclusion that as a first step, he needed to invite a firm of marketing consultants to undertake market investigations on a global scale. He envisaged that these investigations would entail a two-phase approach.

Phase 1. A quick analysis of available data on every country with the view of pinpointing a 'short list' of the best opportunity markets. Criteria for selection of 'short list' countries to be defined at this stage.
Phase 2. An 'in-depth' study of the 'short list' countries in order to submit a positive and practical 'input' for planning purposes. Such 'input' to include details of market environments, needs, institutional structure, legal constraints, competitive offers, etc.

Dr Herrmann's expectation was that at the end of Phase 2 he would know everything that a good businessman needed to know in order to plan an effective marketing effort.

With this objective in mind he approached four firms of consultants with a request for suitable proposals.

Topics for Discussion

The firm's 'universe' consists of around 200 countries. It is obvious that no marketer is able to devote sufficient time to each country. The 'universe' has to be screened fairly quickly with the view of identifying the most promising target-countries for attention. Once such a short-list has been determined more detailed studies can be undertaken.

You should therefore approach the case in a number of interrelated phases:

1 Consider a methodology for reducing the countries of the world to a more manageable target-group.
2 Specify the kind of information that you feel MSI requires in its endeavour to develop detailed marketing plans.

Pioneer International Limited

Background

Pioneer International Limited was founded in 1925 by two brothers John and Charles Royston. The firm started as an engineering company specialising in the manufacture of machinery for bottling liquids. The Company rapidly developed into one of the leading suppliers of bottling equipment and supportive peripheral machinery, in the UK. The products, whilst being on the expensive side, were acknowledged by experts to be of the higest quality, reliability and durability.

Throughout their career the two brothers declared their basic commitment to the philosophy that ultimately 'quality and reliable service were the only formula for success'. Indeed with this philosophy the firm grew from strength to strength.

After World War II the firm entered a phase of remarkable growth both in sales and in profitability. Without too much effort and with very little planning the Company found itself deeply involved in exports to many parts of the world through a network of agents. Pioneer's machinery was in demand and highly saleable.

Profit rose substantially and in an effort to mitigate tax liability the two brothers decided to invest heavily in plant and in businesses. During the decade 1948–58 the brothers acquired almost indiscriminately companies in a variety of businesses. Such acquisitions were not always based on sound investment policy; on occasions the attraction of 'tax loss' advantages outweighed all other considerations. Nonetheless the Company developed into a thriving conglomerate although not all the subsidiaries generated satisfactory results. However, the main activities of the Group were extremely successful and profitable for a large number of years.

By 1965 the Company found itself offering a large number of products to many markets. The table in Figure 77 summarises the most important product/market relationships and the volumes (in cash terms) transacted during the 1964 financial year throughout the world:

In addition to the activities shown in Figure 77 and the markets served, the Company has been operating in many other areas, resulting from acquisitions, representing a turnover of another £6 400 000. This figure is arrived at by adding a host of small activities such as an aerosol filling plant; car washing machinery leasing company; a cold store; a general engineering company; a computer bureau; punch card printing firm; a small plant making

Markets	Bottling Plants and machinery £	Packaging Machinery £	Plastics Machinery £	Tube bending machinery £	Metal office furniture £
Milk	12,000,000	250,000	—	—	—
Oil	3,500,000	800,000	82,000	—	—
Detergents	2,000,000	4,200,000	500,000	—	—
Pharmaceuticals	1,200,000	400,000	200,000	—	—
Convenience Foods	100,000	1,500,000	—	—	—
Furniture makers	—	—	—	3,000,000	—
Tobacco	—	2,300,000	—	—	—
Engineering	—	—	—	1,200,000	—
Cosmetics	1,240,000	420,000	78,000	—	—
Plastics Industry	—	20,000	350,000	—	—
Banks & Insurance	—	—	—	—	275,000
Hotels & Catering	—	—	—	—	150,000
Airlines	—	—	—	—	175,000
Misc. Offices	—	—	—	—	182,000
Total: £36,122,000	20,040,000	9,890,000	1,210,000	4,200,000	782,000
Geographical distribution:	%	%	%	%	%
UK	33	29	56	26	84
USA	27	34	19	32	—
Europe (other than UK)	22	25	21	22	16
Middle East and Africa	7	4	—	5	—
Far East	6	2	—	3	—
Australasia	4	3	3	7	—
Others	1	3	1	5	—
Total	100	100	100	100	100

Fig. 77   Pioneer International Limited—international performance by products, markets and geography

specialised motors, etc. All these activities, a few profitable but most of them not, have gained the title of 'peripheral' activities. For the purpose of this summary they are completely ignored although from the strategic planning point of view their existence is of great importance.

In 1966 James Royston aged 45 took over the Chairmanship of the Company from his father Sir John Royston who retired at the age of 74. The new Chairman decided that the time had come to sort out the Company and consolidate its position.

Production

Pioneer's main product groups were manufactured in the UK, USA, Belgium, Italy and Australia. It owned three plants in the UK; two plants in the USA and one factory in each of the other countries. The plants belonging to the 'peripherals' are ignored here although their number was quite significant and they all employed a substantial labour force.

Basically the main plants consisted of sophisticated engineering shops
capable of producing intricate machines and assembling total systems.
Considerable overlap in skills and equipment existed among the UK factories.
The specialisation of each factory stemmed from the kind of orders entrusted
to it during the years rather than by conscious planning. Through market
conditions and local pressures the division of concentration emerged as set out
in Figure 78:

	Factory	Bottling	Packaging	Plastics	Tube Bending
UK	Stafford	X	—	—	—
	Barleigh	X	X	X	—
	Norton	—	X	X	X
USA	Michigan	X	—	X	—
	Granville	—	X	—	X
Belgium	Antwerp	X	X	—	—
Italy	Boulogna	—	X	X	—
Australia	Mohawk	X	X	—	—

Fig. 78   Pioneer International Limited—plants location

The new Chairman felt that considerable rationalisation could take place
among the various factories especially in the light of Britain's entry into
the EEC. At the same time Royston realised that he possessed very limited
information about the real market potential for his main products. The
Company had always been production orientated; it produced what it felt
was right for the market and with very few failures always succeeded in
achieving the desired results in terms of sales and profits.

Royston had come to realise that market conditions have changed in this
connection and that in the future new or improved products must be based on
a better appreciation of market needs.

Marketing and Selling

Marketing in the modern sense of the term did not exist in the firm until 1966.
The Directors saw no need for what they had always thought was one of the
'new fangled' ideas originating from business schools. They were confident in
their ability to gauge the requirement of their main customers and translate it
into suitable designs. The Company's salesmen, mostly qualified engineers,
and the agents in those countries where the Company did not have its own
subsidiaries, were active and enthusiastic and able to obtain the desired
results. Furthermore, they transmitted frequent reports to the design staff in

the appropriate factories telling them about what was happening in the market. The Directors were convinced that this was the best type of marketing.

In 1966 the Company's confidence suffered an unexpected shock. A European country developed a new type of integrated packaging system for milk utilising a polyethylene/paper laminate. The pack became popular quickly and virtually killed Pioneer's share of the milk bottling business in the country in question. The threat to other markets from this new idea was ominous. Pioneer were totally unprepared for this event and Royston was extremely annoyed that nobody in the European sales force seemed to have noticed such an important threat on the horizon. He was amazed that people who consider themselves as shrewd businessmen could be so blind. He thereupon recruited a young man, Gerald Lee, who had spent a number of years as a marketing executive in the industrial paints industry and appointed him as Marketing Director.

Lee soon became appalled at the size of his job. He asked himself the following questions:

1 'Where do I start? Nobody in the firm understands the marketing concept nor are they prepared to listen.'
2 'The firm consists of so many quasi-independent subsidiaries operating throughout the world; each of these subsidiaries caters for so many heterogeneous markets. Which area should I tackle first?'
3 'Should I start undertaking marketing tasks in the UK in relation to one product and one market? This would mean that I could only scratch the surface and could not achieve the results expected of me in a short period.'

Lee became despondent about his role and was on the verge of resigning. He expressed his doubts to the Chairman who perceived the enormity of the problem and threw all his weight behind Lee and decided to call a firm of management consultants to help in organising a marketing function in the firm to cover the international scene.

Organisation

The organisation of the Company at that point was based more or less on plants in the sense that the plant manager (or in a few instances the person in charge of two or more plants) was the Managing Director of the total activities of such factories including the responsibility for sales. In fact these activities were organised as relatively self-contained subsidiary companies with the Managing Director being responsible to the Chairman. The Managing Directors of the more important units were members of the Main Board.

Pioneer Engineering (UK) Limited

This Company included the Stafford and Barleigh plants and its main turnover was in the bottling plants business. The firm also manufactured a certain amount of packaging and plastic machinery but these were mostly components rather than integrated systems.

The Company was responsible for its own international selling results and had complete freedom to sell in whichever way it thought fit anywhere in the world. The one exception was that in the case of countries which possessed their own manufacturing facilities (for example USA, Belgium, etc.) no direct contact with the market could be made without first clearing it with the local boss.

The Managing Director of Pioneer Engineering (UK) Limited was Albert Smythe who was also a member of the Main Board.

Heather-Price Limited

This subsidiary owned a large factory at Norton. It manufactured packaging machinery, plastics installations (extruders, blow-moulding equipment, injection moulders, etc.) and tube bending equipment. The number of items produced was very large. At the same time the management tried to offer complete systems. If this meant buying components in the open market the firm was happy to do so. The idea was that customers should know that Heather-Price was able to provide a production system as against a collection of components. This meant that the firm acquired over the years considerable know-how in peripheral items such as conveyers, electronic control units, bulk handling hoppers, etc.

Ed Stinnes, the Managing Director, was the man who propounded the theory that the strength of the firm was the 'systems' approach. He was not a member of the Main Board and was rather sore about it.

Like Pioneer Engineering (UK) Limited this firm was free to make its own export arrangements. Stinnes felt that the international marketing situation was chaotic and pressed hard for a serious reappraisal of the prevailing arrangements. He was broad minded about the whole subject and was quite prepared to sacrifice some of his own unit's independence for the sake of achieving a well-planned and well-structured approach to international markets. He had been heard to say on many occasions: 'The way we are going about tackling our international markets we shall one day find our UK factories delivering to USA customers and the Americans will supply the British market—this cannot be good business.'

Pioneer Machinery Inc.

The USA subsidiary manufactured its products in two factories:

1 *The Michigan factory* which manufactured bottling machinery and plastic machinery. The former was very similar in design and capacity to the units manufactured in the UK subject to minor refinements called for by the USA market.

2 *The Granville factory* which manufactured packaging equipment and assembled bending machinery. The outlets for packaging machinery, however, differed considerably from the European scene insofar as the bulk of the output went to the tobacco industry.

The President of Pioneer Machinery Inc. Steve McLean was on the Main Board of Directors of the parent Company in the UK.

Pioneer Europe SA

This Belgian Company mainly assembled machines based on UK or USA components with a certain amount of local fabrication and finishing. The main purpose of the plant was to help the Company to have a Common Market presence thus overcoming duty constraints and also showing a European image.

Whilst logically the Belgian Company was meant to serve the EEC markets it found itself on many occasions competing against the UK and the USA companies who often bypassed the Brussels office and ignored the standard order to consult the local manager in countries that have manufacturing facilities. The truth was that the UK and USA managers hardly considered the Belgian factory as a manufacturing facility and therefore ignored its existence. At the same time they always expected the Belgian set-up to provide the after-sales service whenever necessary. This used to infuriate Jacques Moutier, the Managing Director. He felt that the EEC was the most important single market and that the potential was tremendous. 'The way these Anglo-Saxons treat my market will lead to a catastrophe one of these days.'

Moutier, a well-qualified engineer, believed that marketing was an Anglo-Saxon fad and that in practice all it meant was aggressive selling. 'If you have a good machine you can make people buy it'—was Moutier's philosophy.

Pioneer Italiana

This Boulogna Company was acquired a few years ago. It specialised in packaging machinery for the confectionery industry. The equipment was of highly innovative design and contained many ingenious features. Turnover, however, was quite poor owing to an unsatisfactory marketing and selling effort. The Company's managers were engineers with excellent ideas but these ideas were often totally unrelated to market needs.

The Company's managers were very disappointed that in spite of the fact that they had joined the Pioneer Group with its international ramifications, nobody seemed to care about the Italian Company or the Italian market. They felt lonely and frustrated. They had tried on a number of occasions to get the UK companies and the US subsidiary to distribute their packaging equipment in their respective markets but to no avail. The only sister-company which tried to help in this connection was the Australian subsidiary but their market potential was rather limited.

Pioneer Machinery and Engineering Pty

This Company covered the Australian market and large portions of the Far East market. In its Mohawk factory it produced bottling lines and packaging machinery. Wherever it lacked the facilities or the expertise it bought the appropriate parts from the other companies in the Group. It acted also as an agent for all the other sister-companies including the 'peripherals'. Ed Sullivan the Managing Director was a highly enthusiastic gentleman with a deeply-rooted loyalty to the Group as a whole. He was fully aware of the thought that co-operation among all the Companies in the Group meant strength whereas diffusion of effort and communication could lead to eventual weakening of the firm's international position. He belonged to the school of thought that felt that the time had come to reorganise the Group after appraising fully its global marketing opportunities.

Figure 79 reproduces the organisation chart of the firm.

Topics for discussion

The case presents a useful opportunity to discuss the organisation of the marketing function in a company operating internationally in many products and many markets. The options are numerous and they must be all explored. More specifically:

1 What are the strengths and weaknesses of the present structure in relation to the firm's products and the markets it serves?
2 Explore the corporate structure which might better meet the firm's international aims.
3 Consider how the marketing function could be organised to meet the marketing needs of the product groupings and markets on an international scale.

The advantages and disadvantages of the various options identified should be considered. The answer is not simple and one should not be afraid of exploring creative solutions. Whatever solution is chosen it is important that the interests of the mainstream activities of the firm are fully safeguarded. One must not lose sight of the fact that the peripheral activities are a major distraction for the strategic level and some 'home' must be found for them.

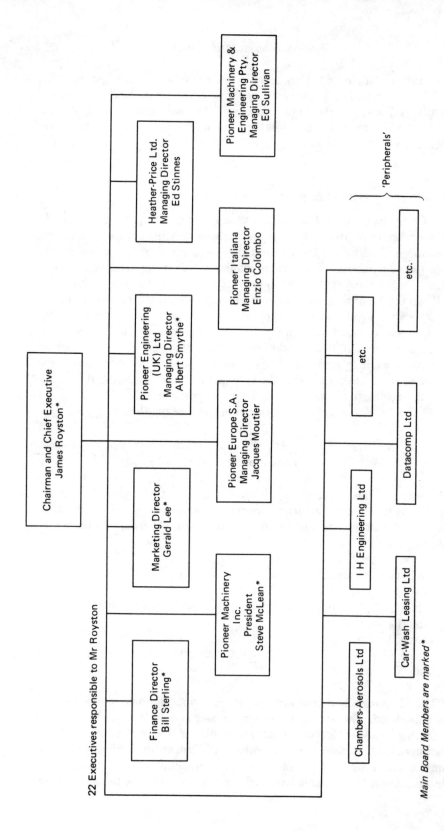

22 Executives responsible to Mr Royston

Chairman and Chief Executive
James Royston*

Finance Director
Bill Sterling*

Marketing Director
Gerald Lee*

Pioneer Machinery
Inc.
President
Steve McLean*

Pioneer Engineering
(UK) Ltd
Managing Director
Albert Smythe*

Heather-Price Ltd.
Managing Director
Ed Stinnes

Pioneer Europe S.A.
Managing Director
Jacques Moutier

Pioneer Italiana
Managing Director
Enzio Colombo

Pioneer Machinery &
Engineering Pty.
Managing Director
Ed Sullivan

Chambers-Aerosols Ltd

Car-Wash Leasing Ltd

I H Engineering Ltd

etc.

Datacomp Ltd

etc.

'Peripherals'

*Main Board Members are marked**

Fig. 79 Pioneer International Limited—organisation chart

References

General

Abel, D. F., *Defining the business: the starting point of strategic planning,* Englewood Cliffs. N. J. Prentice-Hall Incs., 1980.

The American Management Association, New York, Amacom 1975, *A Team Approach to Marketing Planning.*

Barclays Bank Report on export development in France, Germany and the UK: Factors for International Success prepared by ITI Research—Barclays Bank International 1979.

Bartels, R., *The History of Marketing Thought*, 2nd ed., Columbus, Ohio: Grid 1976.

Blake, J. E. (Ed.), *Designing for European Markets—A Management Guide*, London, Design Council, 1972.

British Business in Europe: *Businessmen's Guide to the European Communities*, HMSO for the Departments of Industry and Trade, 1981.

British Overseas Trade Board, *Export Handbook: Services for British Exporters*, 8th ed., London, The Board, 1975.

Drucker, P. F., *Managing in Turbulent Times*, Harper & Row, New York, 1980.

Dunn, S. W. and Lorimor, E. S. (Ed.), *International Advertising and Marketing*, Columbus, Ohio: Grid Publishing, 1979.

Euromonitor Publications Ltd, *International Marketing Data and Statistics*, 2nd ed., 1976/77.

Euromonitor Publications Ltd, *European Marketing Data and Statistics*, 14th ed., 1977/1978.

Fayerweather, J., *International Marketing*, 2nd ed., Englewood Cliffs, New Jersey, Prentice-Hall Inc., 1970.

Hess, J. M. and Cateora, P. R., *International Marketing* (revised ed.), Richard D. Irwin Inc., Homewood, Ill., 1971.

Keegan, W. J., *Multinational Marketing Management*, 2nd ed., Englewood Cliffs, N. J. Prentice Hall 1980.

Kotler, P., *Marketing Management, analysis, planning and control*, 4th ed., 1980 Prentice-Hall Inc.

Kotler, P., Gregor, W. and Rogers, W., *The Marketing Audit Comes of Age*, Sloan Management Review, Winter 1977.

Kracmar, J. Z., *Marketing Research in Developing Countries*, New York, Praeger Publishers, 1971.

Kramer, R. L., *International Marketing*, 3rd ed., Cincinnati, Ohio, Southwestern Publishing, 1970.

Lawrence, R. J. and Thomas, M. J. (Ed.), *Modern Marketing Management: Selected Readings*, Harmondsworth, Middlesex, Penguin Books, 1971.

Levitt, Theodore, *Marketing for Business Growth*, New York, McGraw-Hill, 1974.

Managing Global Marketing—a headquarters perspective, New York, Business International 1976.

Majaro, S., *Marketing in Perspective*, George Allen & Unwin, London, 1982.

Miracle, G. E. and Albaum, G. S., *International Marketing Management*, Irwin, Illinois, 1970.

Readers Digest Association, *A Survey of Europe Today*, RDA, London, 1970.

Root, F. R., *Entry Strategies for Foreign Markets: from domestic to International Business*, New York AMACOM, 1977.

Terpstra, V., *International Marketing Strategy*, Harmondsworth, Middlesex, Penguin Books, 1973.

Terpstra, V., *International Marketing*, 2nd ed., Hinsdale, Ill., The Dryden Press, 1978.

Thorelli, H. M. (Ed.), *International Marketing Strategy*, Harmondsworth, Middlesex, Penguin Books, 1973.

Wainwright, Ken, *Practical Export Marketing*, London, Cassell, 1971.

Weichmann, U. E., *Marketing Management in Multinational Firms*, New York, Praeger, 1976.

Wyatt, D. and Dashwood, A., *The Substantive Law of the EEC*, London, Sweet & Maxwell, 1980.

Yarker, K. A., *International Marketing*, Business Books, 1976.

Articles

Ames, B. C., 'Dilemma of Product/Market Management', *Harvard Business Review*, March–April 1971.

Arpan, J. S., 'International Intracorporate Pricing: Non-American Systems and Views', *Journal of International Studies*, Spring 1972.

Aylmer, R. J., 'Who makes marketing decisions in the multinational firm?', *Journal of Marketing*, October 1970.

Bodinat, H., 'Multinational Decentralisation', *European Business*, Summer 1974.

Brandt, W. K. and Hulbert, J. M., 'Communications in the Multinational Corporation', *Journal of International Business Studies*, Spring 1975.

Buzzell, R. D., 'Can you Standardise Multinational Marketing?' *Harvard Business Review*, November–December 1968.

Davis, S. M., 'Trends in the Organization of Multinational Companies', *Columbia Journal of World Business*, Summer 1976.

Donnelly, J. H. Jr., 'Attitudes Toward Culture and Approach to International Advertising', *Journal of Marketing*, July 1970.

Douglas, Susan P., 'Patterns and Parallels of Marketing Structures', *MSU Business Topics*, Spring 1971.

Doz, Y. L. and Pramalad, C. K., 'How MNC's Cope with heat government intervention', *Harvard Business Review*, March–April 1980.

Dufy, G. and Mirus, R., 'Forecasting Foreign Exchange Rates: A Pedagogical Note', *The Columbus Journal of World Business*, Summer 1981.

Ellison, R., 'An Alternative to Direct Investment Abroad', *International Management*, June 1976.

Gestetner, D., 'Strategy in Managing International Sales', *Harvard Business Review*, September–October, 1974.

Gilbert, M. J., 'Measuring Advertising Effectiveness: An International Approach', *The International Advertiser*, Spring 1971.

Goldstucker, Jac L., 'The Influences of Culture on Channels of Distribution;' 'Marketing and the New Science of Planning', Robert L. King, editor, Chicago, *American Marketing Association*, 1968.

Hanan, M., 'Reorganise your Company Around its Markets', *Harvard Business Review*, November–December 1974.

Hayes, D. J., 'Translating Foreign Currencies', *Harvard Business Review*, January–February 1972.

Institute of Practitioners in Advertising, 'Industrial Marketing and Advertising in Europe', 1970.

'International Currency' Fall 1976 issue of *The Columbia Journal of World Business*.

Keegan, W. J., 'Five Strategies for Multinational Marketing', *European Busines*, January 1970.

Keegan, W. J., 'Multinational Marketing: The Headquarters Role', *Columbia Journal of World Business*, Vol. 6 No. 1, 1971.

McGarrah, R. E., 'Logistics for the International Manufacturer' *Harvard Business Review*, March–April 1966.

'Organisation Design for MNC's' Summer 1976 Issue of *The Columbia Journal of World Business*.

Sethi, S. P., 'Comparative Cluster Analysis for World Markets', *Journal of Marketing Research*, August 1971.

Terpstra, V., 'Selection of Market Entry Strategies in International Marketing'; 'Broadening the concept of Marketing', David L. Sparks, editor, Chicago, *American Marketing Association*, 1970.

'Unilever Ends Production in Mexico But Retains Licensing, Marketing Set up', *Business Latin America*, February 24, 1972.

Widing, J. W. Jr, 'Reorganising your Worldwide Business', *Harvard Business Review*, May–June 1973.

Zani, W. M., 'Blueprint for MIS', *Harvard Business Review,* November–December 1970.

Index